LIVING FOR PLEASURE

GUIDES TO THE GOOD LIFE

Stephen Grimm, Series Editor

LIVING FOR PLEASURE

An Epicurean Guide to Life

Emily A. Austin

OXFORD
UNIVERSITY PRESS

OXFORD
UNIVERSITY PRESS

Oxford University Press is a department of the University of Oxford. It furthers
the University's objective of excellence in research, scholarship, and education
by publishing worldwide. Oxford is a registered trade mark of Oxford University
Press in the UK and certain other countries.

Published in the United States of America by Oxford University Press
198 Madison Avenue, New York, NY 10016, United States of America.

© Oxford University Press 2023

CIP data is on file at the Library of Congress

ISBN 978-0-19-755832-4

DOI: 10.1093/oso/9780197558324.001.0001

Printed by Sheridan Books, Inc., United States of America

For my parents

TABLE OF CONTENTS

SERIES EDITOR FOREWORD

Several ancient philosophers held that the point of studying ethics was not just to learn about ethics—as one might learn about chemistry, astronomy, or history—but to become a better human being. They also recognized that this was not easy to do. In order for thinking about ethics to make a difference in our lives, our habits and inclinations needed to be educated right alongside our minds. They therefore claimed that what mattered to living well was not just *what* we thought but *how* we thought, and not just how we thought but how we emotionally responded to the world and to other people.

The books in this series highlight some of the transformative ideas that philosophers have had about these topics—about the good life, and the practices and ways of life that help us to pursue it. They tell us what various philosophers and traditions have taken to be most important in life, and what they have taken to be less important. They offer philosophical guidance about how to approach broad questions, such as how to structure our days, how to train our attention, and how to die with dignity. They also offer guidance about how to deal with the sort of everyday questions that are often neglected by scholars, but that make up the texture of our lives, such as how to deal with relationships gone wrong, family disruptions, unexpected success, persistent anxiety, and an environment at risk.

Because the books are written by philosophers, they draw attention to the reasons and arguments that underlie these various claims—the particular visions of the world and of human nature that are at the root of these stances. The claims made in these books can therefore be contested, argued with, and found to be more or less plausible. While some answers will clearly compete with one another, other views will likely appear complementary. Thus, a Confucian might well find that a particular practice or insight of, say, Nietzsche's helps to shed light on his or her way of living in the world, and vice versa. On the whole, the idea is that these great philosophers and traditions all have something to teach us about how to be more fully human, and more fully happy.

Above all, the series is dedicated to the idea that philosophy can be more than just an academic discipline—that it can be, as it was for hundreds of years in the ancient world, a way of life. The hope is also that philosophy can enhance the ways of life we already feel pulled toward and help us to engage with them more authentically and fully.

Stephen R. Grimm
Professor of Philosophy
Fordham University

1 | MAYBE WE'RE DOING IT WRONG

Imagine yourself on vacation. Not everyone enjoys beaches, and some people would rather eat sand than sleep in the woods. Maybe you prefer to vacation in your living room. Now that you've figured out where you are, who's there? You, obviously, but people rarely want to be entirely alone for all that long because we're social creatures. You might be with your romantic partner, or maybe your children or some close friends. Maybe you're there with George Clooney because why not?

Think about what it would mean for the trip to go well, like really well. You are in love. Your children put away their phones and are excited about what you are making for dinner. Your best friends gently tease you about that time you threw up outside of Waffle House. You make a playlist, and people say "I love this song" about every song. We've clearly stumbled into my imagination at this point, so your results may vary.[1]

Now, what is the weather like? That one's easy—the weather is "perfect," as is the food. Maybe you see some wonders of the world, or maybe you spend the afternoon reading books and watching movies. You go out dancing or you wear flannel pajamas all day. How long are you staying on vacation? Perhaps forever.

If I were giving a TED talk, I might ask you what single word applies to all of these features of your imaginary vacation. And then, after a pregnant pause, the tone of my voice would soften and I would answer my own question—"Pleasure." Your days are shot through with pleasures. Even your dreams are pleasant! The story doesn't fulfill its ambition unless you are feeling some kind of pleasure at every turn.

You might understand, then, how the Ancient Greek philosopher Epicurus could find himself thinking that pleasure is the source of our happiness and the only truly good thing. The technical term for this view is "hedonism." As Epicurus puts it in his notoriously wooden prose, "pleasure is the starting point and the goal of living blessedly."[2] Happiness begins and ends in pleasure.

But surely that can't be right! Telling someone to aim at pleasure seems like a very unpromising starting point for a self-improvement plan, much less an ethical approach to living. It sounds more like a recipe for insurmountable credit card debt, a series of failed relationships, and a life-long problem with alcohol. Ethics is demanding, but pursuing pleasure seems all too easy and all too destructive. We don't need some old philosopher like Epicurus giving license to our failures of self-control and calling it ethics and happiness.

The last thing we should do is cavalierly dismiss Epicurus as a debauched glutton, but let's not lose sight of how powerfully liberating it can be to hear that pleasure is good. Some people are raised to be ashamed of perfectly natural bodily desires, and others are simply tired of feeling guilty for buying an afternoon latte. Sometimes you just want to ask for avocado on your sandwich without worrying that the person behind you in line is thinking,

"That avocado, son, is the reason you'll never own a home!" More importantly, pleasures both large and small give shape and color to our lives, and any philosophy that denies their genuine value seems to promise little more than a steady diet of cold gruel for the soul. Unlike some other philosophers you might have encountered, Epicurus is no prudish killjoy.

Yet he was also not the ringleader of life-long frat boys in period-appropriate togas. Even while he was alive, many centuries before they put his name on every fancy grocery store in France, Epicurus complained that people were slandering his reputation by casting him as the villainous promoter of unchecked desire. It's true that Epicurus thinks bodily pleasure in moderation is well worth having, and he seemed to have been a devoted fan of cheese. But he insists that his hedonism is not about "drinking bouts and continuous partying" or "consuming fish and other dainties of an extravagant table."[3] While "fish and other dainties" have their place, Epicurus thinks those pleasures are an unnecessary sideshow for the greatest pleasure.

Go back for a moment and reflect on that vacation, cataloguing its many pleasures: the food, the friends, the sounds of the earth, your sudden facility with the guitar. Epicurus thinks all of those pleasures are good, in part because he thinks all pleasures are good, even if some pleasures are best avoided.[4] The best pleasure, though, comes from what is absent from your story—anxiety, or "psychological disturbance." Your imaginary castle of pleasure is built on an anxiety-free foundation, and Epicurus considers that stable, anxiety-free state the ultimate pleasure. We'll call it tranquility, though Epicurus wrote in Greek, so he called it *ataraxia*.

If we understand pleasure as freedom from anxiety, we are often very, very bad at being pleased. Anxiety seems woven into the fabric of daily life, and a host of articles, cultural authorities, and pharmacists report that we are increasingly miserable, lonely, and afraid. You might have even struggled to imagine your vacation without some anxiety creeping in at the margins, recalling perhaps your fear of flying, ticks, or boredom.

Some anxiety has a clear locus—sickness, unemployment, climate change, pandemics, a constitutional crisis. Other anxiety skirts at the margins of our awareness, distracting us like the persistent roar of a great existential leaf blower operated by the world's most zealous lawn maintenance crew. Anxiety tends to come out in force at night, keeping us from going to sleep or getting back to sleep. That kind of feverish insomnia drives many people into the welcoming arms of prescription drugs. Others pass restless hours in the sickly glow of a smartphone, doomscrolling the breaking news of some fresh horror, checking email.

Though we talk about it less, some of our anxiety is about theoretical matters instead of purely practical concerns. We're not simply worried about paying our bills, getting promoted, or keeping our children off the internet after midnight. We are also anxious about truth, science, religion, meaning, and death. These are in some sense the deeper and more perplexing anxieties, but daily life affords few opportunities to discuss them. Seriously, imagine approaching your co-workers tomorrow and saying, "Do you think science makes us more anxious, or less? Sometimes I feel like I don't have any control over what I do, like I'm some sort of puppet. And also, if God's so good, why does Joe's kid have cancer?" Everyone would suddenly remember they have work to do.

It might seem that all this talk of anxiety is taking us far afield from the original discussion of pleasure. Epicurus, though, rightly points out that our anxiety and its attendant emotions largely arise from our desires, what we think will give us pleasure. The best strategy for plumbing the depths of our negativity is something along the lines of "follow the money." When we intensely desire something we aren't sure we can get—anxiety. When we get it and worry we can't keep it—anxiety. When we compete for what we want or want what others have—anxiety, envy, and resentment. When it, whatever "it" is, needs to be perfect, a whole container ship of anxiety. In brief, catalog your unsatisfied desires and you will catalog your pain.

That might seem like a lot of anxiety to address in a short book about how to live like an ancient hedonist, but Epicurus thinks the best advice is brief and memorable. We'll explore what Epicurus thinks most contributes to our anxiety and unhappiness, both theoretically and practically, and how we can change our beliefs, desires, and physical circumstances to put the greatest pleasure within reach. Sometimes we need to change our mind, sometimes we need to change our environment, and sometimes we need to study the world. Because we are anxious about many things, Epicurus has something to say about almost everything, from science and religion, to friendship, ambition, dining choices, gratitude, sex, and politics. Epicurus thinks our anxiety ranges from the stars in the sky to the swerving motions of the atoms in our mind, and so does his philosophy.

Before just diving right in, I should lay out some terms and hedge a few bets. First and foremost, while I am a credentialed Epicurus scholar, I am no kind of life coach. I'm bumbling around in life's wilderness with everyone else, and I don't take myself to be bringing a stone tablet down from the mountain. As far as I can tell, we all struggle to do our best with a life that threatens to overwhelm us. Epicurus was not an elitist, which is one of the many things I admire about his philosophy, and I hope to capture that in the spirit of this book.

I am also not, nor do I think anyone should be, a tireless promoter of "ancient wisdom" as a cure-all for what ails the modern mind. Only a snake-oil dealer or a Google executive would promise to make all your psychological tension disappear. I think Epicurus is right about a great many things, far more than he is given credit for. Along the way, though, I will point out why some Epicurean commitments might give us pause and show how I think Epicurus can best respond to those concerns.

Finally, many books on "philosophy as a way of life" focus almost exclusively on matters of practical import, as if the only thing the ancients cared about was making you better at your job. I will spend some time talking about the heavier stuff—science, religion, truth, freedom, death—because I agree with Epicurus that those things are crucially important for making sense of our place in the world. Epicurus offers by far the most thoroughly modern account of natural science in antiquity, and he thinks our understanding of the natural world has significant bearing on how well we live. It won't shatter my heart if you want to skip those chapters. Perhaps you have no anxiety on those fronts. But if you're curious about ancient philosophical conceptions of the divine, suffering, freedom, or atoms, then Epicurus has something to offer.

I also hope you will occasionally chuckle, perhaps even laugh. Epicurus wrote that "one must philosophize and at the same time laugh and take care of one's household and use the rest of our personal goods, and never stop proclaiming the utterances of correct philosophy."[5] So let's try for all those things. Enough already! Who is this Epicurus, and what does he believe?

2 | EPICUREANISM, THE ORIGINAL CAST

The nature and purpose of this book makes a lengthy account of the intellectual history of Epicureanism a diversion from the core project of exploring how Epicureans live, as alluring as that diversion might seem. Thankfully, there are many excellent books about the history of Ancient Greek and Roman philosophy, some of them focused exclusively on Epicureanism. You can find my suggestions for further reading at the end of the book. In the interim, let me introduce you to the Original Cast and their core texts. Starring role, of course, goes to:

Epicurus: Epicurus was born in 341 BCE in an Athenian colony on the island of Samos, a short ferry ride from what is now Turkey. He was an Athenian citizen by birth, so he traveled to Athens at eighteen to fulfill his civic obligation to serve two years in the military. Epicurus was unable to return home after completing his military service because Samos was asserting its independence from Athens, so he moved to Lampsacus, in then Eastern Greece, where he lived and practiced philosophy with friends. He returned in 306 to Athens, where he spent the remainder of his life. Some of Epicurus' close friends from Lampsacus joined him in Athens, while others remained lifelong correspondents.

Epicurus entered Athens at a time of both political and military instability. Athens found itself knocked down a peg after many years of power and democratic self-rule, the city having been conquered by the Macedonians, their fellow Greeks to the north. They also suffered periodic military incursions from other parts of Greece.[1] Once Epicurus was settled, he founded a philosophical community called the Garden on the outskirts of Athens, not far outside the city's defensive walls. He also seems to have owned a residence inside the walls, in Melite.[2]

Epicurus and his fellow Epicureans lived at the Garden in private households, often with their spouses and children. They had a very active community life and spent much of their time talking, eating, drinking, and socializing together. These shared activities were, they thought, the heart of politics, living as a community bonded by mutual trust and support. In addition to other assorted reasons for celebration, they arranged a regular social gathering on the twentieth of every month, which I consider one of their more charming habits.[3] The Epicureans were by all counts a happy lot, though it seems they might have largely kept to themselves.

Uncharacteristically for his time, Epicurus welcomed women, slaves, and the poor to live, study, and write at the Garden. According to the Roman statesman and philosopher Cicero, Epicurus regularly praised the philosophy and character of Themista, a woman who studied with him in Lampsacus. Another Epicurean woman philosopher, Leontion, wrote a treatise opposing the views of Theophrastus, Aristotle's leading student. Written work by women about matters not concerning household management was exceptionally rare.[4] Cicero expressed disdain that Epicurus would praise Themista over prominent male philosophers, and he cited the existence of Leontion's treatise as evidence of just how "enormous was the wantonness of Epicurus' Garden."[5]

Epicurus ran the school until his death of kidney stones in 270, at the age of seventy-two. The Garden remained active under Epicurean leadership until at least the late 50s BCE. Around that same time, Epicurus' house in Melite fell into the ownership of Gaius Memmius, who seemed determined to construct a new house, despite protestations from prominent Epicureans.[6] More on Memmius in a moment.

We owe Diogenes Laertius a debt of gratitude for much of what we know about Epicurus' biography. His *Lives of Eminent Philosophers*, probably written sometime in the third century CE, documents the doctrines and supposed biographies of important Greek philosophers and their followers. He seasons his accounts with apocryphal tales of the philosophers' temperaments and their deaths, which are often so absurd that they almost seem designed to inject levity. For example, the Stoic philosopher Chrysippus reportedly found his own joke so funny that he laughed himself to death.[7]

Diogenes Laertius plays a starring role in Epicureanism because he copied four philosophical texts by Epicurus that would otherwise have been lost and that now form the backbone of Epicurean scholarship.[8] These include three letters that Epicurus wrote to friends, which were intended as "open letters" to be passed around. In the *Letter to Herodotus*, Epicurus lays out his views on natural science and physics. The *Letter to Pythocles* concerns astronomy and other meteorological phenomena that Epicurus thought needed an explanation based in physics, rather than superstition. Finally, the *Letter to Menoeceus* offers a distilled account of

Epicurean prudence and happiness. Diogenes also includes forty *Principal Doctrines*, which cover the waterfront of Epicurean philosophy. Each doctrine is quite short, often only a single, highly technical sentence.

In addition to the letters and *Principal Doctrines* from Diogenes Laertius, we have another set of Epicurean doctrines called the *Vatican Sayings* that were discovered in 1888 in the Vatican Library, as well as some fragments from otherwise lost works. By scholarly standards, this counts as an abundance of textual evidence. For comparison, we have almost nothing from the early Greek Stoics who were Epicurus' contemporaries.

The heart of Epicureanism remained in Athens, but Epicurus had generations of followers in the east, especially in the vicinity of Lampsacus, where he spent his early adulthood. Other Epicureans took root in the vicinity of Rome, where Greek philosophy became all the rage. Let's turn, then, to the two chief Epicureans working in the Roman sphere, both of them poets as well as philosophers.

Lucretius: We know very little of the life of Titus Lucretius Carus, author of *On the Nature of Things (De Rerum Natura)*, a magisterial six-book defense of Epicureanism in Latin verse. He was born in 94 BCE and likely died sometime in the 50s, making him contemporaneous with the Roman statesman Cicero and the Epicurean Philodemus, both discussed below. Though we can speculate about Lucretius' social status based on his apparent familiarity with the temperaments and predilections of the wealthy and powerful, we know nothing of his material circumstances. All we really know is that he was exceptionally literate, greatly admired Epicurus, and had a biting satirical wit.

On the Nature of Things played such a prominent role in subsequent intellectual history, especially during the Renaissance and Enlightenment, that Lucretius far eclipsed Epicurus in stature, or at least in scholarly and cultural attention.[9] Lucretius wrote in dactylic hexameter, the form used in Greek epics like Homer's *Illiad* and *Odyssey*. Some early Greek philosophers like Parmenides and Empedocles also wrote their highly technical philosophy in verse, and Lucretius seems to have drawn inspiration from them. The poem is addressed to someone named Memmius, likely the same Memmius who found himself in possession of Epicurus' property in Melite. Lucretius apparently hoped to make an Epicurean convert of Memmius, an effort which seems to have been in vain.[10]

Lucretius offers our most extensive account of Epicurean physics and natural science, and here his poem is indispensable. He explains, among other things, Epicurus' arguments for the existence of atoms and void, the physical nature of the mind, the origins of our world, and the infiniteness of the universe. His topical coverage is expansive, including an evolutionary account of survival of the fittest, the development of societies, how magnets work, and an explanation of airborne viruses. He is our key source for Epicurus' argument that atoms sometimes "swerve," such that their movement is spontaneous and non-linear (a view roughly shared by contemporary particle physicists, as well as neuroscientists who study the brain's spontaneous activity).[11] On these matters, Lucretius claims to be working from Epicurus' writings, leading scholars to think he might have been drawing directly from Epicurus' largely lost treatise, *On Nature*.

Much of *On the Nature of Things* is a relatively dry philosophical and scientific treatise, but Lucretius periodically indulges his rhetorical impulses in praise of Epicurus himself and the Epicurean way of life, and here he shines as both a poet and an observer of humanity.[12] He crafts some vivid and biting indictments of those under the powerful sway of desires, whether passionate love or the unbridled pursuit of money, honor, or power. He writes with verve about people wracked by their fear of death and paralyzed by superstition.

Though I will appeal to Lucretius regularly as an Epicurean authority, especially on matters of natural science, I will occasionally register a few reservations about his claims or tone. For example, he might indulge a bit too much in satirizing the opposition and run the risk of conceit. His poetic pride seems at odds with Epicurus' own resistance to rhetorical niceties and intellectual preening. That said, the intellectual world we inherited from the Renaissance would not be the same without him, and he is the most effective advertiser of Epicureanism on record.

Philodemus: Philodemus of Gadara (c.110–c.40/35 BCE) studied at the Garden under the leadership of Zeno of Sidon.[13] He left the Garden and lived for a while in Sicily, though it seems he was asked to move on because of his unorthodox religious views. Philodemus eventually settled on the outskirts of Rome, where he set up a school and library at Herculaneum, perhaps under the patronage of Julius Caesar's father-in-law. Some have speculated that Julius Caesar himself subscribed to Epicureanism, especially to the Epicurean rejection of superstition.[14]

Philodemus' library at Herculaneum contained a treasure trove of Epicurean texts, including Philodemus' own work, but it was regrettably buried under volcanic ash when Mount Vesuvius erupted in 79 CE. The surprising thing about volcanic ash is that it preserves many things, at least if properly excavated. Since the library's rediscovery, some texts have been retrieved, though they are fragmentary and difficult to restore and read. The advent of new technologies has improved matters, but the work is still arduous, like working the most fragile of jigsaw puzzles. Careful and dedicated scholars have gifted us what we have of Philodemus.

Unlike Lucretius, Philodemus seems to have had little interest in Epicurean natural science, which was uncharacteristic for an Epicurean. Market forces might explain his neglect of physics, since Roman patrons tended to care for little else than ethics, politics, and managing their property. If a person were to read only the Roman Stoics, for example, they might never know the Greek Stoics developed propositional logic. Philodemus' treatises tend to focus on how to help novices alter their desires and develop the character of Epicureans, and, as a result, he offers more practical advice for living as an Epicurean than any of our other sources. Among these many fragmentary works, the ones most relevant for our purposes are *On Frank Speech* (how to benefit oneself and others through candor), *On Flattery*, *On Death*, and *On Arrogance*.

Diogenes of Oenoanda: Epicurus transformed the lives of many people, and some of his adherents were proselytizers. Lucretius devoted what was likely the bulk of his creative output to *On the Nature of Things*, and Diogenes of Oenoanda worked to literally carve Epicurus' doctrines in stone. Convinced in his old age that Epicureanism would bring happiness to his fellow citizens and their visitors, he commissioned an Epicurean inscription for the wall of a public building, probably sometime in the second century CE.[15] Diogenes' impulse is familiar to us, of course, as we still carve the words of influential political or cultural figures into marble, but his inscription is distinctive in its magnitude and focus on philosophical argumentation, including a defense of Epicurean physics for the average citizen out for a stroll about town. The wall's remaining sections show not only the geographical reach of Epicureanism, but they also demonstrate that many Epicureans considered their philosophy a kind of political gift to the public. They were not, as their opponents often maintained, a private suburban club for social dropouts, outcasts, and women of easy virtue. Or at least not merely that. Which brings us to Epicureanism's detractors.

The Loyal Opposition

Our other key sources for Epicurean philosophy should be met with caution, chiefly because they were all, to varying extents, hostile to Epicureanism, though they remained eager proponents of Greek philosophy itself. They just played for other teams. Though critics often misrepresent their opponents to make them easier to dismiss, the best philosophers faithfully represent the views they reject. In the process, they play the essential role of drawing our attention to legitimate concerns. Every philosophy needs thoughtful critics lest its advocates fall into complacency, and Epicureanism had some critics who played fair more often than not. We will focus on three of them.

Cicero: Marcus Tullius Cicero (106–43 BCE) fell in love with Greek philosophy and sought to bring it into the Roman intellectual realm and into the Latin language itself. Cicero wrote at length about the major Greek philosophical schools, especially the Stoics, Skeptics, and Epicureans, creating his own Latin vocabulary of philosophical terminology as he went. As an Academic Skeptic, Cicero considered himself in active pursuit of a certainty he suspected would forever elude him. Nevertheless, he believed that philosophical argumentation, at least when conducted rigorously and conscientiously, reveals which views are more likely to be correct. Practicing philosophy involves bringing in the intellectual harvest, then separating the wheat from the chaff. For Cicero, Epicureanism was ever the chaff.[16] He nevertheless sought to remain philosophically charitable, if only because his lifelong best friend, Titus Pomponius, was a dedicated Epicurean. Pomponius won the nickname "Atticus" for his love of all things Athens, where he spent much of his adult life. Cicero wrote regularly to Atticus when they were apart, and a remarkable amount of their correspondence was preserved.

Cicero explains and objects to Epicurean doctrines in numerous texts, central among them *On Moral Ends*, which he wrote in 45 BCE, not long after the death of his beloved daughter, Tullia. *On Moral Ends* depicts an imagined conversation between advocates of competing Greek philosophical schools and Cicero himself. Torquatus, representing Epicureanism, sings the praises of a life aimed at achieving tranquil pleasure, to which Cicero responds with a withering attack. Cicero also touches on Epicurean doctrines in topical works, including *On Fate*, *On Friendship*, *On Duties*, and *On the Nature of the Gods*. *On Moral Ends* will feature most often in this book because it includes a sustained exposition of Epicurean ethics and prudence. Cicero tended to treat the Epicureans as apolitical simpletons, but he has a crowning grace among the Romans—he took the time and care to faithfully represent Epicureanism in terms they would accept. For that reason, he is both a resource for understanding Epicureanism itself and critic worth respecting.

Seneca: Lucius Annaeus Seneca the Younger (4 BCE–65 CE) was a man whose philosophical allegiances were difficult to pin down. He was a devoted and passionate Stoic, but he also embodied the Roman impulse toward *syncretism*, a cafeteria-style hodge-podge of mix-and-match philosophies that was supposed to result in a well-rounded philosophical diet. When in his most generous spirits, Seneca praised Epicurus' own austerity and self-control, even if he considered the followers of Epicurus regrettably indulgent. Seneca also admired Epicurus' tendency to philosophize in letters, which likely inspired Seneca's decision to write philosophical letters himself.[17] If all Epicureans lived like Epicurus, Seneca seems to suggest, their focus on pleasure could almost be passed over as an inconsequential character flaw.

At other times, though, he lets loose against Epicureanism, labeling it "feminine," which, unfortunately, he considered an insult.[18] To be specific, Seneca calls the Epicureans "an effeminate, shade-loving clan of philosophizing banqueters." He compares Epicurus himself to a drag-queen at a festival—unless you look closely, you might not recognize him as a man.[19] Part of this supposed unmanliness stemmed from Epicurus' rejection of the political life that Seneca embraced with enough vigor that it eventually got him assassinated by Nero, the Roman Emperor whose murderous vice Seneca had long ignored, occasionally even enabled. In Seneca's final days, as he tried somewhat desperately to retire from politics, he suggested that Epicurus had perhaps been right. We will focus most on Seneca's *Letters from a Stoic* and his *Consolation to Helvia*, a letter about grief that he addressed to his mother.

Plutarch: Lucius Mestrius Plutarchus (c.45–c.125 CE) is best known for his biographies of Ancient Greek and Roman men of political and military consequence. Plutarch's *Lives* were rediscovered and translated during the Renaissance, and they were effectively adopted as the course texts for Classical History and Leadership Studies 101 for centuries thereafter. What matters for us, though, is that Plutarch hated Epicurus with a fierce intensity. Plutarch wrote a series of philosophically informative hit-jobs on Epicureanism.[20] His *Against Colotes* and *Non Posse* were both responses to Colotes, an Epicurean who maintained that Epicureanism's competitors advocate lives contrary to human nature that lead to disastrous consequences if enacted. For example, Plato suggests that the best people should share wives and children, which has a history of not working well, and some Skeptics seem to advocate believing nothing at all, which could prove dangerous and might very well be impossible.

Plutarch's general aim in *Non Posse* is to show that it is instead Epicureanism that encourages a life contrary to human nature, the philosophical equivalent of "I'm rubber and you're glue." Plutarch rejected Epicurus' hedonism as fit for beasts, and he considered Epicurus' highly unusual account of piety and rejection of the afterlife contemptible. As one might expect given the sheer magnitude of Plutarch's biographical project, Plutarch also criticizes Epicurus' rejection of the active political life. Plutarch considered political leadership the pinnacle of human intellect and virtue, and he could not make sense of anyone who preferred the quiet life.

Plutarch will play a key role in our discussion of Epicurean religion and politics.

A Note on the Texts and Quotations

No other work is necessary for understanding this book, though you might find yourself curious to consult the relevant sources in their full context. To help us avoid the inside baseball of academia, I decided to choose scholarly translations in readily accessible, cost-friendly editions and use them consistently when I quote.

- Quotes from Epicurus are drawn from *Hellenistic Philosophy: Introductory Readings*, 2nd edition, edited by Inwood and Gerson, Hackett Publishing, 1988, unless the passage only appears elsewhere.
- For Lucretius' *On the Nature of Things* (*DRN*), I use Martin Ferguson Smith's translation, Hackett Publishing, 2001.
- For Cicero's *On Moral Ends* (*DF*), I use Raphael Woolf's translation, edited by Julia Annas, Cambridge, 2001.

Citations of less frequently referenced primary texts and of scholarly work can be found in the notes and bibliography.

3 | HAPPINESS, THEIRS AND OURS

Epicurus is part of a tradition of Ancient Greek philosophy that grounded ethics in a fundamental assumption about human psychology—we want to be happy! The dispute among the competing schools (including the Platonists, Aristotelians, Stoics, Cynics, and Skeptics) arises from their divergent views about the nature of happiness, its necessary ingredients, and how we might achieve it. Epicurus' hedonism sets him apart from the crowd, but like all his competitors, he thinks the central ethical question is how to be happy.

Note how strange that sounds to us, though. We tend to think that ethics and happiness are largely unrelated, or perhaps like two people with some overlapping interests who occasionally show up at the same parties. The landscape of our culture seems well populated with happy people of suspect or even depraved morality. Fewer in number, but nevertheless in evidence, are the beleaguered and miserable moral saints. While we might concede that true happiness and moral excellence can coincide, it seems undeniable that many bad people are happy, and many good people are miserable. So much, one might think, for an ethics based in happiness.

Or, as the ancient ethicists might respond, so much the worse for our modern conception of happiness. An example might help.

Imagine that a private detective is meeting a prospective client for the first time:

DETECTIVE: And what kind of work are you hoping I can do for you?

CLIENT: Well, see, I need someone to tell me whether my husband is happy.

DETECTIVE: Hmmm ... so you would like me to find out whether he's cheating, whether he's unhappy in the marriage?

CLIENT: No, no, I know he's not cheating on me, and he would never leave. I'm just not sure whether he's happy.

DETECTIVE: Well, have you asked him whether he's happy?

CLIENT: Sure, and he says he is. He says he's exceptionally happy.

DETECTIVE: So, you think he's lying to you?

CLIENT: No, I'm certain that he's being honest. And I'm sure he would say the same to you and everyone else. But what I want to know is whether he's happy.

You can understand how the detective might find himself perplexed. What sort of investigation is he supposed to carry out, and what sorts of things would count as evidence? The reason this conversation seems a little odd is that we generally allow other people to be the authorities on their own happiness. If someone reports that they are happy, it would seem bizarre to bellow without hesitation, "No, you're not!" We might ask, "Are you sure you're happy?" Or maybe, "I thought this wasn't the sort of thing that would make you happy." Or even, "I don't like the person you've become that *this* is making you happy. I don't even know who you are anymore."

But we generally take people who are offering honest reports of their feelings to be authorities on whether they are happy.

The Ancient Greek ethicists, though, think that the detective has work to do and evidence to collect. Here's how our friend The Ancient Ethicist Detective might proceed:

DETECTIVE: Ah, yes, I see. Well, if it's alright, I'll need to get some basic information.

CLIENT: Sure.

DETECTIVE: So does he have any close friends I might talk to?

CLIENT: No, not really. I mean, people like him okay, I think. And he's got a few guys from work he drinks with occasionally. But he's not really a reliable friend, to be honest, so he doesn't seem to keep friends all that long.

DETECTIVE: Alright, well, is he generous?

CLIENT: Not really, no, at least not with money.

DETECTIVE: Yes, and, on that same topic, how much does he care about money?

CLIENT: Sometimes it seems like it's all he thinks about. He spends a lot of time managing our wealth, and to be honest, it has made us quite wealthy.

DETECTIVE: What about courage, self-control, and a desire for knowledge? Does he have any of those?

CLIENT: Sometimes, maybe? He likes the History Channel. But he denies climate science for reasons I don't fully understand. And it drives me crazy that he won't stand up for what he thinks is right, like last week when this guy at his birthday said something super offensive and he just chuckled awkwardly.

DETECTIVE: Any problems with anger?

CLIENT: He swears at the television a lot these days.

DETECTIVE: Good with misfortune?

CLIENT: He hates to lose.

DETECTIVE: Okay, one last question. Does your husband have an intense fear of death?

CLIENT: OMG, how did you know?!?!

DETECTIVE: Well, you don't need my services, since it's more than obvious that your spouse is miserable, whatever he says to the contrary.

Now, some of you might find yourself quite reasonably wondering whether anyone who fits this spouse's description actually insists on their happiness. I promise you that, yes, they do. And they will be very upset if you suggest otherwise.

What we have, then, are two conceptions of happiness which, for lack of flashier terms, we might call "subjective" and "objective." On a subjective account, the only thing that matters is the self-report of the person whose happiness is under scrutiny. If they say they're happy, then they're happy, regardless of any other life circumstances. Their report is incorrigible. On an objective account of happiness, while a self-report counts for something, it is only one data point among many in determining whether someone is in fact happy. There are other things on the list, and if those criteria are not sufficiently satisfied, then a person is not happy, whatever they claim.

I have been assuming, you might have noticed, that we actually do share a conception of happiness that we might consider "ours." I have called the objective account of the Greek philosophers "theirs" and the subjective account of happiness "ours." It's true that the objective account is theirs. But we might wonder whether the subjective account is really ours. Or, as a more direct appeal to you, the reader, is it yours?

Many people are very uncomfortable with the idea that happiness has objective features, often for good reason. The objective account could easily prove socially awkward and possibly dangerous. On a personal level, it would be very painful to hear from someone you love that they don't think you're happy. I think it's only normal that it would sting to hear my friend say, "Oh, Emily, you are definitely, definitely not happy. Look at yourself, will you?!" By the same token, I'm not chomping at the bit to notify a friend that their attitudes and choices have made them miserable. In fact, that seems like a very good way to lose a friend.

A less personal reason to resist the objective account of happiness is that it can be, and often has been, morally pernicious. The list the ancient detective ran through above was largely benign (in fact, it's pretty much an Epicurean list): friends, a generous spirit, fairness, self-control, courage, good-spirits, resilience, love of the truth, equanimity about death, etc. But what if the list included things like being physically attractive, college-educated, able-bodied, or wealthy? Suddenly the objective account of happiness doesn't just unsettle our confidence that we are happy—it becomes a weapon in the arsenal of elitism. Anyone who adopts an objective theory of happiness, then, needs to show why each item on the list is a genuine source of human flourishing against which we should be willing to measure ourselves. It might be better not to even try developing such a list for fear of causing lasting damage.

Despite these concerns, I think most people are more objective about happiness than they let on. One way this comes out, to borrow an example from the philosopher Richard Kraut, is when we wish new parents future happiness for their child.[1] We are not simply wishing that their child will feel good however she lives her life, even if she passes her days as a friendless narcissist who sells drugs to children. Wishing someone happiness comes with rich details that include things like healthy relationships, virtuous actions, and meaningful pursuits. This is even more clear when we imagine happiness for our own children.

There is a story from Book I of Herodotus that does a good job of illustrating another reason we might be more objective than we think. Solon, renowned for his sagely wisdom, was chosen to write the Athenian constitution. After he finished this important legislative task, he decided it was time to take a well-deserved vacation. During his travels, he came across Croesus, the fabulously rich King of Persia, who was weighing the option of entering a war to expand his empire. Croesus, excited to be in the company of someone so wise, got the bright idea of asking Solon to name the happiest human being, clearly expecting Solon to reply, "You, Croesus, of course! No contest!" Unfortunately for Croesus, he didn't even make Solon's medal stand.

Setting aside the details of Solon's answers, which are interesting in their own right, note that the question itself seems to make complete sense to us. Our initial response is not, "Well that's an absurd question, Croesus! Everyone is just as happy as they think they are!" We are curious about what Solon has to say. Answering Croesus' question, though, requires that we subscribe to some modicum of the objective account of happiness. The only vantage point from which a person can reasonably critique or rank anything is by assuming some sort of standard against which to measure it. If everyone is right about happiness ("Happiness is whatever you say it is, Croesus!"), then all grounds for further discussion disappear. For what it's worth, the story does not end well for Croesus because his desire for wealth, power, and territory lead to the fall of his empire and household.

So that's all well and good, you might think. Perhaps most of us are somewhat objective about happiness after all. Maybe selfish and friendless people who scream at the television and deny the truth are not terribly happy because we would not wish such lives for ourselves or our children. We can imagine far happier lives if asked to provide a rank ordering.

But wait, wait, wait! Epicurus thinks that happiness is a pleasant mental state characterized by the absence of anxiety, so doesn't Epicurus have a *subjective* account of happiness? He thinks happiness is a feeling, and feelings seem like paradigm examples of subjectivity. Think back to the first part of the detective example. This time, instead of happiness, supply "free of anxiety."

DETECTIVE: And what kind of work are you hoping I can do
    for you?
CLIENT: Well, see, I need someone to tell me whether my spouse
    is free of anxiety.
DETECTIVE: And have you asked him whether he's free of
    anxiety?
CLIENT: Sure, and he says he is. He says he's got no anxiety at all.
DETECTIVE: So, you think he's lying to you?
CLIENT: No, I'm certain that he's being honest. And I'm sure he
    would say the same to you and everyone else. But what I want
    to know is whether he's free of anxiety.

It might seem that the detective again has nothing to investigate. We feel our own pain and anxiety in a way that other people cannot, and that might seem to make us authorities on whether we are in pain or anxious. If happiness simply *is* the absence of anxiety, and we report that we're not feeling any anxiety, then doesn't that end the conversation?

Epicurus thinks the same questions are relevant. For Epicurus, being friendless, angry, willfully ignorant, and selfish are simply manifestations of anxiety that is lurking below the surface. Look closely over a period of time, he says, and you will find that such people are never secure in themselves or in the world, whatever they tell you or themselves to the contrary. Vice, especially in the long term, is horribly painful and psychologically disfiguring. Managing the fear and anger that drive aggressive, cowardly, self-centered, and willfully ignorant actions is like keeping check on a beast whose only desire is to eat you.

Let's set aside for a little while whether he's right about the anxious unhappiness of the morally vicious, though I think he's basically spot on. Either way, that is not really what is most at stake for you, my readers, at least in your own lives. I take it that you are all largely decent people! So, the more pressing question is whether and how Epicurus thinks decent people can make themselves less anxious and thereby happier. First, we explore the role of pleasure in a good life, and then we take a cold, honest, and unflinching look at our desires.

4 | NATURAL HEDONISM

Epicurus considers it obvious that we, like every other animal, pursue pleasure and avoid pain by nature. The point requires no rational demonstration—we observe it in other animals and feel it in ourselves. We have never asked for a reasoned argument that fire feels hot and snow feels cold. We just feel it. Epicurus considers it likewise self-evident that pleasure and pain serve as the motivational starting points for all sentient creatures. Torquatus, the Epicurean spokesperson in Cicero's *On Moral Ends*, puts it this way:

> Every animal as soon as it is born seeks pleasure and rejoices in it, while shunning pain as the highest evil and avoiding it as much as possible. This is behavior that has not yet been corrupted, when nature's judgment is pure and whole. Hence [Epicurus] denies there is any need for justification or debate as to why pleasure should be sought, and pain shunned.[1]

The desire for pleasure and an aversion to pain come as standard operating equipment in animals. Epicurus, though, thinks the greatest pleasure is tranquility, a stable psychological state characterized by the presence of pleasure and the absence of pain. That we want tranquility by nature does not seem self-evident, so it might require something more closely resembling an argument. This, too, Epicurus concludes from observation, in particular of animals from their earliest stages, "when nature's judgment is pure and whole."

Picture a human infant cast screaming from the womb into the great hurly-burly of this world, red with rage. It is hungry, over-stimulated, and suddenly very cold and uncomfortable. And all these horrible sounds! As Lucretius puts it, a human newborn is like "a shipwrecked sailor tossed ashore by savage waves" that finds itself "naked, speechless, and utterly helpless." And "how it fills the place with its woeful wailings!"[2] What it wants, and what we want to give it, is whatever will chill that baby out. It needs sustenance, a warm embrace, snuggles, music, the sound of the tap running, to be bounced around, a soft hat. Epicurus thinks that this brute de-sire for secure comfort never leaves us. An infant who lacks foun-dational security struggles to experience easy joys, and Epicurus thinks the same is true for humans at all stages.

The Epicureans and their chief rivals, the Stoics, call this a "Cradle Argument," according to which we can read the funda-mental motivation of a human being from observing its early, un-corrupted state. Epicurus thinks the "Cradle Argument" shows us that infants want freedom from pain, as well as the assorted pleasures consistent with maintaining that tranquil state. Adults, then, are essentially infants grown large and intelligent, facing an immensely more complex world, now largely responsible for pro-viding that precious and pleasant secure state for ourselves. Cicero reports that the Stoics, by contrast, think that "as soon as it is born," an infant "is concerned with itself, and takes care to pre-serve itself."[3] I have admittedly not met any self-preserving infants.

Epicurus advances a bolder claim here than you might at first think. It makes sense that pleasure feels good, and that pain feels bad, and we do often choose pleasures and avoid pains. No controversy there. Epicurus, though, thinks that *all* our actions ultimately aim at our own pleasure. Epicurus is what we will call a "psychological hedonist" because he thinks that we always choose what we think will provide us the most pleasure overall. We have one fundamental motivation—pursuing pleasure. He writes that pleasure is "the starting point for every choice and avoidance."[4] As he thinks the greatest pleasure is freedom from pain and anxiety, he can restate our motivation as pain avoidance: "We do everything for the sake of being neither in pain nor in terror."[5] Cicero puts the point as follows: "Pride of place he gives to what he claims nature herself approves, namely pleasure and pain. For him these explain our every act of pursuit and avoidance."[6] Our every action.

But that seems, at least on the face of it, insane. Consider some of your most recent actions. In the past few hours, you have likely done many things. Perhaps you washed the dishes, opened a bottle of wine, answered some work emails, talked a friend through a crisis, ate an ice cream sandwich, turned off your mind to binge-watch a show. Now you are taking at least a moment to peruse the contents of this book. Each action foreclosed other options. Your reading this book means you are not currently strolling through the night. If I asked you to explain your motivations for these assorted actions, how might you respond?

It would make sense for you to say that you opened a bottle of wine and watched a television show because it was pleasant, but that you washed the dishes reluctantly and resented writing to your boss in what should be your spare time. Sure, you allow yourself to choose what pleases you when possible, but other times, far more often than you would like, you must act from a sense of obligation. In these cases, duty hovers over your shoulder like a scold reminding you that if you always acted for pleasure, especially for the greatest pleasure on offer, the dishes would eventually smell of rot. You might be watching the sun set in Greece, but you would be doing it without a job.

Epicurus denies there are two competing motives at war with one another—pleasure and duty. That's not because he wants to convince you that action done from duty is actually pleasant, like you're foolishly overlooking the joy of dutifully mowing the lawn or changing diapers. It's the Stoics who encourage finding joy in acting from duty. The Epicureans deny that we act from duty at all. If you think you're acting from the motive of duty, you are incorrect. But again, how can this be?! Epicurus needs to show that we choose even the unpleasant actions, like cleaning up vomit, from the motive of pleasure-seeking.

A distinction might help. We often pursue pleasure "directly," in the sense that our path to pleasure appears free and clear, and we choose the unimpeded pleasure of the moment. Sometimes an unalloyed pleasure is right there in front of us, and Epicurus considers it well-worth choosing. Epicureanism's commitment to savoring the joys of leisure is part of what distinguishes it from more austere philosophies. Harmless pleasures within easy reach are in fact the better choice in some circumstances.

Other times, we must pursue pleasure "indirectly," in the sense that we recognize that the only way to reach the city of pleasure is to pass through the hamlet of inconvenience or struggle. Direct pleasures are like low-hanging fruit. Indirect pleasures require deliberation with the future in mind, recognizing that some pain is a necessary part of the process. They require building a ladder to pick the fruit otherwise out of reach. That reluctant feeling of choosing displeasure for the sake of pleasure is, for Epicurus, a mark of "indirect hedonism" at work.

We can conjoin these two thoughts—that we seek a mature version of an infant's security and that we tolerate displeasure to build a secure foundation for varied, more sophisticated pleasures. Securing tranquility sometimes requires inconvenience, even pain, in the short-term. Work and practice can pay long-term dividends in the kind of pleasures that make life joyful. Both security and joyful pleasure occasionally require us to choose pains for a greater payoff.

For example, Epicurus thinks humans benefit from the pleasant security of being a member of a community of friends bonded by trust and mutual support. In fact, nothing diminishes our anxiety more than a community of trustworthy and supportive friends.[7] Maintaining good standing in a community of that sort, though, requires that we respect agreements and demonstrate a willingness to sacrifice for others. Without trustworthy friends, we cannot experience the secure confidence of mutual protection against peril or fully appreciate the anxiety-free joys of time spent together at leisure. Such friendships depend on a willingness to sacrifice for the sake of long-term stability and joy.

In the same vein, we work through long hours of study so that we can experience the pleasant confidence that results from replacing confusion with understanding. We shoulder physical burdens because that gives us confidence that our strength will help us meet unexpected challenges, but also because it can help us survey beauty from the summit of a mountain. Our struggle with foreign languages makes it possible to communicate with people otherwise beyond our comprehension. In short, we willingly do painful or challenging things for two sorts of pleasure—a pleasant peace of mind and, that having been secured, the unalloyed pleasures that prudence endorses.[8] No need for duty, then, when the strategic pursuit of secure pleasure explains it all.

For a practiced, more sagely Epicurean, some exertions can produce their own kind of current mental pleasure that distracts from the pain or inconvenience itself. Epicurus thinks, as we'll explore later, that reflection on past pleasure or anticipation of future pleasure can help counteract pains. But Epicureans do not think painful activities themselves are particularly fun. They need not say, "I am pleased to be cleaning up the rotten trash that the raccoons spilled all over the deck!" It's enough to say, "Well, won't we feel better when we get this cleaned up, and won't it make a good story!" People do the dishes together not only because it is faster, but also to distract from the inconvenience and enjoy one another's company. We can gain some mental pleasure from anticipating the pleasure of completing a difficult project and by remembering how many pleasures our life contains overall, this being a blip in the radar.

Epicurus, then, thinks we are all very much hedonists, like it or not. That presents another problem, though. Someone might say, "Look, if I'm really always pursuing pleasure, then why am I so often displeased?" For Epicurus, that we are all motivated by pleasure does not entail that we are particularly *good* at hedonism. As a "psychological hedonist," Epicurus considers it a point of psychology that all our actions aim at pleasure. Nevertheless, we can be very bad at hitting the target, at pursuing the tranquility and joy we seek. Epicurus thinks we go wrong because we set out to get what we want in life—happiness—without art or strategy, often imprudently choosing whatever pleasure is closest and easiest. We fall into the easy habit of unreflective "direct hedonism," rather than playing the long game of "indirect hedonism," which requires deliberation and some measure of inconvenience.

For Epicurus, hedonistic prudence is the crowning art of living well. Departing from a long line of his philosophical predecessors, Epicurus claims that "prudence is a more valuable thing than philosophy."[9] Aristotle, for example, considered theoretical philosophy the crowning human achievement, practical reasoning always the second fiddle.[10] Epicurean prudence is a calculating art that conjoins a knowledge of human psychology and the natural world with a keen eye for the future consequences of competing options. It requires understanding what will provide human beings the secure pleasure we naturally desire. So, while we are all "psychological hedonists," Epicurus thinks we often fail as "prudential hedonists." We do pleasure wrong.

There are at least two significant ways we mess up the prudential calculation. The first is that we discount the future, granting the nearby pleasure or pain greater resonance than the long-term pleasure or pain that results. Take a standard case of perception. Imagine that we need to find higher ground because the authorities have warned of dangerous flooding. If we have not learned how perception at a distance works, we might climb something big nearby rather than trekking to the mountain that appears small from where we stand. What is nearby seems both bigger and undemanding, but we would be safer by taking a walk.

When distance is measured in time, future pains can seem smaller if we fail to respect the distorting effects of temporal distance. We choose the extra drink now despite the hangover tomorrow. We know that unnecessary purchases now can result in avoidable debt nourished on the toxic fertilizer of compound interest. We burn through carbon for trivial goods, knowing those choices poison the planet and the diverse and beautiful creatures that occupy it. In short, we choose the nearby, direct pleasure and usher in the larger, later-arriving pain, which looks pretty small from here.

In the other direction, we discount the size of the future pleasures that can only result from choosing current pains, which seem especially painful in the moment. We recognize that exercise is good for the heart and mind, that acknowledging and fighting an addiction would improve our lives, how good it would feel to possess a new skill or have completed a project. Yet sometimes we so resent the effort necessary to develop the talent or craft the project that we convince ourselves the greater, more satisfying benefit is smaller than it really is.

Epicurus seems to characterize many prudential miscalculations as just this kind of visual distortion. In *Vatican Saying* 16, he writes that "no one who sees what is bad chooses it." Instead, they are "lured by it as being good" by comparison to something that appears worse, and then they are "caught in the snare." In other words, they think tomorrow's hangover will hurt, but not as bad as not drinking now. Or they think healthy air is good, but not as good as the stuff we get from burning coal. If we see things correctly, we do not choose the more harmful thing. We avoid "the snare."

Our failure to weigh considerations accurately with the known future in mind is made worse by the fact that we are often not that great at recognizing the results of our current actions to begin with. It is not merely that we focus on what seems bigger now, disregarding the higher ground in the distance. Sometimes we do not even look at what lies ahead. The link between drinking and hangovers should be obvious to anyone who has experienced both, and young people often learn all too quickly about how credit card interest works. Long-term results of other current pleasures, though, are not manifest to all, sometimes because social forces actively encourage us to overlook or ignore those connections.

For example, Epicurus thinks we struggle to recognize the deleterious effects of greed for money, power, success, and admiration because we are so often sold on their benefits. The riches and recognition from long hours at work look great now, but we might find ourselves with grown children who resent us because we never got to know them. Power gleams until we get it and realize we have compromised our integrity to pander for a status that we worry we could lose or have stolen from us at any moment. We might win money and fame from hamming for YouTube subscribers, only to discover that we have turned over the rudder of our life to the whims of whatever it turns out millions of other people want to watch.

Discerning and measuring the long-term consequences of indulging some powerful desires is more challenging because the error is so pervasive and so few people encourage us to look out into the distance. That sex can lead to pregnancy is commonplace. That greed is inconsistent with satisfaction is not often acknowledged. Challenging the social understanding of what counts as most desirable and pleasant requires forethought and a commitment to clear-eyed assessment and measurement. The peer pressure of youth too easily transforms itself into the adult groupthink of ladder-climbing, envy, and conspicuous consumption to mask an insecurity we often deny.

Epicurus thinks we also overlook that failing to study science, evaluate our religious beliefs, or confront our mortality can diminish our prospects for long-term, secure pleasure. When we think about it, though, that sounds right. Denying climate science will only unleash the long-prophesied fire next time. The inconvenience of wearing a mask or getting a vaccine during a pandemic can pay dividends in lives saved. Putting fluoride in the water helps keep the teeth in your kid's head. Focusing on justice and happiness in the afterlife could tempt us to delay seeking justice and happiness now. Failing to confront and accept our mortality might leave us unprepared to make important decisions about our medical care or protect the long-term interests of our family.

Prudent Epicureans, then, need to stop discounting the future they can already see with great clarity. As a greater challenge, they must develop their capacities for predicting a future more difficult to discern and correctly measure. Epicurus has lots of advice to offer based on his own understanding of what kinds of desires and pleasures benefit human beings, and that's where we're headed in the next chapter.

You might start to wonder, though, why this brand of hedonism should strike anyone as psychologically or ethically controversial. If hedonism can consistently maintain that we do everything for pleasure *and* explain why we should go to the gym, clean the kitchen, weather the onslaught of a toddler's tantrum, patiently listen to our partner complain about work, and put in the hours to practice a foreign language, then why do so many philosophers, theologians, and neo-Stoics hate hedonism?

Well, the first thing to note is that any knock-down critique of Epicureanism on this front requires showing that "psychological hedonism" is false. If Epicureanism's opponents maintain that we should at least occasionally pursue something ultimately opposed to our own pleasure, they must show that we *can* act for entirely altruistic, other-regarding reasons.[11] I cannot rightly demand that you do something impossible, that you jump out the window and fly unassisted. Human beings are not sparrows. Epicurus might respond that humans simply cannot choose virtuous or admirable actions for reasons not ultimately rooted in their own pleasure.

The critics do admittedly have good reason to push back against psychological hedonism. In particular, it might seem that hedonism cannot explain why people choose some emblematically virtuous actions that they know will lead to their death or a significant measure of pain (for example, joining the military, running into a burning building to save children in peril, standing up to a tyrant, jumping on a grenade). Some of the most praiseworthy actions do seem to set aside any long-term calculation about one's own pleasure and security for the simple reason that they result in death. Cicero who generally preferred Stoicism objects that psychological hedonism cannot make sense of these extreme sacrifices, so psychological hedonism must be false.

Opponents also claim that Epicurus' psychological hedonism leaves him without good reason to prohibit injustices like theft and even murder if those injustices produce greater pleasures or conduce to tranquility. In other words, if injustice is expedient to my own pleasure, then Epicurus seems to encourage, even require, injustice. Epicurus has answers to these objections about virtue and self-sacrifice that we will explore in the chapter on Epicurean courage and justice, but they are certainly legitimate worries.

Before closing, I want to call attention to another possible conflict, not between hedonism and virtue, but between hedonism and prudence. Specifically, the hedonistic calculus might vary widely depending on a person's particular social or psychological circumstances, which could make it difficult for us to arrive at shared principles of good judgment. This comes out most forcefully when people must make decisions under scarcity or when it is difficult or impossible to reliably predict the actions of others with whom we interact.

Consider a famous experiment that you can try at home with your very own child or your rose-colored memory of the child you once were. In the original experiment, an investigator offered children two options—a marshmallow now, or two marshmallows if they hold off eating the first marshmallow until the investigator returns from a trip outside the room.[12] The children are left behind to contemplate the decision. All things being equal, choosing to wait for double the marshmallow is the clearly the prudent choice. Yet the single marshmallow right now in front of us exercises a powerful allure. By hook or by crook, many kids refrain from eating the marshmallow, some of them hilariously prodding and sniffing it without consuming it. Some of them close their eyes and sing. The other kids just eat the first marshmallow.

The experiment was initially thought to show that children with greater self-restraint would succeed in an adult life that requires powers of prudence and self-regulation. The conjecture was reasonable, and they were right that many one-marshmallow kids struggled in adult life. But later researchers who sought to replicate the study introduced a wrinkle. Maybe the one marshmallow kids were in some fashion being prudent, even though they lost out on a marshmallow. Some children have reasons to lack confidence in the investigator's promise of a second marshmallow, possibly grounded in formative experiences of empty promises or unexpected misfortune. A track record of disappointment resulting from unlucky or untrustworthy adults makes it reasonable to eat one marshmallow while you still can because the second might never arrive and even the first might be taken away in the interim.[13] Immediate indulgence becomes prudent pleasure-seeking as a general rule of thumb, even though it might produce bad long-term consequences in terms of marshmallow maximation and life success.[14]

Many of these one-marshmallow kids bring out a worry for Epicurean hedonism. Namely, successful prudence depends on being able to predict the future, and our predictions often depend on the rationality of trusting others in light of our past and current circumstances. While some people have reason to trust others and have confidence that the future will reward their current efforts, others do not. That lack of trust skews their calculations in a way that is simultaneously prudent and, in some meaningful sense, not in their long-term interest. If you have little reason to trust the banks because bank policies disadvantage people like you, then you lack good reason to invest. But if you don't invest, you don't get the benefits of investing.[15]

The most pressing challenge for Epicurean hedonism, then, might not be accounting for virtuous self-sacrifice, but that it leaves itself open to cases where it is prudent to choose something not in our long-term best interest. Such cases arise most often when we lack confidence in others, or when we face conditions of scarcity or poverty. I think that is one reason Epicurus spends so much time talking about mutual trust among close friends and members of a community. An Epicurean must spend time reflecting on how to establish trust, definitely with a few close friends, but ideally in the larger community. Otherwise, successful hedonism for individuals could require what looks from the outside like objective imprudence.

We will revisit these concerns later. Next, though, let's turn to the driving force behind our pleasure-seeking deliberations and choices—desire. Epicurus thinks the first step to improving prudence and diminishing our anxiety is getting a grip on our desires. We should transform ourselves into botanical taxonomists of desire, listing, examining, and classifying them so that we know what to nourish, prune, and root out.

5 | WHAT DO YOU WANT?

Epicurus thinks the key to unlocking our tranquility is a sober evaluation of our desires. Now, you might be thinking that a tidy solution to anxiety would be to adopt a scorched earth approach to desire. If desires produce anxiety, then just stop all that anxiety in its tracks by wanting as little as possible! Some philosophers encourage that kind of austerity, but Epicurus does not. He thinks extreme parsimony is as worrisome as excessive indulgence.[1]

Epicurus sorts desires into three categories: those we should embrace as necessary for our life and happiness, those it's fine to have if we don't get invested in whether we satisfy them, and those we should cut out of our soul root and branch. In his terms, there are "natural and necessary" desires, "natural and unnecessary" desires, and "unnatural and unnecessary" desires. For our purposes, we'll call them necessary desires, extravagant desires, and corrosive desires.[2]

Unfortunately, despite the central role of this taxonomy of desires in Epicurean philosophy, Epicurus himself offers very little in the way of examples. He does, as we'll see below, lay out a few distinctive features of each category of desire, but he doesn't say, "Ah, yes, well the desire for a tasty beer goes in this box here, the desire to be a CEO goes over here, the desire not to outlive one's children goes there, the desire to feel safe from gun violence goes there, and the desire to philosophize goes right here." In this chapter, we'll use what Epicurus tells us about desire in general to lay the groundwork for the book's remaining discussions of specific desires.

Before we start digging desires out of the attics, closets, and basements of our soul, it's worth noting a few things about desires themselves. You might think of each desire as having an object, an intensity, and a likelihood of satisfaction. An "object" is the thing we want, for example a sandwich, pony, or turntable. We can further describe the object of our desire, for example, as an "excellent sandwich," a "spotted pony," or a "high-end turntable." The "intensity" of our desire indicates how much we want it, measured by things like the amount of time we spend fixating on it or its limiting effects on our other desires and actions.

The "likelihood of success" tracks our chances of getting the object of our desire. Given that the future is not in our hands, we often have very little idea whether we will get what we want, but we can usually tell a longshot from a slam dunk. Humans even have the perverse ability to desire something we know is impossible, like for someone not to have died. The likelihood of success on that front is a bitter zero.

In addition to object, intensity, and likelihood of satisfaction, our desires include some prediction about how we will feel when we get what we want. In most cases, we think we will feel great! A lifetime worth of experience tells us, though, that we might be disappointed. Cotton candy was one of the first memorable letdowns of my early life. It was made of sugar and looked like clouds at sunset, but it was full of false promise. Some children, I'm told, would gladly eat cotton candy for breakfast.

Such disappointment continues into adult life. We nurse crushes for people who turn out to be self-absorbed and shallow bores. We think a new house will make us happy, only to discover that we are now just the same person living in a different, usually more expensive space. In some sense, we learn that what we thought we wanted was not what we wanted after all. So, we desire not only that we get something, but that we be pleased when we get it.

Lastly, we have desires about our desires. Unfortunately, what we desire and what we *want* to desire are often painfully at odds. In my experience, a significant percentage of the people seeking relationship advice on the internet say either "I wish I didn't want to sleep with my co-worker" or "I wish I wanted to sleep with my spouse." On the less romantically dramatic front, we want not to desire what we cannot afford, not to desire another drink, not to covet what others have. We want to want to go to work, attend the opera, eat vegetables, or give to charity.

In sum, a sense of reflective satisfaction about the objects, intensity, and likelihood of satisfying our desires, as well as confidence that we will enjoy their satisfaction, is difficult to come by. If you have already reached mental quietude on such matters, then perhaps this is not the book for you.

With this rough conception of desire in hand, let's turn first to Epicurus' discussion of necessary desires, then to the extravagant and corrosive desires. In his *Letter to Menoeceus*, Epicurus claims that there are three ways a desire might be necessary: "Some are necessary for happiness and some for freeing the body from troubles and some for life itself."[3] Examples of desires that are necessary "for life itself" and for "freeing the body from troubles" are clear—food, drink, clothes, basic life-saving medicine, and shelter. We suffer pain when we lack such things, and left without them long enough, we die.

It's harder to think of obvious examples of desires that are "necessary for happiness." Worse, the criterion just seems to bring us back where we started, to restate the question as if it were an answer. What desires do we need to satisfy to achieve happiness? The ones "necessary for happiness." Epicurus must think that we can get a sense of the desires necessary for happiness by reflecting on his big-picture project, which equates happiness with freedom from anxiety. What, then, do we need for tranquility in addition to the things that keep us alive and our body functioning within the bounds of tolerable pain? A more austere philosopher might think that would be enough for tranquility!

And it probably would be enough for any other animal. As we know, Epicurus grounds his hedonism in his empirical account of human psychology, or humankind's distinctive "nature." Humans, like other animals, hate pain and pursue pleasure, so we share with them the necessary desires that keep us alive and free of unnecessary physical pain. Unlike most animals, though, humans have abilities and needs that arise from our rational capacities and our particular social nature. We see ourselves as beings in time with a past, a future, and a present. We can deliberate about our short and long-term aims, and we can communicate our needs to others using speech and symbols. Most importantly, humans are prone to a deep sense of puzzlement about the world that gives rise to a desire to understand our experience, and we depend on social interactions for our rational and social development.

A full belly, peak hydration, and a dry cave do not suffice for mediating the anxieties that stem from these refined rational capacities. If natural puzzlement about how the world works counts as anxiety, and Epicurus thinks it often does, then we need to figure out how to abate that anxiety. If we have the capacity to use our powers of practical deliberation to minimize future anxiety, then we need to hone those skills. If we need to learn life-lessons from others while not feeling endangered in the process, then we need experienced and reliable elders, friends, and acquaintances.

For Epicurus, then, psychological tranquility for human beings requires, among other things, some rudimentary understanding of how the world and human psychology work, a capacity to deliberate about the future in light of our experience of the past, a community of trustworthy friends, and a commitment to virtues (especially those that build trust). The desires "necessary for human happiness" are those that, when satisfied, can produce tranquility for beings with a human nature. Note, though, that our list of necessary desires has now grown quite lengthy.

You might find yourself tempted to get off the necessary desire train here for a couple of reasons. Perhaps some of those desires sound "extravagant" rather than necessary. Take, for example, friends. Someone might agree that friends can produce great pleasures, but are friends *necessary* for happiness? Does happiness really depend on regularly taking time for study and reflection? Surely, you might reasonably think, happiness doesn't rise or fall on one's appreciation of the central principles of physics! In a similar vein, you might worry that the more requirements we put on happiness, the less likely we are to achieve it. If the things that happiness requires lie outside of our control, then happiness becomes a matter of luck and good fortune rather than something in our power to achieve. As the list grows longer, and the items less accessible, our chances of happiness diminish.

Epicurus would not be troubled by such concerns. He thinks the objects of necessary desires, at least on his conception of "necessary," are (in most circumstances) within reach if we and our friends spend our time and energy effectively. Unlike extravagant or corrosive desires, necessary desires do not require, in Epicurus' words, "intense effort."[4] Instead, Epicurus claims that

> He who has learned the limits of life knows that it is easy to provide that which removes the feeling of pain owing to want and make one's whole life perfect. So there is no need for things that involve struggle.[5]

To put that in normal words, understanding the difference between what we need and do not need produces two good results: (1) getting what we need becomes easier, and (2) we achieve satisfaction by realizing happiness requires nothing more, though we will enjoy other pleasures should they come along without anxiety and struggle.

As we will see, Epicurus thinks the objects of necessary desires are on offer in their most basic forms if we avoid distractions, especially if we join forces in communal effort. Making trustworthy and genuine friends, gaining a decent understanding of the world and human psychology, developing virtuous habits, and taming our negative attitudes are all possible if we prioritize those aims. Using our terminology from above, proper pursuit of necessary desires has an exceptionally high likelihood of success.

And yet . . . and yet . . . we struggle and feel unsatisfied, confused, or lonely. Epicurus, then, needs to explain how we can consistently fail to get things we all say we want if, as he claims, those desires are relatively easy to satisfy. Again, it's not that we do not want good things. If I asked whether you want genuine and supportive friendships that you maintain through your adult years, and you replied, "No, I only want a lot of strangers to follow my social media account," I would worry for you. Most of us readily admit that we want to set aside our phones so that we can explore our world and enjoy meaningful human interaction.

Epicurus thinks that if we're honest with ourselves, though, it's more that *we want to want* greater understanding, freedom from our phones, time to cultivate and maintain close friendships, etc. Or, to be more precise, we wish our desire for these things were more powerful than our desire for less important things. Epicurus might say, "Now, of course you want to walk out the door to enjoy the beautiful fall afternoon with your friends, and it's in fact quite easy to walk out the door, but people often do not leave because they want to stay alone indoors on their phone more."

In most cases, our failure to satisfy the desires necessary for happiness results from giving too much time and attention to the other desires, the ones we have labeled extravagant and corrosive. We inflate the importance of our extravagant desires and give rein to the corrosive ones, the two joining forces to crowd out the necessary desires we rightly cherish. Pursuing the corrosive desires in particular exhausts and terrorizes us. To get a sense of how this works, let's turn to Epicurus' general discussion of extravagant and corrosive desires.

Extravagant desires, the ones Epicurus calls "natural and un-necessary," are not always bad. The objects of extravagant desires can contribute genuine joy to a tranquil life, though they are not at all necessary for happiness. Most scholars agree that Epicurus thinks extravagant desires are usually for fancier or more specific versions of the necessary desires. For example, instead of a bread and water, you might want a gourmet sandwich and a good IPA. Instead of basic shelter, you might want a house with a porch swing near a body of water not susceptible to flooding. You might want to live in a particular part of the country, get a top-notch educa-tion, or have earth-shattering sex. As we know by now, Epicurus has nothing against good sandwiches, hoppy beer, excellent educa-tion, great sex, or mild and sunny climates.

Unfortunately, we often let extravagant desires run amok, granting them oversized importance in our deliberations, letting them dominate our mental economy at the expense of fulfilling our necessary desires. We move far away from friends, family, and aging parents so that we can live in a popular town. We work jobs we hate to finance the lifestyle that we have very little time to enjoy with the few friends we have. We go to restaurants that are too loud and popular for a long and intimate discussion with friends. Pursuing the objects of extravagant desires can come at the sizeable cost of time better spent on our relationships or on developing our capacities for understanding ourselves and the world.

Unchecked extravagant desires can also sap the joy of extrava-gance itself. As Epicurus puts it, "those who least need extravagance enjoy it most."[6] The person who eats great food on occasion appre-ciates it more fully than the person who indulges often, takes it for granted, or expects it. Too much experience with extravagance also risks raising our standards to such a level that most things prove disappointing. One of the unfortunate ramifications of our penchant for measuring and ranking extravagances is that few things are ever entirely satisfactory. We have all spent time with the most tedious bores of consumption, some of whom are at times regrettably ourselves.

Another distinctive feature of extravagant desires, as opposed to necessary desires, is that they are more likely to have varying effects on individuals. For some of us, otherwise benign extravagances give rise to damaging addictions. A good cocktail for one person is a potential life-wrecker for an alcoholic. The idle pleasure of a video game for one person turns into a relationship-destroying time-suck for another. For that reason, our response to extravagant desires might vary due to individual disposition. While we can all prudently desire clean water, we cannot all prudently desire alcohol. As long as we are content to indulge our extravagant desires when appropriate, Epicurus thinks they can for the most part stick around, idling away in our mind's background and producing great joy if their objects become available.

The corrosive desires must go. While both necessary and extravagant desires earn Epicurus' endorsement as "natural," corrosive desires are both unnatural and unnecessary. Recall that when Epicurus says "unnatural" here, he does not mean something like "artificial." Instead, he means contrary to our nature, or not conducive to human well-being. While Epicurus recognizes both necessary and unnecessary natural desires, he thinks all unnatural desires are unnecessary. Nothing contrary to our well-being is necessary, a claim we will critically evaluate throughout the book.

Unfortunately, Epicurus again gives very little by way of examples, but it's clear that corrosive desires must work against our tranquility by their very presence. We will explore individual corrosive desires in greater detail in future chapters, but for now it's helpful to mention some of their shared features. Epicurus thinks that corrosive desires take as their objects things that extend without natural limit—things about which someone might say "you can never have too much." For example, "you can never be too wealthy, too popular, or too powerful." One result of having limitless desires, though, is that those desires remain perpetually unsatisfied. People under the power of a corrosive desire always have an unfulfilled desire for more. What they want recedes into the distance, forever at least one step ahead.

The greater problem with corrosive desires is that their objects are usually highly unstable and require great effort. They are hard to get, difficult to maintain, and easy to lose. As such, anxiety attends them at every stage of getting, keeping, and increasing. Some of their objects, like youthful beauty, are by nature inevitably lost. The objects of corrosive desires are also competitive, and significant success usually requires, in less than elegant terms, screwing over competitors or abasing yourself to less than savory characters for power, gain, honor, or money. Corrosive desires transform people into bullies and lackeys.

Because the objects of corrosive desires come in degrees, people will also find themselves prone to comparing themselves against others, measuring themselves by metrics that give rise to envy or conceit. Epicurus calls attention to the dim prospects for genuine friendship and trust among bullies, lackies, cheaters, and those wracked by envy and resentment. Not to mention that being a lackey makes a person feel cheap, and cheaters are always at least a bit afraid of getting caught or suffering retaliation from those they cheat. Bullies fear encountering a bigger, stronger bully.

For these and other reasons, Epicurus thinks tranquility is out of reach when we give ourselves over to corrosive desires. What sort of things does Epicurus have in mind? The best examples, each of which we will explore in greater detail, are the desire for great personal wealth, power, and honor, as well as maximum profit and endless life. For Epicurus, when corrosive desires gain ascendency, we risk becoming slaves to whatever or whomever satisfies them, and we never reach satisfaction. Nothing we have, no matter how much we have, is ever enough.

The real work of Epicureanism, then, is cataloguing, organizing, and minding the store of our desires. Remember that Epicurus doesn't think happiness results from mere subtraction of corrosive desires. We must keep the store stocked with necessary items, which means devoting the time and energy we once expended in corrosive arenas to cultivating the prudence, habits of mind, knowledge, virtuous dispositions, and close relationships with like-minded people that make tranquility possible for creatures like us.

Epicurus would probably still be worth reading if he merely aimed to develop a plausible and insightful categorization of human desires. Epicureanism, though, is a philosophy for living well, not just a way of describing how we live. As we will see, Epicureanism offers practical advice and strategies for recognizing, fostering, and satisfying the necessary desires, while either developing healthy attitudes about extravagant desires or pruning them back entirely for the health of the plant. Corrosive desires are like a multi-headed beast munching away at the fresh green foliage of our well-being. That beast needs to be shown the door, whether kindly or by force, freeing us to devote our time and energy to getting what we really want—tranquility. For Epicurus, the first and most important step to tranquility is, it turns out, making friends.

6 | WHY CAN'T WE BE FRIENDS?

Epicurus loves friendship so much that he devotes some of his only florid prose to praising it, writing that "friendship dances around the world announcing to all of us that we must wake up to blessedness."[1] Reverting to his usual arid tone and style, he claims that "of the things which wisdom provides for the blessedness of one's whole life, by far the greatest is the possession of friends."[2] Friends do not merely contribute to one's happiness—they contribute the most. That seems about right to me.

Yet critics of Epicureanism claim that Epicureans cannot even be friends, or at least not good or true friends. In *On Moral Ends*, Cicero tells Torquatus, "The position you defend and the precepts you have been taught and espouse completely do away with friendship, however much Epicurus may, as he does, praise friendship to the skies."[3] Cicero concedes that Epicurus had many close, lifelong friends, but he thinks that only shows that Epicurus conducted his life in contravention of his own doctrines. Epicurus' flesh and blood friendships serve to refute his abstract philosophy. According to Cicero, someone who always looks out for their own pleasure and advantage will prove a fickle friend, ready to jettison the relationship the minute things become difficult or unpleasant. No dedicated hedonist, Cicero insists, can be a good friend.

To get a sense of Cicero's criticism, think of the two questions that risk casting any relationship into discomfort, even peril: "Why do you love me?" and "Can you help me move?" An Epicurean, it seems, must reply as follows: "The reason I love you is that this relationship is conducive to my overall pleasure and advantage, though I might eventually revise that assessment if you begin to produce more pain than pleasure," and "Yes, I will help you move, mainly because over the long term this inconvenience will lead to greater pleasure for me overall, especially should I myself need to move in the future." If either of those answers makes you uneasy, then you might find yourself sympathetic to Cicero.

Epicurus, though, could be tempted to turn the biographical critique around on Cicero, who formed and abandoned many relationships during his political career to gain power or save his life. While I'm not fond of using a person's life to critique their philosophy, in this case Cicero started it. Cicero's Epicurean friend Atticus was perhaps his only lifelong reliable friend, Cicero referring to him as a "second brother." It was Atticus to whom Cicero turned for support when his beloved daughter Tullia died. Atticus invited him to stay at his villa, where Cicero spent much of his time in the library reading and writing about philosophy to distract himself from his grief. While many of Cicero's Stoic friends derided, even openly mocked, his grief over something so trivial as the death of a daughter, Atticus gave him respite.

If a single person's hypocrisy were enough to sink a philosophy, we would have no philosophies left. That one person fails only matters if it shows that no one can succeed. Remember, though, that Epicurus considers it impossible to act contrary to what we consider advantageous. He advocates psychological hedonism, which means that Cicero can't help forming friendships in pursuit of pleasure and avoidance of pain. The same is true for everyone. We have left the matter of psychological hedonism an unsettled question, chiefly because the question has yet to be settled empirically. But if Epicurus is correct that humans are psychological hedonists, then Cicero's criticism is a complaint against the natural constraints on being a human being rather than against Epicureanism itself.

Even if psychological hedonism were wrong, though, I think Epicurean friendships stand on their own merits as stable and long-lasting. Close Epicurean friendships are joyful and intimate, encourage self-growth, and offer reliable social support in times of need. Far from cheapening friendship, Epicureanism's account of human flourishing better explains why we need friends and of what sort. We need friends with whom we can gain trust, knowledge, security, shared personal reflection, and joy. Close Epicurean friendships are jointly secure attachments enriched by shared joys and a concern for each other's personal growth. At root, the guiding principle of Epicurean friendship is that *friends don't make friends anxious.*

There are two key features of a fundamentally sound Epicurean friendship—trust and a shared conception of what matters in life. That might sound a bit boring or austere. True, there's perhaps nothing so austere as a solid foundation, yet no one would want to build a house on anything else. The intimacy and joys of close friendships necessarily depend on bedrock trust and a shared understanding of what makes life go well. Without those things, we have at best a sub-par or volatile friendship, perhaps merely a relation to another person unworthy of the word "friendship" at all.

For Epicurus, the key indicator of trust is that friends inspire mutual "confidence." That we have confidence in a friend does not mean we feel confident that they will always remember our birthday or never be late to the party. We might have good friends whose driving or navigating skills fail to inspire any measure of confidence. Instead, Epicurean friends are confident that their friendship is secure and that they can rely on each other for support when it matters, especially in the times of crisis that inevitably arrive in life. In other words, not so much when you move house as when you grieve or face hard times.

While Epicurus thinks life and friendship present both brief and extended opportunities for joy and gratitude, he does not deny that misfortunes happen. Epicurus thinks the pain of misfortunes can be managed, but he thinks we can lose some things in life that cause unavoidable pain. Epicurus ties this point about managing inevitable misfortunes to friendship:

> The same understanding produces confidence about there being nothing terrible which is eternal or even long-lasting and has also realized that security amid even these limited bad things is most easily achieved through friendship.[4]

Epicurus, I think, overstates his case for the claim that none of life's harms are "long-lasting." Some harms last the rest of one's life, even though he might be correct that many significant harms are manageable or diminish over time. We will take up that question in the later chapter on misfortune. What matters for us here is that the best way to prepare for and make it through these misfortunes is to cultivate friendships marked by mutual trust and confidence.

It might sound like the Epicurean friend is needy or insecure, the sort of person constantly asking for assistance or reassurance. That's not what Epicurus has in mind. He thinks we do "not need utility from our friends so much as we need confidence concerning that utility."[5] We need to feel confident that they will be there if, though more likely when, we need them. Remember also that Epicureans have their own sense of what counts as a genuine need—the objects of necessary desires—so friends prove willing to step up when a friend's necessary desires are unmet. When a person fails to inspire confidence of assistance in the pains of life, then they fail to meet the first key requirement of friendship—trust. If, in turn, we fail to provide that for our friends, we are not well-qualified for Epicurean friendship.

Reliability is not merely the willingness to show up at the hospital. Epicureans respect and care for each other by following through on their promises, not engaging in gossip and slander, and, as we explore below, not entering or leaving a relationship because of a corrosive desire for status, power, beauty, or money. Developing these shared capacities for practical and emotional support, as well as confidence that the friendship does not depend on either party's ability to satisfy corrosive desires, makes an Epicurean friendship run. When trust falls away, then so does (or at least Epicurus thinks so should) the friendship.

Note that Epicurus thinks relationships of trust happen within communal networks of trust. If we break trust with one friend, and our other friends discover we are the sort of person to break trust, then we likewise diminish their confidence in our genuine, reliable friendship. Epicurus claims that a friend will even suffer death to avoid betraying a friend because otherwise their "entire life will be confounded and utterly upset from a lack of confidence."[6] Betraying a friend is worse than death because we lose not only the confidence of our friend, but also of our community.

The second component of a stable and meaningful Epicurean friendship—a shared conception of what is good and valuable in life—reinforces trust. Epicurus does not mean that we and our friends must desire exactly the same things, as if we need to share our friend's relish in eating oysters, their love of dance clubs, or their taste for avant-garde cinema. Those are extravagant desires, and not sharing specific extravagant desires does not undermine the ability of a friend to inspire confidence. As it happens, friends will often share many extravagant desires, but it's far more important for them to share the same *attitude* toward extravagant desires—namely that their objects are fun, but not necessary for happiness or friendship.

A friend who sneers at people who lack a taste for foreign cinema transforms what should be merely an extravagant desire for a certain kind of pleasure into a corrosive desire for status and exclusion. That sort of attitude reeks of the cultural and intellectual snobbery that Epicurus maligns, as we will see in a few chapters. People who treat extravagant desires as criteria for narrowing the field of friendship will often struggle to find friends at all, much less to form stable friendships. Only so many people like avant-garde cinema, and only so many of them inspire confidence as friends. The candidates for friendship could dwindle into an almost guaranteed loneliness. Worse, harnessing extravagant preferences to corrosive desires for status, power, taste, or attractiveness cracks friendship's foundation itself.

Epicurus could borrow a key component of his predecessor Aristotle's theoretical framework for friendship to show how corrosive desires destabilize friendships. For Aristotle, all friendships have explicit or implicit severance conditions that mirror the reasons the relationship was formed in the first place.[7] "Drinking buddies" are a paradigm case. While drinking buddies might enjoy many things together when drinking, the relationship began because of shared drinking and usually dissolves if one friend gives up alcohol. Nothing sorts drinking buddies from proper buddies like one person getting sober. The same goes for friendships based on mutual business advantage should one party become a drag on the business. In sum, Aristotle thinks that if the reason a person enters a relationship no longer holds, then the friendship will be dissolved, at least barring the discovery of a new reason for friendship.

For Epicurus, corrosive desires are fundamentally unstable, so friendships founded on or infected by corrosive desires are necessarily insecure. Recall that corrosive desires are "limitless," and they are unstable in the sense that their objects are difficult to attain and keep. "Cool" knows no limit, and neither does rich or beautiful. This feature of corrosive desires is often expressed by sentences like, "You can never be too rich," or "You can never be too beautiful." The objects of corrosive desires are scalar and comparative. Some people are richer, cooler, or more beautiful than others. Some objects, like being young and beautiful, are inevitably lost, despite all best efforts. Other objects are gained and lost, subject to the whims of fashion and fluctuations of public interest.

We are all familiar with the fact that allegiances among friends change with the tides in early youth because young people are insecure and focus excessively on coolness, attractiveness, and volatile power dynamics—the "queen-bees and the wannabees," both of them riddled with anxiety for different reasons.[8] I could probably catalogue the sadness, unkindness, even cruelty from this time in my life, but I suspect we can all call our own readily to mind. George Saunders has termed these "failures of kindness," but in some cases that term is a far too charitable euphemism.[9]

Truth is, many adults never outgrow those junior high impulses, though they might be more adept at hiding their desires, even from themselves. We probably all know someone who casually ignores us socially who would come out of the woodwork with invitations and open arms if we grew in status, much like those long-lost relations who appear at the doorstep of lottery winners. We also know they would again cast us aside if that status diminished and someone else's star rose, whenever someone else more effectively fulfills their desire for status, wealth, or power. Epicureans must learn to see this status-dependent attention for what it is, not only in others, but in ourselves. Remember that we do not need to merely seek out good friends; we need to be a good friend.

Good Epicureans, then, reliably inspire confidence in their friends because they recognize what matters for happiness and for friendship. They do not allow the pursuit of extravagant desires to wreck mutual confidence in the stability of the friendship. They eliminate corrosive desires, never even asking themselves, "How does this friendship advance my status, power, or wealth?" They do not pursue or enter new friendships that violate the terms of Epicurean friendship.

Let's return now to the puzzle that opened the chapter—can an Epicurean be a genuine friend if they pursue friendships from a desire for their own tranquility? We have so far established that Epicurean friends do not desert one another and that they inspire mutual confidence because their friendship is built on a stable foundation of necessary, non-corrosive desires. By contrast, friendships built around corrosive desires are unstable because they depend on the friend's ability to secure the objects of corrosive desires as well as or better than others. Someone under the sway of corrosive desires will often, perhaps always, be on the look-out for a friend or partner who better satisfies those desires.

The fact that Epicurean friendships are stable, though, does not address the more pressing question of whether transactional friendships, stable or otherwise, are genuine friendships. Is Cicero right that Epicureans are using their friends? Again, Epicurus thinks we cannot help but pursue our own well-being because he is a psychological hedonist.[10] But even if we could pursue friendships for other reasons, he would consider it imprudent to ignore our long-term well-being. Human beings have needs, and willfully ignoring those needs leaves us unnecessarily vulnerable. Pursuing friendship without recognition of human dependency might prove short-sighted, a hedonic miscalculation resulting from discounting the future. Being cast aside or neglected is the later-arriving pain resulting from the unstable pleasure we overvalue in the moment.

More importantly, I suspect friendship pursued without recognition of our own needs might prove not only short-sighted, but also more self-serving, as counterintuitive as that might at first sound. In his *Letters on Ethics*, Seneca complains that Epicurus needs friends "to attend to him when sick, and to help him when he is thrown into prison or is impoverished."[11] Now, it might seem that Seneca aims merely to join Cicero in accusing Epicurus of using his friends as instruments, but what he says next reveals the true nature of his complaint. Seneca objects to the fact that Epicurus admits to having needs and vulnerabilities at all, that he depends in any meaningful sense on friends.

A Stoic, by contrast, has no such needs. Since Stoic virtue alone suffices for happiness, Stoics do not need friends for happiness, nor do friends impact their happiness. Friends are an example of what the Stoics call "preferred indifferents," when "indifferent" means that the Stoic is just as happy alone. Why, then, you might reasonably wonder, does a Stoic pursue friendship at all? What makes friendship "preferable" if a person could just as well do without it? In brief, Seneca claims friendship offers him welcome opportunities to display his own virtue. A good Stoic seeks a friend upon "whom he himself might attend when that person is sick and whom he might free from imprisonment by his enemies."[12]

Note that this Stoic approach to friendship, which might at first seem admirably selfless, also risks treating people like instruments, and as inferior instruments at that. Seneca's friend becomes a useful tool for displaying Seneca's own vulnerability-free virtue. Sure, Seneca does not request or hope for anything in return. Instead, he seeks to display a sort of excellence. Imagine yourself, then, as Seneca's friend, hearing that you are a welcome opportunity for his virtuous action, even though he will never need you, would in fact be ashamed to ever need you. Upon reflection, that sounds pretty condescending.

At least Epicureans enter the friendship on equal terms as creatures with shared needs and vulnerabilities who can genuinely benefit each other. The fact that Epicureans keep their needs and vulnerabilities in mind does not mean they navigate relationships as shrewd calculators of advantage out to exploit a resource. Epicurus thinks we can err in two ways—we can look for personal advantage in each action or we can imprudently ignore our long-term needs. He writes that:

> The constant friend is neither he who always searches for utility, nor he who never links friendship to utility. For the former makes gratitude a matter for commercial transaction, while the latter kills off good hope for the future.[13]

Friends do not always ask themselves, "But what's in it for me?" They do not seek an even ledger of requests and favors, as though an Epicurean should never pay for a friend's drink without first receiving an offer to "get the next round." Epicurean friendships are characterized by shared confidence in facing the future together, not by a history of equal assistance.

I find myself agreeing with Epicurus that human beings are vulnerable creatures with needs and that entering friendships without acknowledging those vulnerabilities is perilous. We should not pretend that we are so self-reliant that we will never need the assistance of friends, and we should select our friends with our human frailty in mind. Making great sacrifices for a person we have reason to believe will abandon us is imprudent. Neither the short-term benefits of someone's transient attention nor the pleasures of performing one's virtue are worth the long-term pain of neglect.

In sum, Epicurean friendships should be formed on a foundation of mutual trust, a shared sense of what truly matters, and a confidence of assistance in times of need. With that foundation set, friends can experience unalloyed pleasures of shared extravagances, untainted by the corrosion that poisons the well of joy. I leave it to you whether you consider that an alluring conception of friendship. Cicero did not, but his best friend was an Epicurean who did.

Now let's turn to one of the most important ways our friends improve our lives, albeit it by causing us pain.

7 | LET ME BE FRANK

For most of us, our first impulse when criticized is to get upset. That makes sense because criticism is painful, and pain is upsetting. We do not enjoy having our small mistakes corrected, much less having our core values challenged. I confess having bristled when someone pointed out that I do not use space in the dishwasher efficiently (never my strength, but does it really matter?). We can find ourselves stung even when we solicited the advice to begin with. For the record, I did not ask for tips loading the dishwasher.

Epicurus thinks our resistance to criticism and correction is only natural. We pursue pleasure and avoid pain by nature, just like every other animal. Being right feels good and being wrong does not. We prefer to be admirable and above reproach, at least about the important things. When we suspect we are not, it is very uncomfortable. Epicurus gets that.

Unfortunately, we must accept some pains in order to improve our physical, intellectual, and psychological well-being so that we can better navigate the world and have more fulfilling relationships. We exercise to get stronger and to prepare for physical challenges. We swallow bitter medicine to fight infection. We practice for hours so that it eventually becomes natural. We study boring things because boring things save lives.

Epicurus thinks we cannot achieve tranquility unless we develop the strength to acknowledge our weaknesses and work to counteract them. He also recognizes that we are vulnerable creatures, that change happens slowly and imperfectly, and that we often risk doing more harm than good by criticizing ourselves and others. We should proceed with caution and choose partners in such conversations carefully because vulnerability done wrong can cause long-lasting damage.

The Epicurean Philodemus devoted a treatise to what he called "frank speech." *On Frank Speech* was buried under volcanic ash, though devoted scholars have uncovered and stitched together fragments to determine its central questions and claims.[1] The work seems to be something like a guide for having candid conversations about personal impediments to living well without harming each other. Some of these frank discussions might address the correction of intellectual or practical errors, while others cut closer to home and concern weaknesses in character or behavior toward others.

Most of what remains of *On Frank Speech* offers advice about how to interact with Epicurean novices, likely the sorts of people who came to Philodemus for study or advice. Judging from the text, Philodemus thinks a significant portion of frank speech happens between people in an advisory relationship who are at different stages of life or intellectual development. In other words, the discussants are not close friends, but they do have a relationship that involves mutual respect and concern. Examples of such relationships might include parents and children, teachers and students, bosses and employees, ministers and congregants. Frank speech of a personal nature is best avoided between strangers, a point explored below.

More fragmentary sections of the text make clear that the most valuable frank speech happens in open conversation among close friends. In one passage, Philodemus claims that "there is nothing so grand as having one to whom one will say what is in one's heart and who will listen when one speaks. For our nature strongly desires to reveal to some people what it thinks."[2] Philodemus notes that Epicurus and Metrodorus, the two great pillars of the Epicurean community, had a close friendship characterized by frank speech.[3]

As we have seen, Epicureans consider mutual support a core feature of genuine friendships. Philodemus claims that while we strengthen friendships by displaying our "good qualities" when offering support and assistance, we strengthen friendships just as well through revealing our weaknesses and vulnerabilities.[4] In other words, disclosure and support in genuine friendships goes both ways. Some of that support takes the form of helping each other think about and navigate the challenges of life, and another part includes admitting and working through vulnerabilities. If we want to improve, Philodemus thinks we inevitably need help and "sympathy" from friends.[5]

To get a sense of why frank speech is often painful and uncomfortable, even among friends, we might consider some of the sorts of conversations Philodemus has in mind. As examples of intellectual correction, you might tell someone that a virus is not a bacterium and so cannot be treated with antibiotics, that carbon emissions contribute to climate change, that they have made an adding error, that their argument has structural flaws, or that they lack the relevant expertise to claim authority.

On the practical and ethical front, you might tell someone that they should leave their abusive spouse, that they have chosen to pursue a career for which they are ill-suited, that they are an alcoholic, or that they are buying a house they cannot afford. You might tell someone that they seem to care more about money than their friends, that they often become arrogant when drunk, that they are disturbing others by talking too loudly, that their temper is driving friends away, or that they have been unkind or self-involved. Well, doesn't that all sound so very comfortable!?

I assume most of us have initiated or been on the receiving end of conversations about errors or personal weaknesses that have gone horribly wrong, whether at work, with friends, or with strangers. We have solicited advice only to leave feeling worse or have offered advice that alienated the person who asked for it. More often, we have received or offered entirely unsolicited advice, and that did not go well at all. Perhaps we handled it poorly, they delivered it poorly, or everyone involved made a mess of things.

As a result, some of us prefer to avoid difficult discussions entirely, even as we acknowledge that dodging them limits our personal and intellectual growth, as well as the depth of our relationships. Others run to the opposite extreme, diving headlong into correcting almost everyone, thinking perhaps that the world should welcome their wizened commentary, their clever and best version of "just being honest." If their honesty wounds, they rarely consider themselves at fault, as if everyone should be prepared for a hard punch in the face, perhaps in view of an eager crowd. While some people retreat to a deficiency of candor, others transform themselves into pugilistic zealots for honesty.

If Epicureans think that the most effective way to grow and improve ourselves is to have conscientious and productive conversations about the intellectual and ethical challenges of life, then they better provide some guidance about how to not screw it up royally and leave everyone worse for the effort. While Philodemus offers some general prescriptions and rules of the road, he denies there are tidy answers. He thinks that people, situations, and relationships vary so widely that rough heuristics are the best he can offer. However, we should always keep a few things in mind, and there are some things we should rarely, if ever, do.

<u>"You Don't Even Know Me"</u>: Frank speech is for people who have some sort of relationship or mutual understanding, not for strangers on the internet. It is a well-tailored garment, not one-size fits all, and good tailors schedule an in-person fitting. We should know our audience for three reasons, and the less we know, the more carefully we should tread.

First, Philodemus makes it clear that background, life circumstances, and personal history greatly affect how people should interact with one another about difficult matters. We cannot know these things without knowing the person, often without knowing them quite well. Philodemus, for example, notes that some people were criticized too much as children, and some criticized too little.[6] Some find friendship easier because they grew up in households with good will, while others were shown little concern and struggle to trust others.[7]

Some people have been sheltered and so are unwittingly ignorant of the world's evils, while others know the world all too well and need no reminders of their trauma. Some have a stronger educational background that makes them haughty, while others have a weaker education that makes them anxious or defensive. Some people had a parent die when they were young. Some are anxious around peers because they have been bullied, while others have been encouraged to dominate rather than listen.

All of these biographical features play a role in the dynamics of frank speech and govern the likelihood that the conversation will go well.[8] We would never expect the same behavior from a shelter dog as from a dog who has known nothing but love. We cannot expect knowledge from someone who has never had an opportunity to learn. If we have no idea about the person's circumstances, then Philodemus thinks we should hold our tongue. Given that frank speech can prove painful, it is not only useless, but can be sadistic, if employed without careful consideration of what counts as a genuine benefit in the circumstances.

Second, people struggle with participating in frank speech not only because of their background or personal history, but also because of their psychological and physiological circumstances. In short, some people's brains work differently from the get-go, before background and circumstances ever kick in. Epicurus is an atomist who believes our conscious mind depends crucially on our physical nature, and some features of our psychology are not readily malleable.

Lucretius claims that each of us has a "natural disposition" that makes us "differ in character and consequently in behavior." Some people, for example, are by nature "excessively prone to sudden fits of rage," while others give in "a little too readily to fear."[9] Some of us meekly accept what we should resist. Ever the physicalist, Lucretius speculates that those naturally disposed to anger have, like lions, more fiery atoms, while the fearful, like deer, have "chill minds."[10] Helping someone improve requires recognizing these individual dispositions and keeping them in mind during frank conversations.

Some of our struggles, then, are built-in, and Lucretius cautions that "we must not suppose that faults of character can be extirpated." We will always have "surviving traces of our natural dispositions" that even "philosophy is unable to erase."[11] The best we can do is engage in ongoing regulation of the challenges our nature presents. Lucretius remains optimistic that we can quiet such impulses, but he acknowledges that we cannot change everything. Some dispositional traits will persist because they cannot be eliminated, even if we can find work arounds for managing them. For example, we might, as Lucretius puts it elsewhere, "divert the motions" of our minds "into some other channel" to distract ourselves from an unwelcome emotion, or we might avoid environments or people we know risk bringing out the worst in us.[12] These are practical strategies, not fundamental shifts in our personality.

Current psychological research supports Lucretius' view that our power to change ourselves and others is far more limited than we might like. Worse, our efforts often prove dispiritingly ineffective or counterproductive. Personality studies, at least when conducted on Americans, usually rely on a self-reported sorter called the Big Five, which measures five traits that occur on a spectrum between two poles. For most traits, one of the two poles correlates with practical or social success, so people are generally drawn to improve in those directions—to score higher on extraversion, conscientiousness, agreeableness, emotional stability, openness. One facet of conscientiousness, "grit," has recently become an object of great practical desire.[13]

The problem, though, is that our capacity to change seems limited at best. Significant trait-change usually occurs, if it does, as we first enter the workplace or college, and then maybe again when we retire and grow old.[14] Sandwiched between those two points, we stay pretty much the same. It makes sense that we want to improve ourselves. It just remains unclear exactly how much we can improve, and data suggests we should tread cautiously and temper our ambition with a healthy dose of realism.

In a study of undergraduates who expressed interest in changing one or more of their Big Five personality traits, many students who accepted and met a weekly series of trait-specific challenges did manage to improve as they had hoped, at least to some extent, for some traits, and for that window of time.[15] However, those who accepted but failed to meet challenges often made their situation worse. They regressed, likely because they hoped to accomplish more than their time or capacity permitted. Failed attempts at change did not leave subjects innocuously at their starting point.

The study's authors use the fitting word "backfired" and the somewhat contradictory phrase "negative growth" to describe this regression. The lesson seems both optimistic and cautious—we can probably change some things but getting too ambitious might put us in a worse place than where we began. They concluded that perhaps not all attempts to improve are "advisable."[16] As frank speech is at root a kind of advising, we need to know people well to have a decent chance of recognizing when encouraging improvement risks making matters worse.[17]

Finally, frank speech should usually happen in a personal relationship where both parties have a stake in the relationship continuing. Otherwise, there will be little motivation for apologies and forgiveness when frank speech misses the mark or is handled poorly. Philodemus claims that even the most careful conversations between the closest of friends can go wrong. Frank speech is so difficult that missteps are inevitable because of a lack of information about the person, their situation, a failure of reasoning, or some other sort of misunderstanding. Maybe simply because everyone's tired. Even LeBron James occasionally airballs a free throw or overthrows a pass.

Both parties, then, need enough mutual concern and knowledge to acknowledge errors, mend fences, and talk through what went wrong. Philodemus writes that "we do not rightly consider that [someone] has simply been discredited toward the whole because of a former slip."[18] He reports that Epicurus "consistently maintains" that friends are keen to "pardon" each other "for the things in which they slipped up."[19] Strangers lack the incentive and the mutual concern to maintain a relationship that founders due to inevitable errors.

<u>Keep Your Own Imperfections in Mind:</u> Every professor has had at least one earnest student show up holding a graded paper who says, "But my high school teacher told me I'm a very good writer." The professor must, in other words, have made a mistake of some sort. Whenever that happens, I remind myself of the time I was that student who visited two different professors on the same day in my first year of college. As our own failings recede further into the past, we can grow impatient with people making the very same error.

Philodemus recommends reminding ourselves of our past mistakes whenever we find ourselves engaged in frank conversations. He writes, "For how is he going to hate the one who errs, though not desperately, when he knows that he himself is not perfect and reminds himself that everyone is accustomed to err?"[20] Most of us have a past littered with mistakes large and small, times we wounded someone, overstepped our bounds, lashed out at minor criticism, or lost a friendship due to negligence. Philodemus encourages us to keep that in mind, which can admittedly prove challenging because remembering our failings is no joyride.

He thinks we should even openly disclose past errors when appropriate, in part because it humanizes us and indicates we understand weakness. Yet he cautions against using our own mistakes as a way of "showing off." He says that "the wise" will "communicate their own errors to friends with frankness," but he recognizes that other people might disclose past and present errors as a way of boasting.[21] I have encountered the occasional person who responds to an anxious disclosure by treating it as a "one-up" exercise on past failures. "You think you were stupid, let me tell you about myself!"

The Road Goes Both Ways: Of course, some people fail to recognize or remember their errors at all. These same people, Philodemus notes, are usually the ones keen to criticize others. He writes that people often prove obstinate because "they are not aware of their own errors," yet go on to "reproach others" because "they believe for the most part they have not erred."[22] Needless to say, he thinks we should not be that person.

When such people find themselves on the other end of the candor they eagerly offer to others, they often prove the most sensitive and volatile. To be fair, Philodemus thinks some people mistakenly believe they are good at receiving criticism, so they fancy themselves invulnerable. Nevertheless, when they are corrected or criticized, Philodemus thinks such people "have their pretense exposed."[23] They resemble "those who make jokes but do not endure others making jokes at their expense."[24]

In the same way that it would be foolish to think we cannot be burned by a hot stove, Philodemus thinks we should never assume we are indifferent to criticism. He notes that even the wise are stung, despite having the most experience with frank speech and having developed a strong sense of gratitude for its power to improve us.[25] Everyone is by nature a "snowflake," even if some people grow more accustomed to recognizing their errors in the way that some people grow more accustomed to physical exercise.

<u>Most Things Don't Matter</u>: I loved my grandmother, but she tended to criticize almost everything, from grammatical errors to an uneven hem in a pair of pants. Philodemus suggests we should only concern ourselves with the truly important things, which are fewer in number than we often recognize. He writes that "to reproach [someone] for everything is unfriendly to his security and a foolish harshness."[26] The Greek term for "security" here is the word Epicurus employs to describe the sense of confidence we get from friendships built on mutual concern.[27] Anything that undermines a friend's confidence in mutual respect or shared support is harmful and "unfriendly." We should keep to those things that threaten the relationship itself or core features of our friend's well-being. Other comments are "a foolish harshness."

<u>Avoid Irony</u>: Philodemus recognizes that many of us are "enticed" by irony, and it often seems like an effective way to point out foolishness. Nevertheless, he encourages us to "set before our eyes," or picture vividly in imagination, "the difference that exists between caring admonishment and an irony that pleases but stings

pretty much everyone."[28] In its fragmentary context, Philodemus suggests that an instructor employing sustained sarcasm or irony will appear to those "observing him teaching" as if "he will hate all of them in the world."[29] Irony and sarcasm shade into bitterness and cruelty all too quickly, so Philodemus cautions against employing either, whether in the classroom or with friends. Irony, of course, is the currency of the internet, which gives us further reason to take our frank speech offline.

Give It Time: Philodemus thinks one of the most common failures of candid conversations is a failure of patience, both during the conversation itself and in awaiting its effects. Again, Philodemus thinks it is entirely natural in many cases to respond defensively and get upset. The point is not whether being upset is justified—the point is that it is natural. Life is a long game, and we work through things slowly. Philodemus thinks we should not seek instantaneous change or chastise people for failing to eagerly welcome a new way of seeing themselves and the world. Even if the person is exceptionally sensitive, Philodemus thinks little is gained by pointing out their sensitivity and chastising them for it, as if hitting something fragile makes it less likely to break.

Philodemus sums up the ideal practitioner of frank speech as someone who "bears goodwill and practices philosophy intelligently and continually and is great in character and indifferent to fame and least of all a politician and clean of envy and says only what is relevant and is not carried away so as to insult or strut or show contempt or do harm, and does not make use of insolence and flattering arts."[30] We are not and probably never will be ideal practitioners of frank speech. Sometimes we will mess up and need to apologize. Epicurus, though, is confident we can improve, and Philodemus here sets up a target to shoot for.

But what about receiving frank speech? We have thus far addressed conditions on the delivery of frank speech, rather than its reception, in part because Philodemus has less to say about that. We have also not addressed a related danger of frank speech—being on the receiving end of frank speech that is abusive or that we should ignore. I think, though, that we can turn almost all the above points around when we seek advice or support. We should seek frank speech from people we know, who know us, and whom we trust.

While it can be difficult to identify the truly trustworthy, especially quickly or on the fly, Philodemus helps us determine who we should *not* trust. We should not trust someone who uses our background or natural limitations against us or who insists those things are easy to move past or correct. We should not tolerate mockery or the ironic dismissal of our concerns. We should not engage in frank speech with people who correct things of little to no consequence as if they were significant errors. We should avoid those who are unduly impatient with us or do not give us time to sort things out. We should absolutely never engage in frank speech with anyone who criticizes us because of our deficiency with respect to the objects of corrosive desires—that we are insufficiently wealthy, attractive, powerful, brilliant, or high-status. In fact, frank speech used in these domains is a straightforward disqualifier for Epicurean friendship at all.

It bears noting that Epicureanism itself, or really any new philosophy we encounter, asks us to engage candidly with our values and vulnerabilities. This book itself does not count as frank speech because we are not engaged in private conversation about the special challenges of your life. I'm an Epicurus scholar, not an expert in living well, and I don't know you from Adam. That said, controversial ideas themselves, even introduced on paper by someone not directly addressing us, can sometimes feel a bit like the sort of frankness we might encounter in live action. It can feel personal even when it's not.

For that reason, some of what Epicurus says might raise our hackles because it cuts close to home or challenges the psychological benefits of our cherished activities. You might even occasionally feel an impulse to cast aside this book as though Epicurus were trafficking in insults or was simply naïve about the world or the human condition, and he would consider that response natural.

Yet he would also recommend pausing to figure out why some view of his, whether about greed, ambition, politics, status-seeking, science, or religion, has touched a nerve. Perhaps that discomfort indicates that you suspect he might, at least in some respect or other, have a point. And then maybe you could talk about your frustration with a trusted friend who knows you well, perhaps over a meal or a drink, because everything of consequence is better discussed at leisure with a good friend.

8 | THE PLEASURES OF VIRTUE

Like many contemporary American politicians, John F. Kennedy, Jr., set the stage for his presidential campaign by publishing a book. These days, politicians generally write about themselves and why they believe their childhood and adult experiences have molded them into leaders worth electing. Kennedy released a book about other people, in particular American senators he considered especially courageous. The book, *Profiles in Courage*, was a popular success, though it turns out much of the work was not Kennedy's own.[1]

The phrase "profile in courage" is still employed idiomatically, usually negatively to indicate when someone is "hardly" a profile in courage. *Profiles in Courage* is dated in numerous respects and takes a few historical liberties in the service of glory, but it captures key parts of our shared conception of what counts as courage. Courage requires doing the right thing, despite a risk or nearly assured cost to one's interests. The price of courage is sometimes even death, especially when we upset the prevailing norms of society or find ourselves a soldier, a firefighter, a nurse in a pandemic.

This common conception that virtue often requires sacrifice forms one of the core objections to Epicureanism. According to its critics, Epicureanism has trouble accounting for why we should choose justice or courage when acting justly is unpleasant or not to our personal advantage. In *On Moral Ends*, Cicero accuses Torquatus, the mouthpiece of Epicureanism, of espousing a theory that Torquatus' own illustrious and noble ancestors manifestly rejected.

Torquatus, it seems, is the third Torquatus. His grandfather, the first Torquatus, tore a chain from his enemy's neck, fought the Latins, and had his own son beheaded for refusing to fight in hand-to-hand combat.[2] None of those things were particularly pleasant, but Cicero praises him for putting "the authority of the state and of his rank above nature herself and a father's love." Torquatus' grandfather served as a consul, the highest-elected office in Rome, three times.

Abandoning or killing a son on principle seems to run in Torquatus' family. His father, also a consul, gave up a son for adoption and later banished him for taking bribes. The son summarily committed suicide and his father refused to attend the funeral. Cicero claims that such actions, which he greatly admires, could only be carried out from duty, with no thought to pleasure. Given this lineage, Cicero concludes that Torquatus' ancestors would condemn his acceptance of Epicureanism. Hedonism cannot easily justify killing one's son.

Setting aside all this uncomfortably glorified son-killing, Cicero has a point—such actions are not pleasant. Hedonism seems better suited to explain why so many wealthy parents have paid to have their sons exempted from military service, whether legally or through deception. Well-heeled Americans on both sides of the American Civil War purchased substitute soldiers to keep their sons from battle.[3] People who enlist for war because it sounds fun soon discover that the dirty glamour of recruitment commercials is a paradigm of false advertising. Intuition suggests that standing firm when bombs explode is the provenance of duty rather than pleasure.

War is a test at the extremes, but civilian life offers plenty of opportunities to act unjustly or cowardly for one's own gain. A student cheats to get into medical school. An accountant cooks the books to afford private school tuition. A well-executed lie covers up the indiscretion of an affair. A worker stays silent about sexism to keep in good with the boss. A senator compromises personal integrity to stay in office. A police officer covers for an unhinged colleague. A father throws around clout to secure leniency for his law-breaking child. It takes courage to do the right thing when we stand to lose something we value, whether in everyday life or when commanded to join the Nazi party.

We might reasonably think that an abiding commitment to justice and courage is a necessary condition on calling something an "ethics" at all. If Epicureanism requires us to pursue what is most advantageous, and injustice is sometimes most advantageous, then Epicureanism more than permits injustice—it requires it. Cicero's complaint might score a mortal blow to Epicurean ethics, so Epicurus has reason to take the charge very seriously.

Epicurus, as we should expect, denies that vice is advantageous. Instead, he argues that virtue is advantageous and conducive to tranquility, while vice is not. In his *Letter to Menoeceus*, he claims that it is "impossible to live pleasantly without living prudently, honourably, and justly, and impossible to live prudently, honourably, and justly without living pleasantly."[4] It might at first appear that Epicurus is saying the same thing twice, but he is in fact making two points. The first is that virtue is necessary for pleasure, and the second is that pleasure is necessary for virtue. Let's begin with the first—we cannot live pleasantly unless we live virtuously.

Torquatus opens his response to Cicero's account of his noble lineage with the reminder that Epicurean prudence enjoins us to accept pains when a greater long-term benefit results. While the proximate pain might appear significant, the prudent person correctly measures the size of the distant pleasure that results from accepting the pain. Torquatus' ancestors saw that their sacrifices would pay dividends in "security" and confidence. In other words, pain now, but much less anxiety later.

According to Torquatus, when his grandfather bravely yanked away the chain from his enemy, he saved himself from death in full view of others, winning "esteem" and the protection of their respect. When he killed his own son, he aimed to "maintain army discipline at a critical time of war by spreading fear of punishment." In that way he provided "for the security of his fellow citizens, and thereby—as he was well aware—for his own."[5] In other words, the first Torquatus had his own long-term confidence in mind, which required securing the confidence of his community as well. His son was regrettably a threat to everyone's well-being.

Judging from these passages, we might get the sense that the only reason Epicurus thinks we should avoid injustice is from fear of punishment or bad consequences. There is some pain in acting justly, but greater pain in acting unjustly, so justice is the lesser of two evils. Torquatus' grandfather killed his son to maintain discipline, which itself required making his soldiers fear the consequences of injustice. Epicurus concedes the point, at least in part. For many people, the fear of detection and punishment is the only reason to avoid injustice. He writes that "injustice is not a bad thing in its own right, but only because of the fear produced by the suspicion that one will not escape the detection of those assigned to punish such actions."[6]

Epicurus might be right that many people avoid injustice solely from the fear of punishment, but that response presents a few worries. First, what if a person felt sure they could get away with it? Second, is someone who acts justly only from the fear of punishment meaningfully just? After all, they do not want to act justly; they want to avoid punishment. It might seem like a fully just person should not only act justly, but also *want* to act justly. Let's take the concern about getting caught first.

One common Epicurean response is to deny that anyone who commits injustice can be certain that they will never get caught. Epicurus captures this view in two of his *Principal Doctrines*:

> It is hard to commit injustice and escape detection, but to be confident of escaping detection is impossible.[7]

> It is impossible for someone who secretly does something which men agreed not to do in order to avoid harming one another or being harmed to be confident that he will escape detection, even if in his current circumstances he escapes detection ten thousand times. For until his death it will be uncertain whether he will continue to escape detection.[8]

Cicero considers this naïve at best. He admits that the fear of detection might deter "trembling ninnies who torture themselves and fear every shadow." Yet he thinks we should consider the wickedness of "a shrewd calculator of advantage, sharp-witted, wily, a sly old fox, practiced at methods for cheating covertly—no witness, no accomplices."[9] Some thieves, especially the cinematic ones, do seem remarkably clever and unscrupulous.

Torquatus responds that even if someone remains confident that no one will detect their injustice, they might nevertheless fear that they will inadvertently divulge their crimes, as does the paranoid killer in Edgar Alan Poe's "Tell-Tale Heart." Torquatus reminds Cicero that "many wrongdoers indict themselves," an intentional gesture at Cicero's pride in having exposed Cataline's coup attempt.[10] Lucretius reiterates this point in *On the Nature of Things*, writing that the unjust person will fear confessing his injustice in dreams or delirium.[11] These days an unjust person might worry one of their relatives will sign up for Ancestry.com and ignite fire to a cold case.[12] Epicurus thinks the fear of detection will prove sufficient to keep a person who prudently pursues tranquility from committing injustice.

Yet surely acting justly from fear of detection is no more admirable than acting rightly for fear of hell! Torquatus takes a stab at addressing this concern by appealing to shame and guilt. Shame, one might think, could operate independently of the fear of getting caught because it is an internally directed judgment. While discussing cowardice, Torquatus claims that the fear of death has made many people "betray their parents, their friends, in some cases even their country; and in most cases, deep down, *their own selves*."[13] They might betray "their own selves," even if their parents or friends never discover the treachery.

Torquatus adds that "when dishonesty takes root in one's heart, its very presence is disturbing," bringing on the pains of "bad conscience."[14] While Cicero is surely right that some unjust people are shameless, a great deal more feel shame, recognizing that if others knew what they had done, they would be right to disapprove. Avoiding injustice from a sense of shame at least improves on avoiding it from a fear of punishment alone. Either way, Epicurus thinks a prudent person has reason to avoid acting unjustly to avoid long-term anxiety and shame. Still, that might seem a disappointing result—reluctantly choosing justice only to avoid feeling bad.

Remember that Epicurus makes two claims about the relationship between justice and tranquility. We have been exploring the first—that the unjust are necessarily anxious. The second claim asserts that pleasure is necessary for justice. To see why this is both a stronger claim and a harder sell, imagine a banker who decides not to cheat for fear of detection or shame. In that sense, the banker chooses the just and honest action. Yet Epicurus must deny that someone who prefers injustice, but avoids it from fear, is living pleasantly. After all, the banker suffers from a powerful and unfulfilled desire to act unjustly, and people with powerful unsatisfied desires cannot experience tranquility. Epicurus must think, then, that choosing justice from prudence involves more than simply avoiding acting unjustly from fear of detection. Unless we root out the unsatisfied desire to commit injustice, we cannot live a tranquil life.

The desire to commit injustice, though, is rarely a desire for injustice itself. People generally do not commit injustice, or at least grave injustices, for no other reason than to commit injustice. They commit injustices to achieve something they cannot acquire justly. Injustice is "instrumental" to some perceived good. Notice that most of the examples of injustice listed above occur in pursuit of the objects of corrosive desires. The senator chooses injustice to stay in power, and Epicurus considers the desire for power corrosive. The student cheats to feed unchecked ambition, also a corrosive desire. The executive lies for enrichment, yet another corrosive desire. The unfulfilled desire, then, is usually not for injustice, but for what injustice makes possible.

For Epicurus, the successful pursuit of a corrosive desire tends, at some point or other, to require injustice. Achieving wealth, great power, and high-status as efficiently as the crow flies almost always involves minor concessions like pandering and sometimes major injustices like backstabbing, cheating, or violence. Epicureans, though, try their best to root out corrosive desires, which removes most reasons for committing injustice. Epicureans eliminate the desires that make injustice tempting to begin with. By contrast, people who resist injustice only from fear of punishment or shame have remaining unsatisfied corrosive desires that make injustice tempting.

If we eliminate the corrosive, anxiety-causing desires, then we undercut the motive for most unjust action. Epicurus claims that "the just life is most free from disturbance, but the unjust life is full of the greatest disturbance."[15] This freedom from psychological disturbance not only feels good, but it also removes the incentive to harm anyone else unjustly. Epicurus writes that the person "who is free from disturbance within himself also causes no trouble for another."[16] A person who pursues and is content with the objects of natural desires will, Epicurus thinks, rarely have reason to even consider injustice.[17]

We have not yet addressed the greatest benefit of justice and the greatest cost of injustice. Namely, the just deserve the trust of others as a friend and a member of a community. The unjust, by contrast, cannot be trusted and they cannot trust others. As we know, Epicurus thinks trust and confidence are the bedrock of friendship and community, and without a community of friends bound by mutual trust, a person can never be securely happy. In other words, injustice makes it difficult, sometimes impossible, to fulfill the necessary desire for security, trust, and friendship. It puts tranquility out of reach.

Many of Epicurus' philosophical predecessors agreed that stable friendship and community between the unjust is not possible. In Plato's *Republic*, Socrates claims that when injustice "arises between two people," they will "be at odds, hate each other, and be enemies to one another and to just people." Socrates suggests unjust people even harbor disagreement in their own souls.[18] Aristotle thinks friendship is either impossible or very unlikely between the vicious, and like Plato, he suggests a vicious person cannot even be friends with himself, since vice creates a soul divided.[19]

Suppose I am an unjust person who enters a conspiracy with another unjust person to commit some crime. If Epicurus is right, I will worry about detection, even if I act shamelessly and alone. Once I have conspired with someone else, though, the problem compounds. I might worry that the other person will expose my injustices, whether for personal gain or to escape consequences. I will worry they will leave me holding the bag or betray me completely and take the bag for themselves. These possibilities will seem more vivid to me because I have considered doing the same thing to them. If expedient, I would pin the crime on them, and I would cheat them out of their share if I could. There is, as they say, "no honor among thieves." The only prudent attitude for the unjust is to avoid trust. Epicurus considers that far too high a price because trust and friendship are necessary components of tranquility. For Epicurus, the unjust forfeit the greatest good—deserving trust. The just, on the other hand, merit the trust upon which tranquility depends.

One point remains. Cicero thinks the Epicureans cannot willingly die for others, which most people consider among the most courageous actions. "No greater love than this," said Jesus about dying for your friends in the Gospel of John.[20] Cicero's objection to Epicurus hinges on the thought that death is never to a person's own advantage and that the Epicureans are rationally bound to pursue whatever is most to their advantage. Again, Cicero seems to have a point. What possible advantage can an Epicurean expect by dying? As we will see later, Epicurus denies the existence of an afterlife, so no postmortem reward awaits. He thinks death is the absence of experience, so the dead cannot themselves experience anything advantageous, including an awareness of their own reputation after death.

Epicurus, though, insists that Epicureans will die for their friends, even when death would be very painful. He writes that "the wise man feels no more pain when he is tortured than when his friend is tortured, and will die on his behalf; for if he betrays his friend, his entire life will be confounded and utterly upset because of a lack of confidence."[21] Clearly the "pain" in this quote cannot be physical pain, since the physical pain of a tortured and an untortured person cannot be equal. The key point, though, is that the wise Epicurean would rather die than live having betrayed a friend. Betrayal would make life unbearable, not only because of their shame, but also because they would lose their community's trust. Their life would be, as Epicurus puts it, "utterly upset because of a lack of confidence."

When John McCain was held as a prisoner of war in Hanoi during the Vietnam War, his captors offered him the opportunity to be released because he was an admiral's son. He knew, of course, that accepting release before others was a violation of the official rule against taking special favors. In an ABC interview with McCain, though, the primary reason he identified was the following:

> What bothered me most about it was that I knew that if had accepted the release, they would go to other prisoners and say, "See, your country doesn't care about you. They only care about the admirals' sons. And I knew that that's what they would do. And I knew that I couldn't do that to my fellow prisoners."[22]

Accepting the offer would harm McCain's fellow soldiers, leave him with a bad conscience, and undermine the security of his community. He suffered terribly for his refusal, but he decided a betrayal would be worse. His situation was, in the end, not unlike that of Torquatus' ancestors.

The Epicureans also think they are better prepared to sacrifice their life than many people because they deny that death harms them, so they do not fear it. They enjoy living, but they claim death does not deprive them of a fulfilling and complete life, whenever death happens. Remember that Torquatus points out that many people betray their family, friends, and country because they fear death more than injustice. We will explore the Epicurean arguments against fearing death in later chapters. For the moment, we need only note that the Epicureans consider themselves well prepared to view committing injustice as worse than death. Death presents no great loss, but the long-lasting loss of tranquility resulting from a selfish betrayal does.

An additional, somewhat more controversial reason Epicureans might make sacrifices, including their own life, is the confidence that they will live in the memory of the people for whom they risked their lives. Critics have claimed that Epicurus cannot, given his philosophical commitments, concern himself with his reputation after death, and in some ways they are right. A dead person cannot experience the pleasure of a good postmortem reputation because Epicurus thinks a dead person cannot experience anything. In some cases, a desire to be celebrated after one's death is a corrosive desire for fame, so Epicureans cannot die in hopes of achieving fame.[23]

As we will see, though, Epicurus thinks that memories of pleasure and friendship play very important roles in the life of an Epicurean. Among other things, pleasant memories of friendship help us get through times of misfortune. A courageous and just Epicurean might find genuine mental pleasure in knowing they deserve to be, and likely will be, celebrated in the memories of good people and that those pleasant memories will offer their friends consolation in times of their own trials. You do not need to end up in a book titled *Profiles in Courage* to be one for a friend.

9 | IMPOSTER SYNDROME

I was once surprised to discover that Stephen Colbert, longtime host of *The Colbert Report* and current host of the *The Late Show*, grew up in South Carolina. To put it bluntly, he didn't *sound* southern. And, for the most part, neither do I, though I still struggle with some words, tipping my hand for an attentive listener. I occasionally dust off my childhood accent as a party trick or to blend in when I visit Arkansas, my home state. My reasons for becoming what Colbert calls a "stealth Southerner" are apparently the same as his. In an interview with Morley Safer of CBS, he said:

> At a very young age, I decided I was not gonna to have a southern accent. Because people, when I was a kid watching TV, if you wanted to use a shorthand that someone was stupid, you gave the character a southern accent. And that's not true. Southern people are not stupid. But I didn't want to seem stupid. I wanted to seem smart.[1]

I don't know how Colbert feels about his own phonetic transition, but I consider it crucial to my professional success and in some ways deeply regrettable. At a conference in Colorado early in my career, one of the organizers announced to a room full of my peers that southerners were too backward and dumb to employ moral reasoning, and I glanced around the room wondering if I was the only one. I do not know whether any of the laughter was uncomfortable, but I heard laughter.

Keeping check on our accents, though, is only one of the ways that we create anxiety for ourselves by aspiring to be among the select of culture and intellect. We don't want to be caught short not knowing what we think others expect us to know. We fret over learning or experiencing things that are not, upon reflection, all that important for living a good life. We want to talk intelligently about the right music, the right shows, the right books. And we sometimes worry we will be discovered as "imposters."

Worse, if we're honest, or at least if I'm honest about some periods in my life, our desire to be among the "elect" or "informed" can carry along its own exclusionary impulse like a disfiguring burden. We police the borders of these largely artificial standards of intellect and taste against others. We risk making others feel inadequate in the very same way that we fear being judged inadequate. Everyone loses. In sum, arbitrary intellectual and cultural benchmarks increase our own anxiety and tempt us to mistreat those who fall short, including ourselves. This was, for the Epicureans, a matter of some concern.

Epicurus was not what you might call an "intellectual's intellectual." He was by no means an anti-intellectual in the sense of championing ignorance, and he built his entire system around the idea that studying the natural world is necessary to living well. Epicurus did, however, dislike a lot of intellectuals, and they disliked him in return. He claimed, for instance, that "natural philosophy does not create boastful men nor chatterboxes nor men who show off the 'culture' which the many quarrel over."[2] He encouraged his followers to "free themselves from the prison of general education and politics."[3] Epicurus was quite happy to welcome uneducated and maligned members of society into his community, so a solid education in the classics was not a prerequisite for membership.

In some respects, Epicurus was not alone among his philosophical peers in doubting the merits of dedicating your life to what they considered relatively trivial questions of history or literary interpretation. For example, in *On the Shortness of Life*, the Roman Stoic Seneca ridicules Greek intellectuals who whiled away their hours fighting over how many rowers were on Odysseus' ship or whether Homer wrote both the *Odyssey* and the *Illiad*, and if so, in what order.[4] He regrets that the Romans were taking up similar disputes about historical "firsts"—the first emperor to have gladiators fight elephants, for example.

Socrates, as depicted in Plato's *Protagoras*, might give the clearest account of why philosophers were averse to things like literary interpretation, at least as a competitive or performative exercise. Protagoras, of "man is the measure of all things" fame, draws Socrates into a public competition about the meaning of a verse by Simonides. Socrates takes up the challenge and proceeds to make the poem mean exactly what Socrates wants it to mean, Simonides' original intention be damned.

At the end of this bizarre interpretive interlude, Socrates encourages everyone to "put the poets aside and converse directly with each other, testing the truth of our own ideas." He claims that engaging in disputes about poetry is the sort of thing that happens at "second-rate drinking parties."[5] Socrates, like Epicurus, prefers his drinking parties first-rate. The thoughts of a long-dead poet cannot be definitively settled, but we can determine what *we* think. Philosophy is about the ideas of the people in the room. And yet, yes, I am in the process of offering an interpretation of Epicurus, a man long dead, because that is how I make my living. Let's move on, shall we?

The Epicureans departed from their philosophical peers, though, by expanding the territory of their rejection of intellectual and cultural snobbery. Plato and assorted Stoics, for example, argued that appreciating particular kinds of music (and rejecting other kinds) was a mark of the superior person. In fact, they thought childhood exposure to appropriate music was make-or-break for the long-term success of children.[6] Allan Bloom, a Plato scholar who hit the big time when he published a book-length jeremiad entitled *The Closing of the American Mind*, devoted an entire hand-wringing chapter to how rock 'n' roll rots the brains of the young: "But as long as they have the Walkman on, they cannot hear what the great tradition has to say."[7] I spent much of my childhood with "the Walkman on," which probably explains something. The Epicureans, on the other hand, deny there is a benchmark for musical refinement.[8] Feel free to crank up Cheap Trick with a clear conscience. No guilty pleasures when you ride with Epicurus.

Epicurus' point is not that it is wrong to enjoy music and culture, to take pleasure in poetry and fiction, play instruments, or learn to dance. The arts can be both pleasant and useful. The Roman poet Lucretius, after all, wrote a masterful poem in six books that provides the best account of Epicurean physics we have. Lucretius himself acknowledges that he chose to write in meter because the form makes Epicurean doctrines sound more pleasant. He tells Memmius that his verses are like the honey sly doctors put on the lip of a cup filled with medicinal wormwood. In this case, the medicine is Epicureanism, which Lucretius admits "is off-putting to those who have not experienced it, and most people recoil back from it."[9] The bitterness of Epicureanism sometimes needs sweetening, as many people's first taste of alcohol is drowned in fruit punch. Lucretius might very well use YouTube rather than dactylic hexameter for the same purpose these days.

For Epicurus, our mistake is not in finding poetry charming or in using it to make challenging things more pleasant. The mistake is thinking that such activities are marks of excellence rather than assorted extravagances peculiar to individual taste because of familiarity or preference. We generate unnecessary anxiety and hostility whenever we turn culture and intellect into a competition with winners and losers, haves and have-nots. Our ability to live a good life does not rise or fall with cultural refinement or rarified intellectual skills, and sometimes it's just more fun to clown around.

Cicero was especially condescending about Epicurus' lack of educational training. He rarely passes up the opportunity to point out Epicurus' lack of intellectual sophistication, no doubt in part because Cicero so cherished his own rhetorical powers. In *On Moral Ends*, Cicero concludes his opening flurry of objections to Epicureanism with a priggish dig: "For the rest, I wish Epicurus had been better equipped intellectually (you must surely agree that he lacks sophistication in those areas which go to make a person well educated)."[10] Part of Cicero's criticism was that Epicurus did not care for the impractical parts of philosophy, but the other part was that Epicurus lacked the rhetorical grace and the elitist niceties of the well-educated.

Cicero's prose is in fact a joy to read, and he leaves no question that he knows it. He is also admittedly correct that Epicurus' Greek is turgid, clumsy, and sometimes almost barbarous. I once spent a full day translating Epicurus in preparation for a stressful job interview, and by evening I was on the verge of tears. Cicero once gestures at complimenting Epicurus because "his words express his meaning, and he writes in a direct way I can comprehend."[11] Even so, Cicero buries a barb in the worm. He later suggests understanding Epicurus is intellectually undemanding because "it is child's-play to master his doctrines."[12]

Perhaps Cicero and Epicurus are just two people on competing sides of the "sophistication" divide, the one punching up, the other punching down. There might be a temptation to "both sides" this dispute, but I think we have more to gain by siding with Epicurus. Philosophy is in no way the purview of the educated classes, and the people most fluent and graceful in prose and speech often use their talents to destroy good things.

At first glance, the point that goodness comes apart from sophistication seems obvious. Someone can obviously live well without the ability to quote choice lines from John Donne, Gwendolyn Brooks, and Czesław Miłosz. An appreciation for French cinema has no bearing on whether someone is a reliable friend. Dig deeper, though, and we can see how often we orient our own sense of well-being around varying brands of intellectual and cultural snobbery. After all, I got rid of my accent, and I am not alone. A friend informed me of a radio commercial advertising lessons in eliminating Boston's "Southie" accent. The world is littered with people working to mask their natural mode of expression, and I challenge you to watch the musical *My Fair Lady* and see it as anything other than sustained abuse of Audrey Hepburn.

The problem is much bigger than accents, though. Epicureans think valuing talent and intelligence in the wrong way undermines social good will, trust, and a commitment to the truth, all of which are key components of a low-anxiety community. Intelligence is what some philosophers call a "conditional good." The most natural example of a conditional good is a weapon, for example a sword. In isolation, a sword is neither harmful nor beneficial. Its goodness or badness depends on its use, on who uses it and for what purpose. In the hands of someone with intent to do wrong, the sword is harmful. In the hands of someone skilled and trusted to defend others, the sword is advantageous. Independent of its possession and use, a sword is merely a sharp piece of metal shaped to a point.

Intellectual gifts and cultural sophistication are likewise conditional goods. That someone has talents does not ensure that they will use them well, so we should not praise intelligence and sophistication independent of how a person who possesses them uses them. That a horrible person funds opera makes that person no less horrible—it just means horrible people like opera, too. Intelligence coupled with vice is dangerous, in part because an exceptionally talented person often knows how to manipulate others through intellectual sleight of hand and rhetoric.

Plato was especially worried about what happens when argumentation and intelligence fall into the wrong hands. In the *Gorgias*, Socrates talks with a sophist named Gorgias who has set up shop in Athens offering to teach young people to argue and give speeches. Gorgias claims he will give his students the power to persuade people in law courts, council meetings, assemblies, and "any other political gathering that might take place." In fact, he promises his students they will be more persuasive than a trained doctor, physical trainer, or financial expert about medicine, exercise, and money-making.[13]

In other words, Gorgias trains professional imposters, the dangerous sort, like we commonly see on television and the internet. Gorgias' students will sound smarter than the experts, convincing an audience to doubt the doctor, not the imposter. The politician or public personality who effectively casts doubt on the genuine doctor's expertise is clearly a timeless phenomenon, as we saw writ large around the globe during the coronavirus pandemic. Suddenly everyone was an armchair epidemiologist.

The problem is not only that we fall for imposters because they talk pretty. As a result, we ignore or dismiss trustworthy people who know what they are talking about, but who lack style, grace, and rhetorical training. We can fall into the trap of correcting good people's grammar or terminology. Well-educated public figures might use all the right jargon to argue for bigotry, while those who care for their neighbor get chastised for using the less fashionable word. People can value the truth, secure trust, and avoid bigotry without knowing where the apostrophe goes, how to express their ideas clearly, or the most recent academic terminology for marginalized groups whose equality they support. Correcting those things as though they matter risks undermining communal well-being.

In short, it's the truth, trust, and community that matter for Epicureans. The rest of it—mode of expression, dress, and high-status intellectual training—should fall away as domains of consequence. It does not matter if people are smart if they are also vicious. Again, if you find yourself thinking that everyone considers this point obvious, then you might ask why so many people hide the accents that polite society considers stupid or why people so often refer to educational background as "pedigree," like humans are show dogs. Why do some people still consider it clever to mock people for an inability to tell the difference between "your" and "you're" on the internet? Why does subject verb agreement matter when the view is right?

But again, Epicurus is no champion of ignorance. He thinks some intellectual values are strictly necessary to making life go well, but they have nothing to do with fancy speak. Remember that he thinks we have a necessary desire to understand the world, which requires at least a rudimentary grasp of science and psychology that does not advert to superstition. We cannot stopper our ears to reasons or stubbornly reject information that improves our lives. In that sense, he thinks everyone needs to have a general commitment to understanding what makes life go well for the sort of creatures we are. We should not make ourselves gullible to charlatans through resistance to education.

Epicureans also heartily praise natural intellectual gifts divorced of the corrosive desires for status and power. As Torquatus notes in *On Moral Ends*, those who are "well-endowed intellectually" should use their talents generously and justly for the benefit of themselves and their community. He recognizes that intelligence can be used for ill—smart people are best at defending false claims to their advantage, especially to cover up their own injustice. Intelligence, like rhetoric, is a conditional good.

Torquatus claims "generosity is more appropriate" than using intellectual talent solely for personal advancement. He adds that "those who are generous earn themselves the good will of others and also their affection, which is the greatest guarantor of a life of peace."[14] Using one's intelligence for the sake of others is welcome, and it increases good will and trust. Using it to deceive and lie or lording it over others, by contrast, diminishes civic good will and trust.

Having discussed the dangers of over-valuing cultural and intellectual refinement at the civic level, let's return to our private imposter syndrome, the anxiety we suffer when we worry that we will be exposed as ignorant or inexperienced. As we have now seen, Epicureans should not judge others according to standards that are irrelevant for communal well-being. Imposter syndrome, though, comes from judging *ourselves* insufficient according to those same standards. We worry we will be revealed as idiots or rubes and will pay a social or professional cost.

Note, though, that if you agree (and I hope you do) that we should not judge others according to corrosive standards, then we should also extend the same grace to ourselves. If we value the right things, then we meet the only standard that matters. We lack reason to judge ourselves insufficiently intellectual or to envy others for their possession of things irrelevant to living well. We lose reason to pretend to be smarter than experts, or to preen about our own expertise because expertise is just another way of helping a community function, not of being a superior person.

If we see cultural tastes and non-essential intellectual interests as extravagances that can quickly turn corrosive, then condescension, resentment, envy, and imposter syndrome fall away. We are who we are, collectively seeking to navigate the world as best we can. We should focus most intensely on the necessities, expressing ourselves as effectively as we can about the things essential to living well. What matters are pro-social desires and actions that produce trust and well-being. Then all our other cultural charms can decorate life with the harmless extravagances of a satisfied mind.

10 | WEALTH AND WHAT IT COSTS

At a pivotal moment in the movie *Wall Street*, Gordon Gekko addresses a packed audience at the corporate board meeting of a company he intends to take over. While most people consider greed a vice, Gekko casts it as the starring virtue that justifies his relentlessness. In the sort of rousing rhetoric usually employed to inspire unity through personal sacrifice, Gekko says, "The point is, Ladies and Gentlemen, that greed—for lack of a better word—is good. Greed is right. Greed works. Greed clarifies, cuts through, and captures the essence of the evolutionary spirit. Greed, in all of its forms—greed for life, for money, for love, knowledge—has marked the upward surge of mankind." The crowd goes wild.

Let's call this "Gekko's Challenge," which has three key features: (1) greed is natural, (2) greed is advantageous, and (3) greed takes many forms. Those who resist greed in all its glory are, according to Gekko, unnatural and lack proper self-interest. In the evolutionary terms he employs, they are "unfit." While Epicurus endorses the third claim—greed is multi-form—he denies the first two claims. He thinks greed runs contrary to our nature and does not benefit us—instead, it makes tranquility impossible. Greed makes us "unfit."

Gekko's Challenge has a long pedigree, stretching back at least as far as Plato. In Plato's *Gorgias*, Socrates encourages Callicles, a charismatic and ambitious young man on the cusp of political involvement, to moderate his desires. Callicles has no interest in moderation. Instead, he tells Socrates that "this is what's admirable and just by nature—and I'll say it to you now with all frankness—that the man who'll live correctly ought to allow his own appetites to get as large as possible and not restrain them. And when they are large as possible, he ought to be competent to devote himself to them by virtue of his bravery and intelligence, and to fill them with whatever he may have an appetite for at the time."[1] Same story—greed in all its many forms, whether for money, praise, or power—is natural, beneficial, even virtuous.

If this challenge were easy to answer, Gekko and Callicles would not be so enrapturing. Ayn Rand would not still be whispering sweet nothings in the ears of young people, telling them that they deserve everything they can grab. One part of *Dirty Dancing* that always makes me chuckle is when the villain Robbie tells "Baby" that "some people count and some people don't," while shoving a copy of *The Fountainhead* into her hands, adding, "I think you'll enjoy it. But return it. I have notes in there." In this chapter, we'll focus on greed for money. Other manifestations of greed—for power, praise, success, life without end—will be the focus of the next few chapters.

First, though, let's forestall a few possible misunderstandings. While Epicurus argues that greed makes people unhappy, he cannot be dismissed as some sort of commie idealist. While the Epicureans did live together in the Garden, they had private households and unequal quantities of material goods. Epicurus owned the Garden and made arrangements in his will to pass on both the property and his other possessions. Among the will's provisions was financial support for his best friend Metrodorus' children, including a dowry for Metrodorus' daughter. Those are hardly the actions of a man opposed to private property or, for that matter, to marriage, as we'll see later.

By contrast, Diogenes Laertius reports that Zeno, the founder of Stoicism, prohibited the production of "coinage" for any purpose and believed that wives should be held "in common."[2] Zeno borrowed this love of sharing all things from Plato, whose ideal city features the abolition of private families and private property for the powerful classes, lest they tear their city apart. In Plato's *Republic*, the powerful are prohibited from even *touching* gold or silver.[3] Another of Stoicism's influential predecessors, Diogenes the Cynic, was reportedly charged with "adulterating the currency," though the relevant sense of "adulterating" remains unclear (let your imagination run wild!).[4] He committed himself to having as few possessions as possible, casting aside anything he could.

Roman Stoics like Seneca, quite popular with the Silicon Valley set these days, wrote movingly on the evils of money while being as rich as Jeff Bezos. In her excellent book on Seneca, Miriam Griffin writes, "In antiquity and ever since, Seneca has been known best, and hated most, for combining philosophy with wealth. The most persistent charges of hypocrisy centered, then as now, on his fortune and its acquisition, for no one excelled this millionaire in singing the praises of poverty."[5] By "its acquisition," Griffin means, among other things, the part where Seneca likely helped the Emperor Nero justify killing his own mother, Agrippina, the woman who once hired Seneca to tutor her son.[6] The Roman poet Martial referred to him as "Super-rich Seneca."[7]

Though Epicurus considered the desire for great wealth corrosive, he thought the Early Stoic and Platonic impulse to abolish private property was tantamount to telling your friends you don't trust them.[8] For Epicureans, mutual trust is the well-spring of friendship and political tranquility writ large. Epicurus' beef with greed, then, did not extend so far as to make him think money or property poisons the soul or society. In most economies, we use money to acquire the objects of necessary desires like food and shelter, as well as to fulfill extravagant desires for harmless pleasures. Epicurus thinks that people who are excessively abstemious are as bad off as the greedy. "There is," he writes, "a proper measure for parsimony, and he who does not reason it out is just as badly off as he who goes wrong by total neglect of limits."[9] Note the "just as badly off."

Even though Epicurus has more permissive attitudes toward money and private property than some of his philosophical predecessors, he agrees with their central concern that actively pursuing and accumulating great wealth undermines individual tranquility and tears at the social fabric. Greed corrodes. Greed extends beyond the money sufficient for necessary desires, as well as for harmless extravagances. In fact, like most other corrosive desires, it extends further and further into the distance and out of sight. Greedy people are never satisfied because there is always more to want.

Yet it might not seem obvious that Epicurus, a card-carrying hedonist, has good reason to oppose, much less condemn, a desire for great wealth. What if pursuing and accumulating abundant wealth helped secure the objects of our necessary and extravagant desires without undercutting our tranquility or capacity to act virtuously? Why not prefer to live as a tranquil billionaire, enjoying extravagances galore, never an idle worry of being turned out on the street? Perhaps security, stable pleasure, and pleasant extravagances can, at least sometimes, increase in tandem with wealth. A billionaire might seem the most secure of all.

Epicurus agrees that if it were true that people with great wealth achieved security, then he would have no good reason to discourage it. In fact, it would be only natural to indulge greed for money, honor, or power if it made us more secure and less anxious because our core natural impulse is for tranquil security.[10] He thinks possessing adequate resources is a component of security, and adequacy marks the limit of what Epicurus calls "natural wealth." Unlike the Stoics, Epicurus thinks basic material security is necessary for tranquility—the Stoics think we need virtue alone; the Epicureans think we also need food and the money necessary to buy it. Epicurus does note, though, that while money often provides important security, the protection of trustworthy and reliable friends provides by far the greatest security. At the very least, then, we should value our friends more than money when the two conflict, which he thinks they often do.[11]

In our reflective moments, most of us think having enough for our needs is sufficient, and we recognize that only those who lack necessities have genuine cause for complaint. In the hum and buzz of daily life, though, when time for reflection is scarce, we might find ourselves giving in to the desire for, or envy of, great wealth. Even when we don't want to be greedy, it can sneak in unawares. I have admittedly caught myself seriously considering whether to pursue career options that pay more, but that would likely diminish my joy, spare time, and autonomy. Worse, they might require moving away from friends. Speaking only for myself here, I understand that some means of pursuing more money would rob me of things I value more, yet the feeling that money is worth its attendant costs clearly has some illusory power. It can't help that our environment amplifies the illusion.

Epicurus thinks wealth looks good because of hedonistic miscalculation and mismeasurement of the sort we discussed in the chapter on hedonism. Two of the *Vatican Sayings* distill the key reasons Epicurus opposes pursuing, acquiring, and keeping great wealth, the first focusing on freedom and the second on justice:

> A free life cannot acquire great wealth, because the task is not easy without slavery to the mob or those in power . . . And if [a free life] does somehow achieve great wealth, one could easily share this out in order to obtain the good will of one's neighbors.[12]

> It is impious to love money unjustly, and shameful to do so justly; for it is unfitting to be sordidly stingy even if one is just.[13]

These passages share an argumentative form—it is difficult (often impossible) to become wealthy without losing our autonomy or committing injustice. But if, under rare circumstances, we do acquire great wealth freely and justly, we benefit far more in terms of security and well-being from sharing it than keeping it for ourselves. So, either way, getting or keeping great wealth is imprudent and tranquility-undermining.

It might help to distill these arguments into three claims. Greed requires one or more of the following:

1) "slavery to the mob" or powerful,
2) acting unjustly, and
3) destabilizing our community and earning its resentment.

Usually, the extremely wealthy do all three—lose their autonomy, act unjustly, and destabilize their community. Again, Epicurus acknowledges that some individuals might acquire great wealth without compromising their autonomy or acting unjustly (perhaps through art, inheritance, or a divorce settlement). Even so, if these people keep it rather than sharing generously with those in peril, they also destabilize their community and, by extension, their own well-being. None of Epicurus' claims are manifestly true or widely popular.

Early in my teaching career, I unexpectedly struck a hot nerve in my students when it occurred to me to ask them, in the context of teaching Plato's *Apology*, whether Socrates was correct to suggest that no one can gain and keep great wealth without compromising their personal integrity or resorting to dishonesty and injustice.[14] I had merely read a passage from the day's required reading aloud, but they had the punch-drunk look of students who probably had never opened the book. The incredulous look of "it says what?!" often gets a discussion up and running.

None of them, so far as I know, were billionaires, nor were their parents, but they seemed to be taking the question personally. They were good kids who wanted to maintain autonomy and avoid injustice, but they also wouldn't mind being billionaires, or at least fabulously wealthy. They did not want to entertain Socrates' claim that those two desires might conflict as a general principle. They started ginning up counterexamples, increasingly worried that the hunt for exceptions was only serving to shore up the rule.

Following my students' impulse to search for real-world exceptions, let's look at the world as we find it rather than engaging in idle musings about imaginary people living in a fictional society. As I learned from observing my students, we should also consider two different, but closely related sorts of people—the world's roughly 2,750 billionaires and the many millions of other people who wouldn't mind being one. It is far too easy to beat up on the billionaires because they are strangers, but Epicurus would think it also matters that so many people envy billionaires and wealthy executives. For Epicurus, everyone with a corrosive desire for wealth is psychologically unsatisfied, and envy itself is an unpleasant feeling.

Let's begin with Epicurus' claim about the relationship between greed and injustice. Is it true that acquiring excessive wealth generally requires injustice? Call to mind a few titans of business and, more importantly, the companies they have created. In America, a publicly traded corporation's stated aim, backed by the force of law, is to maximize value for shareholders.[15] If investors determine that a company has failed to maximize value on their behalf, they can sue the company for mismanagement. In practice, "value" has largely been interpreted as profit, which means corporate leaders are obligated to seek profit for investors wherever they can find it without breaking the law.[16]

As a result, whenever it increases profit and is technically legal, companies should pay workers as little as the market demands, even if those workers cannot meet their necessary desires with that salary; ignore or even commit human rights violations to secure resources like precious metals, oil, or cheap labor; manifest indifference to environmental degradation; ignore quality control; crush the competition to establish monopolies; market tools for wide-scale violations of privacy to advertisers and foreign governments; undermine political confidence through the complicit or direct promotion of lies; etc. In sum, if the guiding aim is maximum profit, then anything legal that maximizes profit is something you *should* do. There is a point past which the increase in ethical compromise within the bounds of law becomes logarithmic.

If you, like me, prefer to interpret people's actions with good will, you might think most people who launch projects that turn into mega-corporations do not begin with malign intentions because of inherently warped characters. They are often creatives or entrepreneurs out to produce something visionary or transformative, maybe even with some thought that they could avoid falling prey to injustice and greed. Think, for example, of Google's now quaint pledge: "Don't be evil." Stated at length in its initial IPO offering, it almost reads like Epicurus wrote it:

> Don't be evil. We believe strongly that in the long term, we will be better served—as shareholders and in all other ways—by a company that does good things for the world even if we forgo some short-term gains.[17]

That sounds like indirect hedonism at work—short-term costs for long-term gains. Perhaps they honestly believed that would happen, but this ideal was quickly cast aside in practice, then quietly revised, and finally expunged from company policy. Again, if profit is the only "gain" on offer, doing "good things for the world" (or, more narrowly, your employees or community) only makes sense when it produces more money for the shareholders. When "good for the world" and profit conflict, profit wins. So, as a conceptual matter, Epicurus is right: if maximizing profit is your fundamental aim, then other important ethical values drop out.

Let's turn now to Epicurus' claim that those who maximize profit at the cost of injustice suffer from private anxiety and public resentment. A person who makes a killing from immorality that is technically legal has two options—rest easy or try to assuage their conscience, perhaps by using their left hand to quarter-solve the environmental, economic, and psychological crises they set in motion with their right. In other words, they might fly to Davos for the World Economic Forum to brainstorm solutions without discussing whether they themselves played any causal role in producing the problems.[18] Avoiding cause for ill-feeling, though, usually depends on limiting the guest list to those who never chastise the participants. When, for example, Rutger Bregman (a Dutch journalist and historian) and Winnie Byanyima (Executive Director of Oxfam International) once suggested that the attendees at Davos could fix the problem of financial inequality and exploitative labor by giving up significant portions of their personal wealth through taxation, they were met with a silent chorus of, "Who invited these people?"[19]

Borne aloft on the wings of Cicero's undeniably elegant and muscular prose, Torquatus ties together these Epicurean threads:

> Any contribution that wicked deeds can make to lessening the discomforts of life is outweighed by the bad conscience,

the legal penalties, and the hatred of one's fellow citizens that looms as a result. Yet some people put no limit on their greed, their love of honor or power, their lust, their gluttony, or any of their other desires. It is not as if ill-gotten gain diminishes these desires—rather it inflames them. They must be choked off, not reformed.[20]

In other words, the relentless quest for profit requires the kind of ethical sacrifice and injustice that inevitably fosters communal resentment and erodes trust. It also, in some fashion, tends to prey on the conscience of those who benefit financially.

Epicurus thinks that corrosive desires, once given space, become so powerful that they crowd out everything else, even our own well-being. Alcoholics keep drinking even as they ruin relationships, destroy their health, break laws, and lose jobs. Addictions lay waste to good things, and Torquatus talks of greed as though it were an addiction. People indulge greed despite the "bad conscience, legal penalties, and the hatred of fellow citizens." Greed "must be choked off, not reformed."

Remember, though, that Epicurus thinks some people can obtain abundant financial resources without sacrificing their autonomy or acting unjustly. For that reason, they should not feel guilt or suffer a bad conscience about how they came by their money, and he thinks they should use it for their own harmless joys, especially joys shared with friends. Nevertheless, they benefit far more from sharing than keeping the excess. Of those who gain wealth ethically, Torquatus says that "generosity is more appropriate. Those who are generous earn themselves the good will of others and their affection, which is the greatest guarantor of a life of peace." In other words, they themselves gain from giving it away—it makes them happier and more secure.

Tupac Shakur, in a long unreleased interview with MTV in 1992, gives voice to these Epicurean talking points when imagining the possibility of his own future riches. He begins by suggesting that seeking great wealth requires tireless effort, competition, and an indifference to crushing others:

> This world is—and when I say "this world" I mean it, I don't mean it in an ideal sense. I mean it in every day, every little thing you do—it's such a "Gimme, gimme, gimme." Everybody back off. Everybody's taught that from school. Everywhere. Big business: You wanna be successful? You wanna be like Trump? Gimme, gimme, gimme. Push, push, push, push. Step, step, step. Crush, crush, crush. That's how it all is. And it's like nobody ever stops, you know?

The interviewer asks Shakur how he would respond to people who might object that they earned their money fairly and deserve to keep it.

> If they earned it—I think that's good and I think that they deserve it. But even if you earned it, you still owe. Look at me. I'm not—I don't have that mega-money. But I feel guilty walking by somebody. I gotta give him some mail . . . Can you imagine somebody having $32 million . . . and this person has nothing? And you can sleep? These are the type of people who get humanitarian awards—millionaires. How can they be humanitarians? The fact that they're millionaires and

there's so many poor people shows how inhumane they are, you know what I'm saying?

And that bugs me. I'm not saying that I'm never gonna be rich, but I'm saying there's a struggle, and I think everybody deserves, and I think there's a way to pay these people.[21]

Epicurus thinks those who give generously to ensure the fundamental well-being of their community live happier, more satisfied lives because they earn the "good will" of their neighbors in need. They don't engage in complicated mental gymnastics to convince themselves that it is fine that others live in desperation or that a drop in the bucket of generosity makes them a humanitarian. They do not need to avert their eyes in embarrassment or move into a private enclave to avoid seeing the disadvantaged.[22] Running away from the poor is itself anxiety in action.

Again, I suspect most of us do not particularly want to be billionaires or corporate executives for many of the reasons I have canvassed. We might agree with Epicurus that "the more good fortune they have, the more they spoil it for themselves."[23] Yet we can sometimes be taken in by the illusion that great wealth produces greater pleasure. Unless we recalibrate our tool for hedonistic measurement, wealth's pleasures will always look bigger and better than they really are, like we can get there with our values intact.

Epicurus thinks that people content with enough have a peace of mind that is its own kind of wealth, the natural kind. To borrow from an old country song, "the wealthiest person is a pauper at times, compared to the man with a satisfied mind."[24]

11 | LIVING UNNOTICED: POLITICS AND POWER

Epicurus advised his followers, somewhat enigmatically, to "live unnoticed."[1] What, though, does that even mean? After all, Epicurus himself lived very much noticed. He founded a school, wrote down his views, responded to his opponents, and handed his community down to be managed in his spirit in perpetuity. While the Garden might have been on the bucolic outskirts of Athens, it was not literally hidden. More importantly, Epicurus thinks we absolutely need close friends, and we surely want *them* to notice us! If Epicurus considered it prudent to live unnoticed, he must have believed it was possible to live unnoticed in plain sight. He does not encourage us to don the camouflage of wallflowers.

Opponents of Epicurus at the time correctly interpreted Epicurus' injunction to "live unnoticed" as, at least in part, a caution against getting involved in high-level, competitive politics. Cicero and Seneca, both of whom were deeply enmeshed in Roman political intrigue, did not welcome the criticism. Had Epicurus been their contemporary, he would no doubt have enjoyed discussing the topic in their company. Cicero's best friend, Atticus, was an Epicurean, and the two regularly disagreed on the question of political involvement, Atticus skirting politics, Cicero diving in headlong.

Atticus at one point won the upper hand in the dispute. Cicero flirted with the Epicurean stance when he was legally prohibited from political engagement, though his misgivings were more likely "sour grapes" than a proper conversion.[2] He set those qualms aside and eagerly re-entered the political fray when he was invited back to Rome. Seneca likewise expressed a newfound appreciation of Epicurus when he at long last attempted to withdraw from politics, too late in the end to save himself from a politically motivated assassination.[3]

As Cicero fled Rome and his executioner, perhaps he found himself again thinking of Epicurus. Cicero's head and his right hand were cut off and nailed to the rostrum in the Forum where he had gracefully delivered many powerful and eloquent political speeches.[4] Seneca was ordered to kill himself or an executioner would. Suicide was the better option for practical reasons because citizens who died by their own hand were buried intact and could transfer their property to heirs. In this respect, Nero showed a perverse kind of mercy by offering Seneca a choice.[5]

From an Epicurean perspective, the problem is not so much that Seneca and Cicero were killed by their political rivals. Recall that Epicurus considers it noble to die protecting your friends or in defense of your values.[6] He's no shrinking violet, and death is sometimes the better option. His concern would be that Cicero's and Seneca's deaths came on the heels of an adult life spent pursuing power and pandering to vicious people, some of whom eventually came for their lives. Even those sympathetic to their philosophy cannot overlook Cicero's fickleness and self-aggrandizement or Seneca's naïve attempts to reform the cruel and sadistic Emperor

Nero. Epicurus, by contrast, lived out his natural life with friends, all his limbs left intact at death. The question for this chapter is whether that kind of quietism comes with its own ethical costs.

We of course have our modern stand-ins for Cicero and Seneca, people with intermittently good intentions willing to pander to tyrants at the cost of their integrity. High-octane politics remains much as it has always been, an invitation for life-long participants to hold their nose and toss aside their scruples in hopes of eventually building their fort at the top of the hill. We sometimes lose sight of how readily politics can still get you killed, especially when politicians are brave enough to advance views that make other people uncomfortably aware of their ethical shortcomings. Epicurus' advice to "live unnoticed," then, is sometimes read as a caution against getting involved in politics altogether, but it is perhaps better read as a caution against selling your soul for power.

When most of us consider the role of politics in our lives, though, we do not weigh whether to compete for the highest offices in the land. Instead, we think of politics as a way of advancing and protecting our own interests, as well as the interests of our community. It might seem at first glance that here, too, Epicureans have some reason to "live unnoticed," to drop out of political involvement altogether whenever they reasonably can. An Epicurean concerned to minimize anxiety might not even read the news, much less join a movement. Caring deeply about politics can seem like opening the door wide to the overlord of anxiety, pessimism, and resentment. Here, too, "live unnoticed" might mean we should avoid investing in political causes and tend to our own personal affairs for the sake of tranquility.

That is certainly the reasonable response of many people. When describing his experiences at the US Capitol Building on January 6, 2021, DC Metropolitan Police Officer Michael Fanone said, "I think I'm a pretty apolitical person. You know, my preference is— I look at politics the same way I look at the Olympics. Like I like my politics every four years and only for the month that the election season has taken place. The rest of the time like I don't give a (muted)."[7] He was being interviewed because he was almost killed while fighting off a political insurrection, so he had just learned up-close what political violence and anger looks like when it rides the wave of massive deception. The lesson—some politics comes even for the apolitical.

So, what kind of politics does Epicurus oppose? Well, it depends on what you mean by "politics." The foundation and fulcrum of a healthy political body is justice, and Epicurus definitely has principled views about natural justice and fairness. He writes that "the justice of nature is a pledge to reciprocal usefulness, neither to harm one another nor to be harmed."[8] While the details of that contract might vary by location, Epicurus thinks the basic outlines of a contract for "reciprocal usefulness" and against mutual harm are the same for everyone.[9] So in that sense, Epicurus is decidedly political—he thinks justice is an agreement among all rational creatures not to harm one another, and a healthy political body is one that respects and enforces that contract. Many contemporary political philosophers agree with Epicurus on this front.

Lucretius recounts the origins of justice in political society, starting from a time when humans "were unable to look to the common interest, and had no knowledge of the mutual benefits of any customs or laws. Individuals instinctively seized whatever prize fortune had offered to them, trained as they were to live and use their strength for themselves alone."[10] No one helped anyone else, so they died alone of starvation or devoured by beasts. Lucretius briefly indulges his characteristic pessimism by pointing out a silver lining for this race of imprudent loners—at least they didn't die by the thousands in war, chasing riches on the sea, or victims of their own gluttony.[11]

On Lucretius' telling, justice came into being when the children got cute. Once the men for whatever reason stayed around long enough to see their children born, these "children with their charming ways easily broke down the stern disposition of their parents. It was then, too, that neighbors, in their eagerness neither to harm nor be harmed, began to form mutual pacts of friendship, . . . indicating by means of inarticulate cries and gestures that everyone ought to have compassion on the weak."[12] It worked, if imperfectly. Lucretius writes, "Although it was not possible for concord to be achieved universally, yet the great majority kept their compacts loyally." Otherwise, he claims, we would not be where we are.

Justice was not merely theoretical for Epicurus. He built a diverse community bounded by trust and mutual concern, surrounding himself with people committed to shared values. It makes sense that trust would be central the Garden's culture because pacts and contracts are essentially pledges of trust. Epicurus has a conception of political happiness that puts civic tranquility at its center, so it was essential that no members fell into life-threatening material distress or insecurity. For the record, Epicurus was also an Athenian citizen by birth, subject to whatever obligations followed from that status.

In sum, Epicurus was political, at least in some important senses of the word. Living unnoticed is clearly consistent with forming a community committed to justice and fairness, which many people might count the heart of politics. Critics, though, contend that Epicurean politics remains relatively narrow and insufficiently public-facing. In other words, the limits of Epicurus' political action might not stretch all that much further than the bounds of his own Epicurean community.[13]

Here they are not entirely wrong. Epicurean politics is more likely to be local, not necessarily out of selfishness or an indifference to helping others in the wider world. As I take it, Epicurean politics are limited by three considerations—the rejection of corrosive desires, the relatively limited set of political priorities, and the desire to put their energies to best use. Nevertheless, Epicureans do have political interests, and they will pursue those interests in a way consistent with their tranquility, even at grave risk. They do not drop out so much as refuse to play the game on terms that require them to abandon their core values. Their view is controversial, but it is, I think, an interesting perspective.

The starting point for all things Epicurean is desire. At this point you can probably sing along—there are three kinds of desire. Necessary desires are the ones required for the tranquility of creatures like us. These include not only food, drink, shelter, and protection from violence and poisons, but also a basic understanding of the workings of the natural world, friends, and some free time to enjoy these pleasures. While the category of necessary desires is restricted, it is also far more expansive than we often recognize. Without confidence that we can satisfy our necessary desires, Epicurus thinks we cannot be tranquil or fully happy.[14]

Thankfully, Epicurus thinks we can satisfy the necessary desires of our community without great effort *if* we get our priorities straight, both individually and collectively.

We just tend not to get our priorities straight, both individually and collectively. The most common impediments are that we overvalue extravagant desires or feed rather than starve corrosive desires. Most extravagant desires are for fancy versions of necessary desires, and Epicurus thinks they should be heartily enjoyed when available, but we can achieve tranquility without them. Overvaluing extravagances undermines tranquility because they are often scarce, competitive, and difficult to obtain. In addition, pursuing them can detract from time better spent fulfilling necessary desires.

The political effects of corrosive desires for wealth, power, and status are even more worrisome than the distractions of extravagance. Corrosive desires are unlimited and undermine tranquility by their very nature. They are unlimited in the sense that people think more is ever better, so corrosive desires can never be sated— more money, more respect, more power. People under the sway of corrosive desires are anxious to get more, to keep it longer, to never lose it. They pander, commit injustice, and neglect more meaningful pleasures like genuine friendship. The taxonomy of desires, as we have seen, serves as the foundation for Epicurean happiness, both individual and political.

Returning, then, to the question of political priorities, the first, and possibly only, genuine Epicurean political priority is protecting members of one's community from the avoidable peril of unsatisfied necessary desires. No political cause is more important for an Epicurean than ensuring that people have protection against physical violence and grave mistreatment, as well as confidence that they will not be left hungry, unhoused, without access to a fundamental education, life-saving medical care, or the liberty to pursue harmless personal and private relations. Those are the core domains of Epicurean tranquility, so they are the backbone of mutual aid and protection.

Now, some people might label this fundamental shared concern for necessary desires "socialism," as though Epicurus would know that word or how it is currently bandied about in political theater. Remember, Epicureanism is a theory of happiness, not a model of government or a taxation policy. It is not an attempt to reform the desires of the rich for the benefit of those less fortunate because it is an attempt to reform *everyone's* desires for everyone's benefit. Corrosive desires are not the exclusive purview of any group, class, or political party. Greed for money, reputation, or power can be found among the poor and among big-hearted liberals who hoard their wealth. Politicians are power-hungry across all aisles and in all quadrants. Corrosive desires can crop up in any of us.[15]

Epicurus thinks corrosive desires are the greatest impediment to securing political confidence about the satisfaction of necessary desires. Feed and fertilize the corrosive desires and the necessary desires starve. Shared trust and the will to sustain collective action depend on the satisfaction of necessary desires, so a community that neglects them kneecaps itself and undercuts its chances for political tranquility. Societies enthralled with corrosive desires while members lack necessities are anxious and unsatisfied. Trust withers. For an Epicurean, then, other political projects take a back seat to necessary desires, whether those projects involve lowering taxes or debates about statues, maximizing profits or wrangling over language, bitter disputes about pet theories more abstract than practical.

You can see why Epicurean political engagement would not be often welcome because it takes Epicurean frank speech into the political arena. It challenges people, not political parties, by asking everyone to assess their priorities and adopt a willingness to sacrifice. Telling large numbers of people that their corrosive desires leave them miserable and undermine community trust can put a mark on a politician's back, even when kindly expressed. Telling them they are wrapped up in political disputes of little consequence while refusing to make material sacrifices to take care of others is also not a winning message because it, too, challenges people, not political parties. It snags the person who fights abortion but resists supporting poor mothers, as well as the person who correctly points out oppression without a willingness to give up resources to remedy that oppression.

Let's return, then, to the question of what Epicurus means when he tells his followers to live unnoticed. While he clearly rejects corrosive political aims, he also claims that Epicurean commitments make a person "unhesitant in the face of life's necessary duties" and "fearless in the face of chance."[16] In some cases, then, Epicureans might find themselves obligated to enter the political sphere to help their community secure the objects of necessary desires. Engaging in some forms of political action might turn out to one of "life's necessary duties," and a failure to fulfill that duty might constitute a betrayal of trust. When such circumstances arise, the Epicurean will choose their cause wisely, pursue it without hesitation, and recognize it might fail because of circumstances beyond their control. They will, in sum, choose "necessary duties" and be "fearless in the face of chance."

If we were to devise some sort of rough heuristic for when and how an Epicurean might get politically involved without sacrificing tranquility, we might propose the following three tests:

The Necessity Test: Does my political involvement help people get the essential things they need?

The Status Test: Would I be happy to see my project succeed even if absolutely no one knew that I supported it and even if I received absolutely no recognition or advantage for the cause's advancement?

The Chance Test: Can I emotionally accept that my project will meet resistance and might never be accomplished, at least in my own lifetime?

The Necessity Test is, I suspect, the most controversial. When people turn blue in the face over things that have no significant bearing on remediable distress, Epicurus would think their cause at best extravagant, but more likely just corrosion wrapped in the veneer of political concern. When political action moves away from physical security, food, housing, life-saving medicine, fundamental education, and liberty for meaningful relationships, Epicurus thinks it moves away from the necessities of individual and political happiness. The only necessary political interests for Epicureans are necessary desires. Other things are nice, but not the first priority.

The Status Test is the test perhaps most closely tied to the original spirit of "live unnoticed." It keeps us honest about whether we have harnessed our cause to corrosive desires for status, power, and money. With respect to status, we can sometimes care that others recognize our participation in a cause as much as, even more than, we care that the cause itself succeed. Some instances of caring about recognition are relatively harmless, though they demonstrate that political activity is often performative. For example, we turn our Instagram picture black for a day. We donate to charity because we can wear a t-shirt that makes our generosity visible. We film ourselves pouring ice over our heads. Performing our concern is not in itself wrong, and it even proves beneficial in some cases.

It becomes a problem, though, when we do nothing other than pursue attention or, worse, when we draw attention toward ourselves and away from the cause itself, encouraging others to do the same. A concern for status becomes deeply corrosive when someone, especially a leader, risks subverting the aims and interests of the cause to increase their private resources, fame, or power. As people climb the ranks of a movement and gain access to shared resources, it can be increasingly tempting to bend the rules. Ethical failures on this front, though, have dreadful consequences for a cause because they demoralize the proponents and strengthen the opposition. People who struggle to contain their greed or competitive desires can wreck admirable pursuits.

Lastly, the Chance Test requires a delicate balance between caring about a cause and not giving in to bitterness, hostility, and despair when it meets resistance or failure. An Epicurean's political activity must operate within the bounds of their own tranquility. Some might believe important causes are worth sacrifices in psychological well-being and that we should be angry when admirable aims fail because of bad actors. Epicurus acknowledges, as we will see, that many things lie outside of our control and that some misfortunes are justified reasons for genuine disappointment. Yet he also thinks the things that lie within our power give us reason not to despair. He writes that we should never assume success, but we should also "not despair of it as unconditionally not going to occur."[17]

On my reading, then, Epicureans "live unnoticed" not by withdrawing from society or focusing only on themselves. Instead, they "live unnoticed" by ignoring status, refusing to clamber for personal attention, and being very careful around power. The critics are correct that Epicureans will generally avoid mainstage politics because that kind of political success usually requires feeding rather than starving corrosive desires. Power politics perpetuates itself by sowing discord and eroding trust.

For these and other reasons, Epicurean political involvement is more likely to be smaller scale, local, and far less glamorous. It will involve a willingness to give up unnecessary resources to secure the necessary desires of others because necessary goods improve people's lives fundamentally, not cosmetically. The efforts of Epicureans will often go unnoticed because most decency and small-scale generosity does, but honestly, they're fine with that. In fact, they prefer it that way.

12 | LIVING UNNOTICED: THE TYRANNY OF THE "LIKE"

I usually serve as an academic adviser for a group of first-year students, and the advising office encourages us to conduct an "ice breaker" at our first meeting before diving into the boring nuts and bolts of the curriculum. Every normal and well-adjusted person hates ice breakers, but they do, regrettably, serve their purpose. So, I usually resort to that old chestnut, "Tell us something distinctive about yourself." In my twelve years at my university, only one response has elicited the sharp intake of breath that indicates genuine surprise, followed by a chorus of "No way!" One student said his name, his hometown, and reported, "I have never had a social media account." It was apparently entirely by choice. Minds blown.

Epicurus thinks we all need a social life. Friends are necessary for tranquility, and friends want to spend time with one another and keep up with each other's lives. Epicurus would endorse any tool that facilitates friendly interaction without otherwise increasing anxiety because he thinks *anything* conducive to tranquility is naturally good. If seeking attention on the internet sustained tranquility, then Epicurus would not object.[1] Some people on social media are tranquil. Most people are not. Epicurus, of course, could not have anticipated the internet at all, much less the many ways we have devised to turn it against ourselves, but here his enigmatic advice to "live unnoticed" has perhaps its greatest contemporary resonance.

In our collective defense, the whole thing is engineered to make us miserable. Social media is itself the outgrowth of its designers' corrosive desires for power and profit, and they designed social media to target our corrosive desires for recognition, status, and acquisition. As we know, Epicurus thinks corrosive desires are the ones that extend without limit. More profit, more power, more honor. More clicks, more likes, more followers.

The designers of social media want to make a limitless amount of money, and they know that the best way to do that is to feed their subscribers' limitless desire for attention. They understand that people under the sway of corrosive desires are like dogs tirelessly chasing the metal rabbit at a racetrack—no dog ever catches it, but they just keep running. In this case, the people who own the track are trying to keep as many dogs in the race as possible, and they seem to have set up not only a dog race, but also a dog fight. A dog war.

Remember that for Epicurus, corrosive desires have other features resulting from their limitless nature. Feeding corrosive desires undercuts our ability to satisfy our necessary desires—a person relentless in their pursuit of money does not have time for their family, and neither does someone always on the internet. In addition, corrosive desires are competitive and comparative, so that one person has more or less than others, making them subject to conceit or envy. Everyone has a follower count and a tally of likes that, under the right circumstances, sometimes turns into a quantity of dollars.

Lastly, while most people under the sway of corrosive desires believe they are the ones in control, someone else is almost always driving the car. Epicurus says we can rarely acquire great wealth without "slavery to the mob or those in power," but he would likely think the point applies equally well to status on the internet.[2] The person who wants money chases whomever will give it to them, and the politician chases the voter. The person who markets themselves for likes and followers conforms to the transient whims of other people, convincing themselves that they, somehow, are the "influencer." Everyone thinks they are in control, but few, if any, really are.

When we feel a powerful need for attention, we do what will get it. If anger gets attention, we get angry. If mocking people gets attention, we mock people. If outrage gets attention, we are outraged. When attention is the currency, we do what other people want to see, try to become whatever other people want to watch, admire, and envy. Instead of figuring out who we want to be or what we enjoy, we want to satisfy the desires of others.

In other words, we turn *ourselves* into the product, testing out consumer feedback to improve ourselves according to the market. Some of us convince ourselves this market is just a necessary evil of daily living, of doing business. We act like New York stockbrokers or supermodels in the 1980s, telling each other, "To do our job well, we really need to sign up for cocaine accounts and consume a steady diet of cocaine." Success at living require success at social media.

An Epicurean opponent might reasonably push back in defense of social media from exactly that purely practical standpoint. After all, many successful stockbrokers and supermodels probably did need the cocaine to succeed. More broadly, though, we might imagine someone saying, "Look, the hard truth is that humans are in the business of satisfying other people's desires to stay afloat—I have to satisfy my boss, the professor has to please the students, the writer has to satisfy the reader, the barista makes the coffee exactly as the customer wants. That's the way of the world, Epicurus! Great that you dropped out, bully for you, but the rest of us have to live our lives as wage slaves and people pleasers. We have no choice but to be walking advertisements for ourselves or pawns in someone else's game. Social media is a necessary evil."

This objection has some fierce teeth. We do in fact satisfy the desires of others all the time in our public and private life. We do a lot of things we do not want to do because we would otherwise lack the necessities of life. That is certainly the situation of most "essential workers," the tireless souls who had to venture out during COVID-19 lockdowns. They serve the desires of customers and their boss, and they would suffer genuine loss without those funds, even by Epicurus' standards. They would be cast out on the street. They please or drown. Note, though, that essential workers rarely need a social media account to do their job, nor do most people who work most jobs, honestly. We do not usually need social media to keep a roof over our head.

And even if some social media is necessary for functioning in the modern world, much of our time on social media is, truth be told, recreational and status-seeking. It feeds our pride, and Epicurus opposes feeding pretty much anything that does not convert food into energy. He endorses self-confidence, but he thinks it should be self-sustaining so that it does not depend on others. He writes that "natural philosophy," by which he means the art of living well within limits, "does not create boastful men nor chatterboxes nor men who show off the 'culture' which the many quarrel over, but rather strong and self-sufficient men, who pride themselves on their own personal goods, not those of external circumstances."[3] Ouch. If you took the boastful chatterboxes who pride themselves on culture and external circumstances off social media, who would be left?

Epicurus' more biting point, though, is about freedom and joy. He thinks people who seek things from strangers for reasons outside their control cannot be free. They want something that requires "slavery to the mob."[4] Worse, chasing fame and honor is not a solid long-term strategy for pleasure because of fame's instability. Epicurus writes that "the disturbance of the soul will not be dissolved nor will considerable joy be produced . . . by honor and admiration among the many, nor by anything that is the result of indefinite causes."[5] We never quite know what will win admiration, what will go viral, because that sort of sudden fame or notoriety results from "indefinite causes." Our friends are reliable, know who we are as people, and want what is best for us. We can experience the unalloyed joys of companionship and extravagances with our friends. They trust us and care for us. Anonymous strangers do not, and if we want their affirmation, we turn over the reins to our freedom and pride.

Perhaps we might offer instead a defense of social media on the political front. We have some reason to believe that social media is an effective mechanism for important social movements that aim to secure the necessary desires of those who are desperate. Years ago, especially during the "Arab Spring," many thought social media was a promising tool for political change that would empower the dispossessed. People have hoped, and still hope, that social media can change political structures that stand in the way of the autonomy and security of members of oppressed groups. Epicurus cares about the necessary desires of the desperate, so he would have reason to hear out the point. Again, he believes that any mechanism that secures necessary goods for a community is a useful tool for obtaining a natural good.

Social media, though, is merely a tool, and like most other tools, it can be used effectively by both good and bad people. Earlier we explored the idea of "conditional goods," things that are good in the right hands and bad in the wrong hands. A hammer in the hands of a good person builds houses, and in the hands of a bad person cracks skulls. Social media's status as a conditional good was, in retrospect, one of the long-game lessons of the "Arab Spring."[6] Rhetorical powers are good when used to convince others of the truth, bad when used by tyrants to reinforce the status quo. For Epicurus, then, those who think social media will improve the circumstances of people in need must demonstrate that it does, and if their case is strong, he will endorse it. He thinks humans often pursue power and influence to gain security, and he concedes that "*if* the life of such men is secure, they acquire the natural good."[7]

Epicurus is generally skeptical that power and influence bring security, but again, he concedes it might in some cases. To convince him, we would need reason to think social media makes things better for the disadvantaged. If it makes their situation worse, or if internet activity just sets people up to perform concern rather than act off-screen, Epicurus would reject it. If people post without acting, social media is merely a veneer of social change. Given the rage, the political unrest, and the deadly mob violence, much of it ginned up by well-crafted lies promoted by algorithms to the top of social media newsfeeds, my guess is that Epicurus would opt to steer clear and find another tool, even if that alternative works on a smaller scale. Epicurus might think we are better served by actual conversations with people in our community, building trust in person.

One final point about social media bears mentioning. It can sap the joy from our extravagances and time with friends by encouraging us to flatten and frame our experiences for the edification and admiration of others. We see a field of flowers in the desert and seek out exactly the right photo for social media, the awe of the moment diminished or lost entirely. We walk through museums taking pictures of the art, looking at it on our screens more than on the wall in front of us. We curate our experiences with an eye toward how the camera best captures a rich experience or how we might make even authentic misery look good.

A few years ago, I ended up the glorified female chaperone for twenty-six Duke University students on a trip to Greece. My primary job was making sure no one got left behind. I had never been to Greece before, despite making Greek philosophy my profession, so I took the opportunity for a free trip. I counted to twenty-six at least two hundred times, all the ducklings on the bus or boat before we pulled away to see something else remarkable. Like any month-long trip with twenty-year-olds, it had its ups and downs, but I liked all the kids. Greece is beautiful, and our guide is one of my favorite people ever.

One afternoon toward the end of the trip, I came across a student who had just awakened from a nap in the shade of a yacht docked at the port of a beautiful Greek island (ridiculous, I know, but it was Duke!). For reasons I could not pinpoint, I kept a special look-out for this student's well-being because she was clearly struggling to make sense of adult life. By that point in the trip, the students were all exhausted from burning the candle at both ends, so I was relieved she had gotten some sleep. Upon awakening, though, she was immediately distressed that she had slept through her friends' trip to the beach.

Her reason for distress was not missing her friends or the beach. Instead, she had missed "the pics." It was, she told me in the tone she no doubt usually reserved for her mother, "all about the pics." The experience itself had become the picture of the experience, uploaded each day with relentless regularity to keep a Snapchat streak going. (When we climbed Mount Olympus, some students were so worried they would lose internet reception, and their Snapchat streak along with it, that they gave a friend who could not climb their login credentials to upload a picture on their behalf.) I suddenly understood a chief source of her sadness, which took some of the shine off my day.

I do not mean to sound like the curmudgeon who glorifies growing up before the internet, though I admit being relieved that my juvenilia are not preserved in digital amber. I do not think "kids these days" are any different than the kids I grew up with. Life was hard enough when I was a teenager, back when bullies had to call your home phone. Now, though, it seems that the corrosive desires of the digital architects who built the tools have led young people to construct a prison for themselves and call it friendship and a lifestyle.

As for me, I closed my social media accounts eight or nine years ago, not from some purity of mind or heart, but because it was prudent for my well-being. I was growing increasingly unhappy, and I identified Facebook as one driver of that unhappiness. I decided I could embody my values in my life and my work. There have been some drawbacks. I have heard about the sickness, death, and divorce of old friends later and second-hand. So far, though, someone has contacted me directly to let me know the things that matter most. The friends who need me when they are in distress, and who I need in turn, have my phone number and my email address. I could do without social media, so I did.

Everyone, of course, should make decisions in light of what prudence requires in their own life, but Epicurus recommends ongoing reflection on our desires. In the context of social media, the relevant questions are: Am I performing for other people, or is this who I am? Does this help me forge the relationships that secure genuine happiness, or does it distract from the things that give me confidence and joy—trustworthy and caring friends, an appreciation for truth, and deep, rather than shallow, understanding? Does this help my community understand what matters most, or does it feed corrosive desires through lies or half-truths that undermine mutual respect?

Epicurus writes that "praise from other men must come of its own accord; and we must be concerned with healing ourselves."[8] Social media provides a wealth of opportunities to seek praise from strangers, and it remains unclear whether it makes healing ourselves any easier. I cannot remember the reason that first-year student offered for never having opened a social media account, but I hope he is still out there being a rare bird.

13 | AMBITION, WORK, AND SUCCESS

"Epicureanism has a lot to offer," my students tell me, "but I don't like that he rejects ambition." That might be a bit like saying, "I am a fan of Christianity, but the poor can look out for themselves." Epicurus' views on ambition are so central to his philosophy that excising them is a surgery that risks killing the patient. That said, his conception of ambition is often misunderstood, and critics sometimes willfully misrepresent it to score easy points. Epicurus does not insist that we stop cultivating and using our talents. He does, though, think that we should get clear on the purpose and value of work. In brief, we are probably doing success wrong.

Critics have some reason to think Epicurus opposes setting uncertain goals or competing for scarce goods because he seems to say it explicitly. In *Principal Doctrine* 21, he writes that unnecessary desires distinguish themselves in that they are "for things that involve struggle." He expresses roughly the same idea when he claims in *Principal Doctrine* 30 that desires for things "about which there is intense effort" are "produced by a groundless opinion." What humans need is within reach if we live prudently, and things that "involve struggle" or "intense effort" are unnecessary. That seems, at first glance, to rule out difficult tasks many people consider worthwhile, including perfecting a trade, attending college, or training for athletic competition.

Our broader understanding of Epicurus' philosophical project helps explain his reticence. Epicurus aims to eliminate anxiety, or at least greatly diminish it, and we are often very anxious to avoid failure and loss. We have all experienced anxiety in pursuit of a goal and disappointment when we fall short of it. Competition seems especially risky for an Epicurean because it can give rise to toxic emotions and behaviors. Winners can turn proud and feel superior. Losers can feel inadequate and suffer from envy or resentment. Worse, people dead set on winning will sometimes cheat or even refuse to accept their loss. Since Epicureans see pernicious emotional states, injustice, and delusions about the world as the hallmarks of misery, critics are correct that Epicureans are wary of many competitive enterprises.

But a life without uncertain goals or some forms of competition does admittedly sound like a very unhuman life. If Epicurus tells us not to try for something that stretches our reach or discourages whiling away a pleasant afternoon in sport, then I can see why someone would not fancy that sort of life. Society itself might stagnate because no one would take risks for innovation or improvement. A wide variety of joys, ranging from solving a hard puzzle to scoring a goal for the team would disappear, as would culinary experimentation and rock 'n' roll. If a society of Epicureans could not pursue a vaccine for a deadly virus lest they fail or play ultimate frisbee lest they lose, their society would fumble the future and die of boredom.

Thankfully, the Epicurean approach to goals and competition is not dismal parsimony, as if he thought the only things worth pursuing are those ready at hand and easy to achieve. While most of us more naturally run toward the dangers of excess ambition, Epicurus also worries about those who exercise too much restraint, caution, or fragility. Developing resilience requires failing and losing, and we should not be so abstemious as to deprive ourselves of opportunities for genuine pleasures that are not strictly necessary for happiness. Prudence requires us to seek better ways to satisfy natural desires through, for example, medical innovations. Also, remember that Epicurus loved cheese, and cheese takes time and effort.

We know from our regular discussion of extravagant desires that Epicurus not only permits but encourages us to enjoy pleasures we do not need, so long as we pursue them with the proper attitude. By "proper attitude," Epicurus means that we never think we must have extravagances. Nor, and this is the more controversial point, should we believe that possessing them makes us happier or better than people without access to such extravagances. Unfortunately, when it comes to ambition, success, and competition, we often thoroughly fail to take the "proper" Epicurean attitude. We consider success necessary for happiness, and we think highly successful people live better lives because of their success. As a result, we risk making not only ourselves, but our friends, family, and community miserable.

I can assure you we are making many of our young adults miserable because I teach them. Students tell me, eyes brimming with tears, how much they fear failure, how important it is to succeed. These are, for what it's worth, usually the very same students who tell me that Epicurus is wrong about ambition. Ask them what it means to succeed in life, and most of them struggle to answer.

They are like hunters in the woods in search of a bear, knowing only vaguely what a bear looks like, its size, what make it dangerous, hunters who might very well cry inconsolably if they ever manage to kill one, wondering how they ended up spending so much of their life alone in the woods with a gun to begin with. They look around and think, "Is this all there is? They call this a trophy, I guess?"

For Epicurus, the first problem is that we focus on success rather than satisfaction. Satisfaction is a feeling or attitude that expresses a limit or endpoint, that point at which we have "enough." We can always have more money, more prestige, or more cars. We cannot, however, have "more enough." Enough is enough. Epicureanism encourages us to that draw the line of "enough" at the edge of the necessary desires, seeing that as the limit that surrounds the ingredients of tranquility. Epicurus thinks we can readily satisfy necessary desires if we (along with our friends and community) make them a priority. Note that there are two requirements for satisfaction—having enough and appreciating it as enough. When we have enough, but we fail to appreciate that we have enough, we lack tranquility because we feel unsatisfied.

Recall also that the class of necessary desires for Epicurus is more expansive than we often think, far more than just the bare necessities for survival. The necessary components of happiness include the toolset that helps us understand and navigate the world effectively so that we do not fear the future or suffer from superstition and irrational fears. It includes trustworthy friends who share our conception of what makes life go well, friends we trust not to abandon us if we fall into distress. We also need confidence that our powers of prudential reason will help us choose well in pursuit of our long-term advantage and that, should we make mistakes, we will learn to avoid similar errors in the future.

Fulfilling many of our necessary desires in a larger community requires a division of labor that ranges widely. That means we need farmers, plumbers, electrical and structural engineers, grocery store clerks, doctors, schoolteachers, caregivers, housebuilders, firefighters, and policemen. Concrete pourers and flagmen. We need the "essential workers," as well as the people who make the necessary things that the essential workers use. Collectively, these people make it possible to satisfy our necessary desires, both material and educational, and we could not function without them.

Yet many of these people are often not even counted among the successful. We do not hold necessary workers up as examples of success, at best just as regrettably underappreciated pillars. We celebrate essential workers until we go back to forgetting them. If we ask a teenager what it means to be successful, they will rarely point to a plumber, even though they will inevitably complain about the dearth and cost of plumbers when water gushes out of a pipe on the second floor of their first home. Instead, they generally apply "successful" to someone who, at the very least, satisfies a vast array of extravagant desires—someone with a larger house, a nicer car, a timeshare. Again, Epicurus thinks there is nothing wrong with satisfying extravagant desires, but there is something wrong in confusing extravagant for necessary desires and in thinking that satisfying extravagant desires is what makes a person happy and successful.

Worse, many people consider only those working feverishly to feed their corrosive desires successful—those pursuing excess wealth, squabbling over trivial honors, whipping up rage in a political sphere for profit for power, winning the competition for most "clicks" and "likes." In other words, people who satisfy necessary desires are often counted unsuccessful, while those who are most effectively slavish to their corrosive desires are considered the most complete successes.

As a result, success as judged by society becomes the purview of the few rather than the many, of the wealthy and famous. Success is rarely, if ever, attributed to the people who meaningfully contribute to what makes it possible for us to have enough. And our kids see that. My students claim that they are the most progressive and caring generation yet, and that might be true, but vanishingly few of them are pursuing careers that serve others, at least at my institution.

Those content to have enough are often considered suspicious, as though their failure to work for more makes them lazy or complacent. Working constantly becomes a badge of honor, even as it crowds out more desirable goods like time with friends and family. Alex Williams, in an article fittingly titled "Why Don't Rich People Just Stop Working?," canvassed some candidate answers, some of them distinctively Epicurean—that the rich are "anxious and isolated," that if they stopped they would have to "face the nature of existence," that they compare themselves constantly to others, and that money is simply an addiction.[1] These are not mutually exclusive answers—yes, yes, and yes. Epicureans, by contrast, work to be at leisure with friends and family.

For Epicurus, as we noted earlier, corrosion is not locked up tight in the heart of Jeff Bezos alone. It is among us in those who work tirelessly for diminishing and inessential returns or who reach the pinnacle of the pecking order and remain unsatisfied.

Early in my professional career, I attended an extravagant post-conference reception at the home of a respected member of my specialization. Two of the most highly paid and prominent figures in the field sat on a couch near me and my unemployed friend, and they spent at least thirty minutes complaining bitterly about their situations. You would think their university was starving them of resources, that no one respected them. Despite the largesse of funds and opportunities available to them, the ways they had negotiated better and better situations for themselves, they remained deeply dissatisfied. My unemployed friend was close to tears. What struck me in the moment, though, was how whiny and pitiful they seemed, how much I hoped I would never be that way.

Returning to the initial question of the anxiety surrounding the possibility of failure and loss, we can see how reconceiving success on Epicurean terms can lessen our anxiety. We achieve success by feeling satisfied with having what we need. For Epicurus, the professional opportunities to play a necessary social role or create extravagant (non-corrosive) joys are numerous and within reach of most of us. We should all have opportunities to count as successful by the only objective measure that matters to Epicurus—our ability to contribute to a community of trust. Other models of success are recipes for dissatisfaction.

Now, some will object that counting everyone successful who recognizes and appreciates enough as enough is like giving every kid a trophy, watering down excellence. Epicurus might very well grant the point—"Yeah, by your standards I have watered down excellence." He understands that he swims against the tide. But he might just as well push back, noting that by his standards of success, very few people are successful. After all, Epicurean happiness is satisfaction with having enough, and very few people are satisfied with enough. If trophies were offered for satisfaction, then it seems that trophies are forged from a rare metal. Epicurean success is available to many but achieved by very few.

Epicurus would also perhaps point out that some people who would be content with enough are left without it because of social conditions that exclude them from sufficient resources. This chapter is not about how much Epicurus would compensate necessary workers to put life satisfaction within reach.[2] Whatever the appropriate amount, he would think a community that can but does not pay necessary workers enough to satisfy their own necessary desires is a community that fails to respect the people it needs. A society that unnecessarily consigns hard-working people to an anxious life behind the eight-ball should not be surprised that it founders, especially when it labels those people the failures.

Epicurus would, to be frank, look about and see many manifestly unsatisfied people who mask the odor of psychological rot and dissatisfaction with the oversweet perfume of ambition. For Epicurus, success lies at the limit of understanding and appreciating what counts as enough and, when possible, stretching our capacities and talents to embellish our success with the extravagant joys of life. Failure is thinking that we need more to be happy. And anyway, what is success other than happiness?

14 | GREED FOR LIFE

A central conceit of Tennessee Williams' *Cat on a Hot Tin Roof* is that no one should tell the wealthy family progenitor, Big Daddy, that he has terminal cancer. "You will be back on your feet in no time," they all insist. This collective mendacity is exposed when his bitter, alcoholic, and favorite son, played in the film version by Paul Newman at his most beautiful, divulges in anger what Big Daddy probably suspected all along. Yep, he's dying.

Big Daddy's response to this disheartening news might seem a bit off-topic to a non-Epicurean. Looking around him at a basement filled with the many expensive things he and his wife have accumulated but rarely used, he tells his son Brick that "the human animal is a beast that dies and if he's got money he buys and buys and buys and I think the reason he buys everything he can is that in the back of his mind he has the crazy hope that one of his purchases will be life everlasting!—which it never can be."[1] In other words, Big Daddy concludes that our desire to live longer, perhaps forever, is somehow tied up with our urge to spend and acquire. Big Daddy surveys his abundant possessions with an Epicurean's eyes, or at least so says Lucretius.

Epicurus considers the fear of death one of the greatest impediments to the tranquil life. Deep and persistent fear puts tranquility out of reach. Just to be clear, though, Epicurus is like most people—he really enjoys living, and he's therefore in no rush to die. Some contemporaries and predecessors of Epicurus did run around telling people that life is bleak, and that death is a welcome reprieve from human suffering, but Epicurus thinks that's nonsense. The Cyrenaics were a competing hedonistic philosophical school and numbered among them was a man dubbed "Hegesias the Death Persuader" for the power of his argument that life is more painful than pleasant.[2] Hegesias was reportedly run out of town for his effects on the young. That life is unpleasant is an odd view for a hedonist, and Epicurus felt at pains to deny it.

Yet Epicurus also thinks that enjoying life fully does not entail that we must fear death. As he puts it, "the wise man neither rejects life nor fears death."[3] In fact, one central reason Epicureans do not fear death is that they more fully appreciate their life every day, focusing on what they have rather than, as Epicurus puts it, "what is absent."[4] In this case, tomorrow is "what is absent," and Epicureans do not strictly need it, even though they would welcome it. Epicurus claims that living well as an Epicurean is the very same thing that enables us to die well whenever that should happen.[5]

As we will see in the last section of the book, Epicurus thinks that some forms of the fear of death arise directly from scientific or conceptual confusions. For instance, we might mistakenly think the dead can suffer harms, overlooking that the dead cannot experience pain, which Epicurus considers a necessary condition on harm. We might fear, for example, being in our casket or rotting. Epicurus argues that we will not experience those things, so we should not fear them.[6] If we fear being trapped as a ghost or suffering a dismal afterlife, Epicurus argues that natural science precludes either option. Again, we will explore that argument against fearing death later.

Other fears of death, though, stem from the fact that death puts out of reach the satisfaction of desires that we think give our life meaning. The philosopher Bernard Williams called these "categorical desires," but we will just call them "meaningful desires."[7] Meaningful desires provide us with reasons to desire more life. For example, you might desire to have a child, see your child fall in love, finish your book, and grow old with your partner. You might consider these the elements that form a complete life, such that not living to fulfill them is a harm.

By contrast, "conditional desires" are for things we will consider pleasant or prudent on the condition that we remain alive, but that we do not consider necessary components of a complete life. For example, I will consider it prudent to have the oil changed in my car in a few months, but I do not consider that a reason I must stay alive. I would not say, "Dying now means I will not be here for jury duty or to renew my car registration!"[8] Desires for pleasure can also be conditional—I can desire to watch a movie featuring my favorite actress without thinking that my life will be impoverished if I miss out on it. Our failure to fulfill some desires, even for genuine pleasures, sometimes has no effect on whether we consider our life complete or happy.

The problem, of course, is that many of us imagine having unsatisfied meaningful desires up until the day we die. In that case, we will always have reasons to stick around and reasons to resent death standing in the way of our satisfaction. Death will harm us because it thwarts those desires, whatever they happen to be at the time, however old we might be. For some people, that might be a minor disappointment. For others, though, the fear that their desires will go unsatisfied might motivate them to do everything they can to avoid death. They might try to live as long as possible, as much life as their money or power can buy.

In Book Three of *On the Nature of Things*, Lucretius writes that many people claim "with bravado" that there are worse fates than death. They say that they fear death less than "dread illness or a life of infamy." However, Lucretius thinks we cannot know whether their pronouncements are aimed to "win applause" or are "prompted by true conviction" until we see those claims put to the test. Some of these very same people, he writes, "though banished from their homeland, driven far from the sight of other human beings, branded with the stigma of some foul crime, and afflicted, in a word, with every kind of tribulation, continue to live."[9] For Lucretius, the real test of how much a person fears death is "adversity."

Lucretius raises an interesting point about how we usually think about the fear of death. We tend not to moralize it, considering the fear of death a matter of psychology, a garden-variety anxiety that manifests in some people as a neurosis. Someone's fear of death is a private and practical matter they might discuss with a therapist, not a way of determining whether they qualify as a suitable friend or trustworthy peer. Upon reflection, though, we can see that the fear of death plays an important role in ethical decision-making. Lucretius thinks a person who is truly terrified of death will do almost anything to avoid it, regardless of what they report to the contrary. The more powerful the fear, the more they are willing to do. If a person fears death more than injustice, death more than cowardice, death more than losing self-respect, then those values take a back seat to preserving their life in times of crisis.

A person's attitudes toward death, then, are manifested in their behaviors, in what Epicurus calls their "choice and avoidance."[10] We generally think a person should accept death in some cases to preserve their commitment to more important values, and we think that kind of prudential calculation underlies paradigmatic cases of courage. People who run into a burning building to save children, who stand up for the truth despite the risk of assassination, who jump on a grenade to save their fellow soldiers all decide that some admirable actions merit a risk to one's life. Many people joined the Nazi party for no other reason than to stay alive, which makes those who refused to join at the cost of death merit the admiration they elicit. A courageous person must be willing to accept death, and the statistical evidence of complicity indicates that that kind of courage is very rare.

Lucretius thinks our fear of death affects more than our deliberations about whether to turn coward or throw a friend under the bus to avoid death. It might not overstate things to say Lucretius thinks the fear of death is bound up with nearly all of our desires. For example, Lucretius claims that "avarice and blind lust for status," as well as the motivation "to strive night and day with prodigious effort to scale the summit of wealth—these sores of life are nourished in no small degree by dread of death."[11] Corrosive desires, especially when relentlessly pursued, are "nourished" by the fear of death. Big Daddy, in the quote that opens this chapter, seems to entertain a similar connection.

We need not turn to fictional characters, though, when we can follow the million-dollar exploits of some of the world's richest men seeking to triumph over death. Just check their expense ledger. In a 2017 *New Yorker* article, Tad Friend makes the rounds with scientists and their billionaire Silicon Valley supporters working to extend life indefinitely, perhaps forever.[12] Jeff Bezos, Sergey Brin (co-founder of Google), and numerous other Google power brokers have ponied up funds for a wide variety of tech start-ups aiming to "crack the code" of aging. While some of them intend to merely live longer and better, others, Peter Thiel included, want to live "forever." Friend reports his interaction with "Arram Sabeti, the thirty-year-old founder of a tech company called ZeroCater," who tells him, "The proposition that we can live forever is obvious. It doesn't violate the laws of physics, so we will achieve it." Sabeti's inference, of course, is nonsense—that something does not violate the laws of physics does not entail we will achieve it.

A donor-pitch from one Google power broker to another indicates that these efforts bear the hallmarks of corrosive desires: "Imagine you found a lamp on the beach, and a genie came out and granted you a wish. If you were clever, your first wish would be for unlimited wishes. Let's say you're going to live, at most, another thirty years. If each day is a wish, that's only between one and ten thousand wishes. I don't know about you, but I want to add more—I want to add wishes faster than they're taken away." The pitch sells "more and more" time to make "more and more" wishes, which is definitionally a desire to eliminate limits.

The problem with always wanting more is that we are never actually satisfied, and we look forever into the future for a satisfaction that never comes. Those things currently in our possession are never "enough." Lucretius thinks the greedy see those content with enough as having prematurely acquiesced to death. He claims that people who chase more and more consider satisfaction "a sort of premature loitering before the portals of death."[13] In

Plato's *Gorgias*, Callicles echoes this characterization when he tells Socrates that those satisfied with what they have are no better than "stones and corpses."[14]

The more things we want, however, the more time we want to pursue and enjoy those things. As such, Lucretius thinks that the threat of death makes us want more, and the more we want, the more we resent death. Wanting more stuff means wanting more time, but time is a limited commodity for mortal creatures. Death forces a natural limit on the unlimited desires people pursue, at least in part, to escape their fear of death in the first place.

Still, we might think Lucretius overlooks that death threatens the fulfillment of some desires that Epicurus himself considers genuinely good for us. Some people do not need countless wishes for more and more. They would simply welcome more time with friends and family. Death threatens time spent in the company of the people even Epicurus recognizes make life genuinely pleasant. While Epicurus might not consider it important that we finish the Great American Novel, he does think some things we desire are natural and valuable. Their loss at death might understandably cause a sense of impending loss.

Epicurus agrees, as we will see in the next chapter, that the loss of a friend is a genuine misfortune. He thinks we can weather the loss over time through gratitude for what we had and currently have, a recognition that the past cannot be undone, and the support of caring friends.[15] Unlike the Stoics, Epicurus considers it unnatural to not feel grief or a sense of loss. Proper grief indicates that we understand a friend's contribution to our well-being. However, Epicurus thinks that intense grief or over-powering fear of loss keeps us from fully appreciating what we have now and have had in the past. It encourages us to think that happiness is lost or lies only in the future, when what we need for happiness is with us already.

Here again, the importance of limits for psychological well-being plays a role in Epicurus' claim that happiness does not require more time. He writes that "unlimited time and limited time contain equal amounts of pleasure, if one measures by the limits of reason."[16] On the surface, this appears false. If our pleasures are additive, then when I combine yesterday's pleasures with today's pleasures, I have more pleasures because I have lived longer. That means that the me of today has experienced more pleasure than the me of yesterday. If life were unlimited, then pleasure would be as well.

Epicurus claims, though, that our reason tells us that tranquility is a stable and complete state, not an additive state. Enough is enough at every moment we have it. We do not have more tranquility or more happiness by having it longer. In that sense, we do not have more "enough" tomorrow. We have enough all the time we live. He develops this thought at greater length in *Principal Doctrine* 20. Note the difference between the "flesh" (body) and the "intellect" (rational mind):

> The flesh took the limits of pleasures to be unlimited, and [only] an unlimited time would have provided it. But the intellect, reasoning out the goal and limit of the flesh and dissolving the fears of eternity, provided us with the perfect way of life and had no further need of unlimited time. But [the intellect] did not flee pleasure, and even when circumstances caused an exit from life it did not die as though it were lacking in any aspect of the best life.[17]

Despite the elaborate, technical nature of this doctrine, its upshot is simple—if you are always satisfied, then you do not die dissatisfied. Epicurus thinks that our unreasoning body craves unlimited time, but our reason can correct for that error, telling us that happiness is tranquil pleasure within the natural limit of a human life. An Epicurean who has reached confidence about the satisfaction of their necessary desires and recognizes that situation as sufficient for happiness lives a fully good life at all times. Death deprives them of nothing because they already have everything they need. Epicurus' additional claim that we have no reason to fear the afterlife will be the focus of a later chapter.

Remember the distinction between meaningful and conditional desires. Meaningful desires are those whose satisfaction death threatens. Satisfying meaningful desires depends on our having more time. Conditional desires, however, are pleasures we will enjoy should we be living at the time. For Epicurus, it seems we should learn to treat even our meaningful desires as conditional, counting them as desires we will greatly enjoy satisfying should the opportunity arise, but whose objects we do not need for our happiness.

In that sense, our desire for future pleasures is what we have been calling an extravagant desire—a naturally desirable thing we should welcome given the opportunity and that we will appreciate more because we do not need it. As Epicurus puts it, "Those who least need extravagance enjoy it most."[18] The future, when we do not need it, is a continuing source of joy. Epicureans think each day offers everything they need for happiness, and their days are decorated with the various joyful extravagances of human life. One of those extravagances is more time with friends, which an Epicurean best appreciates.

It only makes sense that we struggle to adopt this Epicurean stance. We almost can't help seeing more time as more pleasure, longer tranquility as greater tranquility. Epicurus, though, thinks that those fortunate enough to gain confidence about the satisfaction of their necessary desires can and should use their reason to correct that misperception. For Epicurus, we have two options. We can appreciate each day as enough and as a reason for complete joy. Or, we can view every day as never quite enough, never fully joyful. Epicurus thinks we have reason to aim for steady satisfaction because that state is more pleasant, not because it lowers our expectations for pleasure.

Epicurus does not, of course, think we can or should eliminate all varieties of the fear of death. It would run counter to nature and prudence to ignore an oncoming bus or fail to clearly label bottles of rat poison. We put the rotten odor in natural gas so we can smell it. Some varieties of the fear of death, though, undermine our happiness, and to the extent that we can control or eliminate them, we should. We should not allow our fear of death to undermine our commitment to our principles, friends, and values. We should not allow our fear to convince us that living well requires greed for more things and more time. Using science to improve our quality of life makes good sense, but we should not waste riches chasing the fool's errand of never dying when we could spend that money more generously building a community of trust.

Let's return to Gekko's Challenge, which kicked off our exploration of corrosive desires. In the past few chapters, we have seen that Epicurus believes that the various manifestations of greed leave us dissatisfied because we always want more, we want to keep it longer, and we worry about losing it. In addition, prioritizing greed often requires us to sacrifice our competing commitments to virtue and self-respect. Greed alienates us from those with whom we share bonds of trust because it makes it tempting to cheat and short others of what they need to get more for ourselves. It gives rise to the envy and resentment, pride and conceit that make it difficult to see each other as equals and friends. Greed wrecks not only individual tranquility, but also undermines social stability.

For these reasons, Epicurus thinks that if we want to achieve and maintain tranquility, we should root out corrosive, unlimited desires. He thinks our fundamental desire is for secure pleasure in a community of trust, for joy both private and shared. Epicurus contends that greed is a recipe for unhappiness because it undermines those values. We must starve desires for more and more so that we can focus on getting, keeping, and appreciating what is enough. Then we can wake each morning to find ourselves pleased to welcome the extravagance of another day. As Epicurus' best friend Metrodorus writes, "He who least needs tomorrow will go with greatest pleasure to meet tomorrow."[19]

15 | MISFORTUNE AND RESILIENCE

A good friend of mine was in his early twenties when his long-time friend shot him in the gut with an arrow fired from a compound bow. It was a workplace accident. They were temporary employees quality-testing the bows for a sporting goods company. My friend underwent numerous surgeries, spent fifteen days in the hospital, and now has a sizable scar. We sometimes feel moved to tell the story of our life to others or ourselves, which requires fitting things like frightening workplace accidents into a larger narrative. From perhaps a natural impulse, we are inclined to recast misfortunes as instructive or transformative, and my friend in fact reports drawing a lesson from the experience.

My friend's lesson, it turns out, is decidedly Epicurean. He did not find himself thinking about what he would have missed out on had he died. Instead, he realized that when you are lying in a hospital bed for a month, a situation with ever-increasing likelihood as we slouch toward the end of life, one of the only ways to sustain and entertain yourself is with your memories. He resolved not so much to "live life to the fullest" because he could die at any time (also a famed Epicurean sentiment), but to craft a life filled with as many things worth remembering as possible in case he again found himself in need of remembering them. These two aims are in fact conjoined—we must live joyfully to have memories of living joyfully. My friend needed to prepare himself for adversity and misfortune by building a library of pleasurable memories. He had unwittingly cast himself in the role of an Epicurean.

For Epicurus, our special cognitive powers to remember the past, relish the present, and imagine the future are among our most distinctive features as human beings. We have an awareness of being in time. As we have seen, our capacity to deliberate about future pleasures and pains lies at the core of Epicurean prudence. Epicurus thinks we gain prudence through experience and instruction, much like natural scientists learn about the causal interactions between two chemicals when combined. Sometimes someone just tells us, "Don't eat that. It's poisonous." Other times we regrettably need to experience the pain ourselves. Either way, though, the lesson is useless if we do not remember it and recognize how it should inform our future choices. One experience with a hot stove is sufficient for most of us. For that reason, memory and anticipation are fundamental to Epicurean prudence, just as they are to applied science.

Memory and anticipation, though, play another crucial role in Epicurean well-being, the one my friend discovered. They can help us counteract grief and pain, as well as fight boredom. Even when we are not trapped in a hospital bed or confined to our homes while a pandemic rages, we find ourselves remembering past pleasures, reflecting on current pleasures, and anticipating future pleasures. I can right now remember the meaningful conversation with my friend yesterday and think about how grateful I am that I currently have such a friend. I can imagine the pleasures we will share in the future during the time we are both alive and able. Epicurus thinks all three of these mental states are themselves pleasant. In such cases, I am experiencing pleasures about pleasures, or, as philosophers call them, "second-order pleasures." For Epicurus, these mental states are not merely thoughts about pleasure with no feeling attached. They are themselves pleasures.

Epicurus thinks our power to experience pleasure from reflecting on pleasures past, present, and future is one of the greatest tools for resilience that the human mind provides. It is not a bell and whistle, but an essential feature worth developing to its full strength. Epicurus thinks we need the second-order pleasures of memory and anticipation most when we encounter life's inevitable and unavoidable pains and setbacks. In such periods, our memories and appreciation of pleasure sustain us, chiefly by distracting us. Epicurus apparently used this method during his own painful final days. He wrote to his friend Idomeneus about his condition:

> On this blissful day, which is also the last of my life, I write this to you. My continual sufferings from strangury and dysentery are so great that nothing could augment them; but over against them all I set gladness of mind at the remembrance of our past conversations.[1]

Epicurus here recounts this strategy of cultivating "gladness of mind" and memories of friendship as a method for counteracting his intense physical pain, but other Epicurean texts show that he also endorses using it in response to misfortunes like the death of a loved one. The strategy of recollecting pleasures plays a central role in Epicurus' larger account of how we cope with misfortune, develop resilience, and cultivate gratitude. His views were distinctive and controversial then, and to some extent they remain so today.

It might help to put Epicurus in the context of his time, focusing primarily on his chief competitors, the Stoics. Epicurus distinguishes himself from the Stoics by recognizing that we can suffer misfortunes that are harmful, worthy of grief, and non-providential. When a friend dies, we lose something of genuine value that has contributed to our happiness. Epicurus denies a cosmic justification or purpose for suffering such that it could be reconstrued as good. For Epicurus, misfortune is not a divine will at work, a point we will revisit in the chapter on religion. Nor is it a welcome opportunity to gain strength. Instead, misfortunes are harms that happen without design or intention. While we might in some cases gain personal insight from misfortunes, misfortunes never occur *for the sake of* insight because they do not happen for the sake of anything.

Epicurus, unlike the Stoics, suggests strategies for coping with and counteracting grief rather than encouraging its elimination. The Stoics seek to eliminate grief because they think it arises from a false judgment that something bad has happened. Epicureans, by contrast, manage grief, and they recommend distracting ourselves by replaying pleasant memories, expressing gratitude for past and present pleasures, and engaging with close and caring friends. Taken together, we have three Epicurean points about misfortune: some losses are genuine misfortunes that merit grief, we should cope with our grief rather than seek to eliminate it, and the most effective strategies involve cultivating gratitude and caring friendships.

Before turning to whether Epicurus' coping strategies seem appropriate and effective, we should explore why his claims about misfortune and grief are contentious, even today. Many of us seek a philosophy of living specifically because we encounter pain and suffering in our own lives, and we witness it in the lives of friends and those we do not even know. If we are not currently suffering, we know all too well that we probably will eventually. Every serious contender in the competition between philosophies of living, then, must include some account of what counts as a misfortune and how we should respond to it.

The Stoics generally advocated a providential account of the universe, according to which the gods structure the cosmos for the best and to the benefit of human beings. As such, most of the Stoics thought that everything under the control of the gods happens for a good reason, even things which might at first appear to be serious misfortunes. In contemporary religious discourse, endorsement of complete providence secured by an all-powerful and beneficent God might express itself in phrases like "the Lord works in mysterious ways." Plutarch reports that the Stoic Chrysippus thought that on close inspection, many apparent evils might instead be benefits—wars might rid us of excess population and mice might induce tidiness.[2] On many providential accounts, while the person who suffers might not see the beneficial reason for their suffering, they are encouraged to demonstrate acceptance of the result as evidence of faith, piety, or a commitment to an all-encompassing cosmic goodness.

The Stoics also arrived at the conclusion that we should not grieve by a non-providential route. They believe that the only good thing is virtue, and the only bad thing is vice. Nothing else is good or bad; everything else is "indifferent," neither good nor bad. For the Stoics, happiness is the full possession of virtue, and the gain or loss of "indifferents" contributes nothing to happiness. Things like children, health, and a stable country are not good (only virtue is), so their presence or absence is of no consequence to our happiness. The Stoics think that the only harm a person can suffer is the loss of their virtue, as some religious believers think the only true harm would be losing their faith. If our child dies, our health rapidly diminishes, or our country falls into crisis, the Stoics think our happiness should remain unaffected.

Seneca captures this Stoic attitude toward loss with the story of Stilbo, cast as a model of Stoic virtue. Stilbo survived the destruction of his country and the death of his wife and children. When the man responsible for Stilbo's misfortunes asked how he was holding up, Stilbo responded, "I have lost nothing!"[3] While Stilbo's response does seem admittedly badass, it depends on the underlying assumption that none of the things he lost contributed to his happiness, so their loss cannot diminish his happiness. His children were "nothing." Whether by a providential or non-providential account, Stoic doctrine leads to the conclusion that grief is irrational because nothing bad or harmful has happened.

Epicurus rejects both routes to Stoic indifference. He denies providential accounts of the cosmos. The universe was not designed or ordered for the good.[4] When a child dies, Epicurus does not believe there is an explanation according to which the child died for the good. It was a misfortune without design. Remember also that Epicurus thinks that friends are necessary for our happiness, so he does not consider friends "indifferents." Epicurean happiness takes a hit with the loss of a close friend, a loss that cannot be construed as cosmically good.

Plutarch reports this Epicurean commitment about grief, referencing two now-lost letters of consolation by Epicurus. He writes that the Epicureans "argue with those who eliminate pains and tears and lamentations for the death of friends, and they say that kind of freedom from pain which amounts to insensitivity is the result of another and greater bad thing, savagery and unadulterated lust for fame and madness."[5] The savage and proud people Epicurus opposes here are clearly the Stoics, especially because the word translated as "insensitivity" is *apathes*, the Stoic term describing the absence of all negative emotions. Plutarch reports that Epicurus thinks genuine attachment entails grief at the loss of someone who contributes to your happiness.

As a matter of historical record, critics of Epicurus, like Cicero, did grieve intensely, sometimes much to their own surprise and dismay. When Cicero's daughter Tullia died, he was distraught and left Rome to mourn in the countryside. His grief was viewed by some in Rome as an embarrassment, and he conceded to Atticus that he was at various points beyond consolation. He threw himself into his work as a distraction, writing extensively on philosophy. On the more contemporary front, C. S. Lewis, the notable twentieth-century Christian author and philosopher, was sufficiently uncomfortable with his intense grief at the unexpected death of his wife that he initially published *A Grief Observed* under a pseudonym, N. W. Clerk. A man who once chided others as "perfectly ridiculous" for "whimpering" about nuclear devastation suddenly found himself in religious crisis.[6] After long reflection, he determined that the best way to move past grief was to cultivate gratitude.

In his *Consolation to Helvia*, Seneca writes to his mother to console her about his own exile. While Seneca is confident that she will not give into the "usual noisy manifestations of feminine grief," he regrets that her father failed to train her in the kind of rational thinking in the liberal arts tradition that would allow her to vanquish grief forever.[7] She is, unfortunately, not a proper philosopher. He encourages her to take philosophy up late in life because then, once sufficiently practiced, "never again will grief enter" her mind. Until that day comes, though, Seneca tells her that strategic consolations will have to suffice. As he puts it, "But until you arrive at this haven which philosophy holds out to you, you must have supports to lean on." Specifically, she should take comfort in her family, friends, and memories. She should, in effect, grieve like an Epicurean, not like a Stoic philosopher, who does not grieve at all.

That brings us, in a roundabout way, to the Epicurean approach to grief, which roughly resembles what Cicero did, Lewis concluded, and Seneca offered his inadequately philosophical mother—distraction, gratitude for past and present pleasures, acceptance, and assistance from supportive friends. Epicurus writes that "misfortunes must be cured by a sense of gratitude for what has been and the knowledge that what is past cannot be undone."[8] For those who find themselves comforting the grieving, Epicurus writes, "Let us share our friends' suffering not with laments, but with thoughtful concern."[9]

Epicurus' advice that we come to recognize that "what is past cannot be undone" presumably aims to forestall painful rumination about how the misfortune might not have happened, a fruitless exercise many of us have no doubt struggled to avoid. Rumination involves directly, even obsessively, focusing on the misfortune to determine how it might have been otherwise, when any other result is no longer possible. But acceptance usually takes time, and during that period, Epicurus thinks we should avoid rumination largely by distracting ourselves. Before we reach acceptance, Epicurus apparently suggests drawing our attention away from the misfortune rather than focusing on it with sustained attention.

Epicurus' chief practical strategy for coping prior to acceptance is engaging in a special kind of distractive pleasure—gratitude.[10] Gratitude is what we earlier called a "second-order pleasure," a pleasure about past, present, and possible pleasures. Epicurus encourages:

1) recalling and replaying memories of past pleasure;
2) appreciating our current pleasures, especially with our supportive friends; and
3) when appropriate, cultivating the pleasant awareness that future joys are possible.

In *On Moral Ends*, Torquatus puts all three points together when he tells Cicero that Epicureans effectively combat pain with pleasure because "they recall the past with affection; are in full possession of the present moment and appreciate how great are its delights; [and] have hopes for the future, but do not rely on it."[11]

In his final letter to Idomeneus, quoted above, Epicurus clearly takes himself to be modeling this attitude as he approaches death. He recalls his past pleasures with gratitude in the process of writing with pleasure to a supportive friend. Someone might think Epicurus' impending death precludes the third kind of distractive pleasure, the hopeful ones. Epicurus, though, closes his letter by expressing confidence that Idomeneus will look out for the children of Metrodorus. Epicurus had himself taken on the role of guardian when Metrodorus died, and Epicurus passes on that confidence to Idomeneus. Philodemus suggests in his *On Death* that friends play a crucial role in relieving the natural anxiety that our children will be abandoned should we die.[12] Even when dying, Epicurus takes pleasure in that confidence.

Epicurus, then, recommends gratitude for pleasures and the eventual acceptance that the past is fixed as the best strategies for coping with misfortune. The former encourages positive distraction in private or in the company of friends, and the latter keeps us from fruitlessly wishing to change what cannot be changed. Neither strategy requires reconceiving of horrible events as good, as tests of mettle, or as necessary for a good life.

Unfortunately for Epicurus, distraction as a coping strategy has a very bad reputation, not just in Seneca, but also in most contemporary psychology research. The long-standing consensus among research psychologists is that distraction has harmful long-term psychological, physical, and relational consequences.[13] While distraction is healthier than outright denial that something bad has happened (in other words, Stoicism), researchers consider distraction another form of avoidance behavior. Distraction does not address the underlying pain.

Seneca captures this objection to distraction, again in his *Consolation to Helvia*: "Sometimes we divert our mind with public shows or gladiatorial contests, but in the very midst of the distractions of the spectacles it is undermined by some little reminder of its loss. Therefore, it is better to conquer our grief than deceive it."[14] By conquer, Seneca means eliminate. Yet "public shows" and "gladiatorial contests" are not what Epicurus has in mind when he talks of distractive gratitude, as if he thought the proper response to grieving parents would be, "I bought you VIP passes to Disney World!"

Recent research challenges the consensus that distraction is unhealthy, as it indicates that "positive distraction" is both adaptive and beneficial as a coping strategy. When researchers take care to separate distractions like "stayed drunk all weekend" or "slept around to forget about it" (negative distraction) from things like "had dinner with friends and told stories" (positive distraction), they get widely divergent results for long-term psychological health. I mean, who would have guessed dinner with close friends and getting wasted all weekend would not have the same effects on well-being and relationships?[15]

Current research also indicates that replaying pleasant memories and cultivating gratitude can have a powerful effect on well-being, both in daily life and in cases of misfortune. Studies indicate that people who reminisce and recall their most pleasant memories fare better in times of crisis.[16] Those who anticipate the possibility of future pleasures while handling misfortune are better able to distance themselves from current pain and more likely to think that things will improve. Registering and expressing gratitude seems to make people better equipped to manage stress. Far from proving maladaptive, the Epicurean toolkit for handling misfortune has gained increasingly robust research support, at least as one tool among many.

What does this mean for those of us currently suffering a misfortune or who recognize that misfortune likely awaits? Epicurus thinks we should prepare, but not by anticipating, picturing, or pre-rehearsing misfortunes, as many Stoics suggest. Pre-rehearsing evils is not the Epicurean way. We should not spend our days play-acting the worst-case scenario that might never occur. For Epicureans, the first step, as usual, is to form and sustain relationships with close and supportive friends. Then, we should make it a lifelong project to build a collection of pleasant memories as large, varied, and rich as possible. These two steps dovetail because most of the best memories happen in the company of friends, and shared experience strengthens friendships. We should develop our skill for gratitude, tighten our friendships, and share memorable joys and pleasures.

Epicurus thinks fulfilling those goals requires making them a priority. In many instances, that means we need to set aside time that we might otherwise spend doing things of little consequence or chasing the objects of corrosive desires. When we catch ourselves deliberating about how to spend time, we should choose what will produce shared pleasures, gratitude, and memories. Presented with a choice between a dinner with friends and a lonely shopping venture or between a daytrip and an afternoon surfing the internet, we should choose the memorable option. A consistent failure to privilege joy and those we love over needless ambition or greed risks leaving us without the memories or people that make coping with misfortune manageable. We should choose wisely in preparation by pursuing pleasure, not by, as the Stoics suggest, imagining and steeling ourselves for pain.

One practice that Epicurus might recommend that has research support is keeping a gratitude journal or a daily record of memorable pleasures. Regularly reflecting on and cataloguing things for which we are grateful and moments worth remembering helps us prioritize those options in our daily life.[17] It gets us in the habit of building our library of memories, and it helps us better recognize when we are passing up memorable activities to waste time. Keeping a record helps us navigate our day in search of things worth remembering.

Before moving on from this topic, we should address Epicurus' view about helping others grieve, about communal grief as "thoughtful concern." Epicurus contends that communities of friends are most secure against misfortune because they provide mutual support against material and emotional distress.[18] Epicurus thinks we can seek security in many ways, but the greatest security comes from a supportive group of friends.[19] As we know, he thinks nothing "provides for the blessedness of one's whole life" more than friendships.

Nevertheless, this shared and secure community cannot protect us from all misfortune. As Metrodorus writes, "One can attain security against other things, but when it comes to death all men live in a city without walls."[20] Misfortune strikes, often in the form of the death of someone we love. Just as an Epicurean community shares joys, they also support each other in times of pain. Many of us regrettably live in cultures that do very little to support those who grieve, and some people's deep losses go unnoticed or are actively ignored.

Americans, for example, rarely get dedicated grief time away from work, even for the death of their parents. They must use their "vacation hours." Many of the bereaved report that friends and co-workers avoid their company or fail to reach out to offer support, sometimes because they have so little experience with misfortune themselves that they do not know what to do or what a grieving person would want. Epicurus makes it clear that a community of friends never leaves someone to grieve alone.

At the same time, though, Epicurean communal grief is not borne of pity for the dead because, as we saw earlier, the Epicureans think the dead themselves do not suffer. Epicurus writes, somewhat awkwardly in the past tense, that those who achieved the "greatest confidence" within a community "also thereby lived together most pleasantly with the surest guarantee." Because "they enjoyed the fullest sense of belonging they did not grieve the early death of the departed, as though it called for pity."[21] No one, Epicurus thinks at least, should pity a person who lived a life of satisfaction, a life "most pleasant" that affords "the fullest sense of belonging." Grief is for the living, a natural, painful outgrowth of genuine attachment best handled through memory and appreciation for what one has had. And not handled entirely alone.

Just as we'll be grateful for the support of our community of friends when we lose a loved one, we'll be happy we have cherished memories of the person we've lost. Like my friend, we might one day find ourselves lying in a hospital bed with only our memories to sustain us. The best way to prepare for that possibility is to live a vividly joyful life steeped in gratitude for those who share our lives with us.

Johnny Cash left behind a treasure trove of unrecorded songs when he died, and among them were the lyrics for a song titled "Pretty Pictures in My Mind." Arranged and recorded by The Lumineers, it includes a few verses that capture the Epicurean strategy for getting through hard times. It seems Johnny Cash had his own occasional Epicurean streak:

There are things that I remember,
locked away for other times,
I will bring out, on a down day,
pretty pictures in my mind

I will rerun love and laughter,
from the vaults locked back behind,
on an ugly day, I will do it,
pretty pictures in my mind.

16 | OF SEX, LOVE, AND HARMLESS PLEASURE

At a certain point in every young American evangelical's life, all the adults coalesce around a single purpose—keeping you from having sex. Daniel, though cast into the lion's den, was not devoured, and the hungry lions might just as well represent the desire for sex as anything else. Jesus turned the water into wine—and then finally the groom and bride could have sex. The widow's mite was generous in spirit, and widows also do not have sex. My ninth-grade Sunday School teacher said that while avoiding premarital sex was simply the right thing to do, it would also ensure that our future husband's sexual abilities would never suffer by comparison. In sum, early sex was shameful, and we should not expect married sex to be pleasant.

This problem was compounded because I grew up during the height of the AIDS epidemic, when Arkansas briefly decided that protecting students from HIV was more important than winning top honors in the national teen birthrate contest. Unlike the other kids in my church, I went to public school, where we learned that sex would surely kill us unless we could put a condom on a banana. You can see why I might have been secretly relieved no one wanted to have sex with me, like I was Daniel in a lion-less den.

My experience is, it seems, not a relic of the past. Each year I teach an introductory ethics course that includes two articles on pornography (one a qualified defense, the other generally opposed), and my students, especially those from a handful of states in America, complain that no one talks to them about sex at all. Experts in such matters confirm that many young people's sexual education comes almost exclusively from internet porn, just about the worst place to learn about mutual pleasure and respect. The students' own off-internet educational efforts seem stymied at almost every turn. For example, the Tennessee state legislature has long opposed "Sex Week," an event in which college students over the age of eighteen learn about sex as it happens pleasantly and safely in the wild. The legislature even commissioned a 269-page report on Sex Weeks nationwide and brainstormed legal ways to intervene.[1]

Epicurus is happy to send his calling card to anyone with a bodily desire that they have been told it's wrong to satisfy. After all, sex is an obvious source of intense pleasure! Epicurus is a hedonist who thinks pleasure is the only truly good thing, and sex is pleasant, so surely he must think sex is good! Athenaeus confirms this expectation. In a passage reportedly from Epicurus' lost work, *On the Goal*, Epicurus claims that sexual pleasures are so manifestly good that he cannot make sense of the good at all without sex:

> For I at least do not even know what I should conceive the good to be, if I eliminate the pleasures of taste, and eliminate the pleasures of sex, and eliminate the pleasures of listening, and eliminate the pleasant motions caused in our vision by visible form.[2]

Tastes, sounds, sights, and sex are undeniably pleasant. Sensory pleasures feel good. Epicurus, by his standards, almost waxes poetic, at least until you get to the part about "pleasant motions caused in our vision by visible form." As we know, though, Epicurus does not think all tastes, sounds, sights, and sexual activities are prudent. He thinks that "every pleasure is a good thing, since it has a nature congenial to us, but not every one is to be chosen."[3]

Many scholars have argued that while Epicurus recognizes that sex is pleasant, he is actually largely hostile to sex, even more so to love. If you find it difficult to make sense of how Epicurus could reject sex and love and still have said what Athenaeus claims, then you are in the good company of me, at least. I think Epicurus' concerns about sex and love have been overstated. That Epicurus thinks sex and love should be selected prudently makes complete sense, especially given the many ways it can cause and sustain anxiety. Nevertheless, Epicurus thinks sexual pleasure and committed romantic relationships are natural, but unnecessary, desires (or so I argue). In the terms of this book, they are extravagant desires, and all extravagant desires can adorn the tranquil life if you do them right.

We should, though, not underestimate the many ways in which the desire for sex can be harmful and corrosive. Scholars have a point that Epicurus has very good reasons to proceed cautiously for the sake of sound prudence. At their worst, desires for sex and love turn obsessive, possessive, and violent. Self-styled "incels" cluster on internet chat boards railing against both the beautiful women who reject their sexual advances and the men those women prefer instead—in their lingo, "Stacy and Chad." Incels periodically turn their virtual anger into real-world lethal violence against anyone they assume is having sex. It's terrifying.

Each day, social workers and close friends try to help those suffering from the persistent thrum of domestic and spousal abuse, often fruitlessly assisting the same person over and over. If you visit the National Domestic Violence Hotline's website, it cautions against entry if your internet history could be monitored by your abuser and points out the quickest way to escape the screen in case someone walks into the room. It usually takes seven times for an abused partner to successfully leave an abuser who claims to love them—if they ever can finally leave.[4] Again, it's terrifying.

Many people are sexually harassed in the streets, are sexually abused as children, or fend off advances from those who have power over them at work. Each year, a few students discreetly notify me they will be missing some specific class meetings because of an anxiety I would never ask them to name, though sadly I always know what it is. I ask them whether they have a support network. The percentage of Americans who report having suffered sexual assault or violence during their lives is so high as to induce despair.

Of less dismaying, but still real consequence, sexual desires can lead to indiscretions that upset the trust of relationships through lies and deceit. People ruin their careers or embrace the embarrassing cliché of "it started when we worked together on my political campaign" or "they were my brightest graduate student." Even for the run-of-the-mill, safe, well-adjusted adult, sex and love present ongoing anxieties. Not everyone loves removing their clothing, especially under the glare of bad lighting. We fear sexual rejection even from our most loving partner. Our bodies do not always comply. "We need to talk" makes our heart sink.

Again, scholars are not wrong to think these many downsides might make Epicurus wary of endorsing sexual desire as a force for good, and they have textual evidence on their side as well. One of the longest extant passages about sex in the Epicurean tradition comes from a letter Metrodorus wrote to Pythocles, a young man probably not eager for this counsel:

> I hear from you that the movement of your flesh is abundantly disposed toward sexual intercourse. As long as you do not break the laws or disturb noble and settled customs or vex any of your neighbors or wear out your body or use up the things necessary for life, indulge yourself in any way you prefer. However, it is impossible not be constrained by some one of these things. For sex never profits, and one must be content if it does not harm.[5]

Metrodorus might sound like a fusty advocate of celibacy or prudery, but I think that slightly overstates his intention. He is not entirely hostile to sex. Instead, he points out an Epicurean commonplace about extravagant desires. The objects of all extravagant desires should be pursued only if they do no harm; in other words, we should only pursue extravagant desires when they are relatively harmless. Torquatus asks Cicero in *On Moral Ends*, "[W]ho could find fault with anyone who wished to enjoy a pleasure that had no harmful consequences?"[6] For *every* Epicurean extravagance we should "be content if it does not harm."

To put the point another way, Epicurus denies that extravagant desires "profit" us, so it should not surprise us that Epicurus thinks sex does not profit us. Remember that while Epicurus thinks extravagances can vary or adorn the pleasures of a tranquil life, he denies that extravagances secure or increase happiness.[7] The person who has sex is not happier than the person who does not have sex if both have achieved confidence concerning their necessary desires. Extravagant pleasures only vary our tranquility because we can (and should) be fully happy without extravagances. Like other extravagances, then, sex is fine if we avoid coupling it with corrosive desires for status and power, considering it necessary for our tranquility, or undermining our ability to satisfy our necessary desires.

So much for sex. What about love? Again, I think most critics have overstated Epicurus' opposition to romantic attachment, rendering him more austere and abstemious that he intended. The scholarly impulse to portray him an ascetic sometimes seems like an interpretive overcorrection to the long-standing, much greater misunderstanding that he was a sex-crazed glutton. Epicurus clearly acknowledges that the intense desire to possess a particular individual quickly turns corrosive and upsets tranquility. When romantic love manifests itself in an insecure desire to acquire, possess, and keep a sexual relationship (or anything, for that matter), it can wreck the tranquility of everyone involved. Harnessing romantic attachment to corrosive desires for wealth, beauty, or status makes the relationship unstable in hard times or when beauty fades.

Lucretius captures the Epicurean stance on romantic passion in rich detail. His florid and bitter hostility to romantic passion has been a hard act to follow for poets ever since. He focuses more on how love makes us imprudent fools than on the ways it can lead us to harm others, but his characterization of a lover's folly pulls no punches, a master class in Roman satire.[8] He initiates the passage on love with an admittedly awkward basic sex ed account of the "stirring of the seed" during "adolescence." Once the "seed is ejected from its places of lodgement," it "concentrates in certain parts of the groin."[9] And a chorus of twelve-year-olds say, "Eww . . . ." At one point Lucretius concludes an unnecessarily lengthy argument about women's sexual pleasure with: "So I insist that sexual pleasure is shared."[10] Remarkable that this was considered an open question; glad he defended the correct response.

Like Epicurus, Lucretius thinks sex can be great, though with the caveat that the "pleasure of sex is purer for the healthy-minded than the lovesick."[11] Sex between the "lovesick" is too rough and greedy for his taste, and the calm that follows consummation does not last long. He even claims that sex between the lovesick is so pernicious that it is better to (pardon me) "ejaculate the accumulated fluid into any woman's body rather than reserve it for a single lover who monopolizes you." Better to have sex with "some random-roaming Venus," at least if you cannot manage to "divert the motions of your mind into some other channel."[12] In short, hook-up culture is superior to an unhealthy relationship, though distraction with something else is generally the optimal solution.

Lucretius paints a sad picture of the besotted lover, embellishing his genuine critique with biting mockery. When a man falls into the wrong kind of relationship, his "duties are neglected," and his bank account suffers. "The hard-earned family fortune melts away, transformed into Babylonian perfumes." Not to mention the emeralds, tiaras, headdresses, and the occasional "Greek cloak and stuffs." Also, the expensive parties, draperies, "garlands, and festoons of flowers." In other words, Lucretius complains that "women be shopping."[13]

Unfortunately for the lover, even in the glow of these many pleasures, "there wells up something sour to pain him among the very flowers."[14] He begins to suffer from bad conscience about the waste and sloth. Worse, the onset of doubt and jealousy: "Perhaps his mistress has thrown out an ambiguous word and left it embedded in his passionate heart, where it burns like living fire; or perhaps he fancies that her eyes are wandering too freely, or that she is ogling some other man, while he detects in her face the trace of a smile." And then a whole new set of anxieties are up and running.

We should not conclude, though, that Lucretius resists love or attachment itself. Instead, Lucretius is more like the buddy in a romantic comedy who tries to protect his friend from embarrassing himself over someone who is not, after all, a good person. Lucretius worries that we tend to set ourselves up for disappointment when we transform an ordinary human being into someone to worship and admire at all costs. Taking this tendency to its most absurd extreme, Lucretius writes that the romantically obsessed can even transform a "victim of consumption" into "a slender little darling," a delusion that will eventually lead to the lover's disappointment and likely their very own case of what the Germ Theory taught us to call tuberculosis.

Better, Lucretius suggests, to set your store elsewhere with a clear eye for unadorned, but genuine, goodness. He seems to think that non-impulsive, stable love does not strike immediately, but through a habit of spending time together. This happens even, or perhaps especially, with a woman "with little pretension to beauty" who, through her many good qualities, "easily accustoms a man to spend his life with her."[15] Lucretius, it turns out, recommends both marriage and children, but then Lucretius is quite traditional in the end, a point we will explore further in the next chapter.

For a bit of practical advice, Epicurus seems to recommend the "no contact" method of moving on from an unhealthy relationship, writing that "if you take away the chance to see and talk and spend time with [the beloved], then the passion of sexual love is dissolved."[16] Plato recommends the same strategy, writing that all those who rightly realize their "passion is not beneficial" should "force themselves to stay away."[17] Corrosive desires are always the ones that should be, as Torquatus puts it, "choked off, not reformed."[18]

In sum, Epicurus encourages due caution about sexual desires, which is merely the sort of sound advice that most people acknowledge, but regularly disregard. We often wildly miscalculate the short-term and long-term consequences of choices in the sexual domain. Short-term pleasures loom large, and the distant pains appear small and far away, sometimes out of sight entirely. We mistakenly judge sex as necessary for happiness; we fail to appreciate stable and pleasant attachment when we have it; and we infect both sex and love with limitless desires for status, power, and money. We delude ourselves about the relative perfection of a perfectly normal human being.

For Epicurus, any relationship built on shifting sands proves volatile. Just as with healthy friendships, healthy romantic relationships depend on trust and a shared conception of what matters for happiness. And all the harmless sex you jointly desire, of course.

17 | BUILDING THE TRANQUIL CHILD

Epicurus wrote in Greek, ugly Greek, so his texts present numerous challenges for translators and commentators. A persistent challenge of working with almost all ancient texts, though, is that what we have are copies of copies of copies, and humans are prone to errors in transcription. Anyone who has played the childhood game of "telephone" knows the sort of absurdities that can result when gossip is passed from mouth to mouth, and the written word is surprisingly not all that much better. Translators also make errors, and those errors are themselves copied. Once a mistake takes hold, it can change the whole tenor of our understanding. A philosopher can go from pro-marriage and children to anti-marriage and children in the blink of a "nor." Such, I maintain, is the tale of Epicurus on marriage and children.

Diogenes Laertius seems to have started us out with an Epicurus generally in favor of marriage and children. In his catalogue of the sage's many psychological characteristics and behaviors, he says, "And indeed the wise man will marry and father children, as Epicurus says in his *Problems* and in the *On Nature*. But he will marry only when it is indicated by the circumstances of his life at a given time. And some will be diverted from this."[1] This seems so practical as to be unremarkable. Epicureans will be happy to marry or have children, but they will not get married if the circumstances of life make it imprudent, a good opportunity does not arise, or they get busy with other valuable things. In other words, Epicurus considers it prudent to marry or have children, unless it isn't.

Despite this eminently reasonable position, late-Renaissance scholars concluded that there must be an error in the text because they could not make sense of an Epicurus who actively encouraged any such thing. They decided to alter the received text to reflect their own understanding of Epicurus: "Nor will the wise man marry and father children."[2] The subsequent lines, as they render them, introduce the rare exceptions to the general principle of avoiding marriage and having children. It should come as no surprise at this point that I think Epicurus believes that marriage and children are worthwhile pleasures when done right, and I think we lack reason to change the received text to say otherwise.[3]

Granted, the scholars who propose emending the text have two decent reasons on their side. The first is that they consider Epicurus disdainful of sex and hostile to love, questions we explored in the previous chapter. Sex is the most common way to have children, and marriage seems to indicate a long-term caring relationship with a particular individual that often involves love. If sex and love are best avoided, then so are children and loving marriages. Rather than reconsider whether Epicurus was so hostile to love and sex when treated as proper extravagances, the commentators instead decided to make him generally anti-marriage and children.

One might also find the emendation reasonable because perhaps Epicurus recognized that marriages and children are often sources of anxiety, exhaustion, and drudgery. His atomist predecessor,

Democritus, claims that having children is too risky because you never know what you'll get, so he recommends requesting to take into your possession a child of your good friend.[4] Can you imagine—"Mary, I was wondering whether I might choose one of your charming sons or daughters for fear that I would birth a difficult child." Even before the anxieties of modern parenting, Democritus preferred not to gamble on a child.

As it stands, nearly one-half of American marriages end in divorce, despite almost no couple announcing at the outset, "Pretty decent chance that we won't make it!" Parenting is difficult, and many parents, especially American parents of young children, report significantly lower subjective well-being than their childless peers. I remember a pregnant friend of mine expressing distress over a *New York Magazine* cover story by Jennifer Senior, "All Joy and No Fun." The story included an account of a study conducted by UCLA's Center on Everyday Life of Families, the results of which one of the experimenters summed up as "the very purest form of birth control ever devised. Ever." He already had two children.[5] Words like "duty" and "obligation" seem to roll off the tongue when people discuss the challenges of both social enterprises. This might make even a person who thinks Epicurus is fine with sex and love think it nevertheless best to avoid children and marriage.

The idea that Epicurus thinks marriage and children produce anxiety and unhappiness in many people should not surprise us because he thinks many otherwise pleasant things produce anxiety and unhappiness when coupled with prudential errors or corrosive desires. Marriage and family can be choice-worthy and fulfilling, at least for, as Lucretius calls them, "the healthy-minded."

Before turning to what makes marriage and children healthy for the healthy-minded, I want to point out some commonly overlooked evidence that supports the idea that Epicureans recommend children for those who want them.

As we know, Metrodorus was Epicurus' closest friend, whom Epicurus apparently did not persuade against children. In fact, Metrodorus named his son Epicurus.[6] Two other Epicureans, Leonteus and his wife, also seem to have named a son Epicurus.[7] Then, when Metrodorus died, he chose Epicurus to parent his children. It seems strange to honor a man who opposes having children by naming your child after him and then asking him to care for those children after you die. In Epicurus' will, he expresses the wish that Metrodorus' daughter marry well and sets aside money for her dowry. It seems Epicurus encourages people to marry and have children left and right, naming one of their sons after him should they feel so moved.

Lucretius—and this seems the more overlooked passage—delights in the possibility of children. After pages of condemnation of corrosive passion, he addresses fertility and the desire to have children. He counts it a genuine misfortune if a man or woman who wants children cannot have them, and he resents that they are told their situation results from divine will rather than some biological impediment. He writes that it is cruel to think the gods would "deprive any man of procreative capacity so that he is prevented from ever being called father by sweet children and is condemned to live a life cursed with sterility."[8] He notes that sometimes both women and men struggle to have children in an earlier marriage (or two), yet "at last" they find someone with whom they can "conceive babies and be enriched with sweet offspring."[9] That sounds neither hostile to marriage nor children. In fact, it sounds like Lucretius recommends the serial monogamy of successive marriages.

Lucretius even offers some fertility advice, suggesting, among other things, that "diet plays a part."[10] Not one to shy away from too many details, Lucretius speculates about what sexual positions and motions are more likely to succeed in producing children. Upshot—the absence of the motions prostitutes use to avoid getting pregnant. That's Lucretius for you, ready to dive into that discomfort. In sum, he thinks having children is worth the effort of repeatedly trying for success.

Later, in his account of the development of civil society, Lucretius identifies children as the reason people formed communities to begin with. He claims that children "with their charming ways easily broke down the stern dispositions of their parents." For the sake of protecting their children, neighbors joined coalitions and formed "pacts of friendship," jointly concluding that "everyone ought to have compassion on the weak."[11] These pacts are what make tranquility possible, and if children were the primary impetus for bringing about such pacts, then children might be what continues to hold society together.

Epicurus, then, has no problem with people having children, at least if they adopt a healthy attitude and avoid setting unreasonable expectations. What, though, does a healthy attitude involve, and how is an Epicurean supposed to achieve it? If Epicurus encourages people to have children under appropriate circumstances, then he must think that, at least in those cases, parenting should not undermine tranquility. Given that the data suggests that many modern parents find parenting stressful, even miserable, something about their expectations or social circumstances must be making things more difficult than necessary.

Remember that for Epicurus, everything conducive or opposed to our tranquility begins with desire. I have suggested that Epicurus thinks the desires for marriage and children are natural, but not necessary, desires. In the terms of this book, they are extravagant desires. While many people have these desires, some do not, just as some people do not like the beach, coffee, or ice cream. Epicurus thinks a person should not be forced to pursue an extravagance they do not desire, nor should they be shamed for wanting it. In other words, if children are for you, that is great; if they are not for you, that is also fine.

For Epicurus, if we have the right attitude toward an extravagant desire, in this case a desire for children, then an opportunity to satisfy the desire should provide a pleasant variation in our tranquility. If we do not find a suitable partner or have an opportunity for children, Epicurus thinks our tranquility should remain intact, even if we find ourselves somewhat disappointed. As Epicureans, we might find ourselves in a community that has mutual concern for children, so even the childless will have opportunities to contribute to the well-being of the community's children. Epicurus, after all, had no children, but he was clearly involved in the lives of the children in the Garden.

The problem is that extravagant desires so easily turn corrosive, and the desire for children is no exception. Having and raising children presents itself in some societies as a great, gleaming beacon of corrosive fire. It takes careful Epicurean prudence to avoid lighting our fragile moth wings alight, not to mention the fragile wings of our children. To think of the parenting relationship in terms of Epicurean desires, we might think that parents desire a child, but they also usually desire a particular kind of child. To ask parents what they want for their child is to ask them to define what they consider a good life.

It might help to revisit some common features of desire from early in the book—intensity, likelihood of success, and expected pleasure. With respect to intensity, my desire that my child grow up to be kind and considerate of others might be powerful, while I might not be deeply invested in my child being funny or creative. I might not give much thought to whether they will laugh at my jokes rather than subsist on a steady diet of Will Ferrell movies. For Epicurus, powerful desires can be risky, so the only strong desires worth keeping around should be within reach if we focus our efforts.

Our desire's likelihood of success determines whether we are more or less likely to end up with the kind of child we hope for. If I desperately want to raise a professional basketball player, then my chances are slim. I am far more likely to produce a kind and considerate child than an Olympian. For Epicurus, if we think our child's success or happiness requires obtaining scarce goods (only so many people in the NBA, so many CEOs), then our likelihood of producing the child we "want" diminishes significantly. We also might come to see other children as competitors for those spots and our child as proceeding through life in a quest to top the pecking order. Epicurus, as we know, considers such desires invitations to anxiety and dissatisfaction in our own lives, and as parents we risk extending the volatility of those desires to the feelings and actions of our children.

For Epicurus, then, parenting starts with the parent's desires. Creating and shaping a human without first developing a conception of what matters in life is like climbing into a boat, pushing off from shore, and hoping it will drift someplace nice. Epicurus encourages all of us, parent or not, to take the rudder and navigate life with a plan. He thinks we should develop well-considered views about the importance of money, status, beauty, and power, as well as about what we owe other members of our community and what it means to be kind. We need views about what counts as resilience, autonomy, and self-respect. We should have an answer to the question—what does happiness require, and what does it not require? If we are parents, our answers to those questions can determine a young human's well-being.

Epicurus thinks, as we know, that human beings can achieve happiness if our necessary desires are currently met and if we have reasonable confidence those desires will be met in the future. Remember also that necessary desires are not merely for food and shelter, but also for a foundational understanding of the workings of the world and how to navigate it. Most importantly, Epicurus thinks we need to develop and maintain reliable and caring friendships. For Epicurus, consistent satisfaction of necessary desires is sufficient to afford a person a tranquil life, filled with joys in a community of mutual concern.

At the most fundamental level, then, Epicurus thinks raising a happy child requires three things: satisfying as best we can a child's necessary desires, helping them develop the capacities to satisfy those desires for themselves, and helping them find satisfaction in having enough. That's a tall order! Even meeting a child's necessary desires can present a challenge when the conditions of the world work against you. Unlike the Stoics, Epicurus believes that being in genuine need makes tranquility difficult, perhaps putting it out of reach in some cases.

Epicurus remains optimistic that most people can satisfy their necessary desires if they and their community prioritize them. Healthy friendships within trusting communities help ensure that people do not fall into material distress. In his will, Epicurus directs the executor to ensure that, to whatever extent his funds allow, none of the members of his community who grew old with him and showed him kindness should find themselves without "the necessaries of life."[12] For Epicurus, by far the greatest skill we can give our children is a capacity for friendship.

What, then, of the other things we might want for our children? As usual, Epicurus is fine with extravagances, as long as we adopt the right attitude toward them. Extravagant desires in the context of parenting might include things like fostering special talents and skills for things like sports and creative outlets, birthday parties and vacations, trips to the state park to dig around in the dirt looking for diamonds (in Arkansas, specifically), or visits to castles in Europe. As usual, Epicurus thinks we are all more likely to enjoy extravagances when they are shared with others and when they are not routine or expected. Rare and shared experiences are not only more intense, but more vividly remembered. They are, however, unnecessary for fundamental tranquility.

Corrosive and competitive desires for status, money, and power poison everything, even the most pleasant extravagances. The desire to be the smartest, the best, the most admired transforms things that would otherwise be joyful into opportunities for anxiety and disappointment. Epicurus thinks the worst thing we can do to ourselves is rob ourselves of joy by making everything a chase for an unlimited good—never too smart, never too talented, never too admired. As we should not feed our own corrosive desires,

Epicurus thinks we should not feed our children's either. In fact, he likely thinks that is the worst thing we can do for our children because he thinks it is the worst thing we can do for ourselves.

It might help to imagine what this looks like from the child's perspective. Children, savvy little observers that they are, figure out fairly quickly what kind of child their parents want, and they try to be, at least for a while, that child. They know whether their parents want them to be smarter and more successful in school, in sport, or in beauty (or everything all at once). If they worry that they cannot meet those expectations, then they are filled with anxiety. If they fail, they feel shame and disappointment. While many children grow up to recognize and resent that their self-confidence was cashed out in the currency of their parents' self-esteem and status-seeking, others just renew the cycle of anxious expectation and disappointment with their own children.

Most children, I suspect, feel better if they have confidence that they already have the resources within themselves to be the child their parents want. If the values their parents want for them are available to everyone who makes them a priority, rather than rare or competitive, then children are more likely to feel secure. In other words, psychological security for a child is best built on a foundation of what Epicurus thinks is within reach of everyone not laboring under tragic circumstances—kindness, trustworthiness, and confidence that we understand what is necessary for happiness.

Agreeing with the Epicurean model of parenting's aims depends, of course, on our first agreeing with his conception of happiness itself. Anyone who thinks what Epicurus considers corrosive desires are great for a person's well-being will want their children to have those desires. Epicurus thinks corrosive desires are unhealthy for anyone, but he has no interest in coercing people to value the same things he does. His only aim is to make a case for a particular way of living. Epicurus is just not a "tiger mom."

In the end, I think we should stick to the received text of Diogenes Laertius. Epicurus encourages Epicureans to get married or have children if it happens to fit their life plan and they can take up the project with a healthy attitude. Given that Epicurus considers it a worthwhile project to foster Epicureanism in others, he has reason to encourage people to foster it in children as well. The first step of good parenting is putting order to the house of our own desires. Parents who set limits on their desires are less anxious and more joyful, and their children are more likely to feel secure joy in turn. Life in a community like the Garden offers shared concern for the community's children and confidence that a friend will help your children out if misfortune strikes. We should all be so fortunate.

18 | FOODIES, DINNER PARTIES, AND WINE SNOBS

Philosophers have long been lampooned, by both friends and foes alike. For example, Monty Python, whom I number among philosophy's friends, produced a skit depicting a football match between famous Greek and German philosophers. When the whistle blows, no one touches the ball. The players just walk around lost in thought, muttering to themselves or chatting with each other, gesticulating wildly. Nietzsche receives his third booking in four matches for arguing about free will with Confucius, the referee. The announcer identifies Epicurus as Greece's "tireless number 6."[1] In the final minutes of a nil–nil match in which the ball has never moved, Archimedes has a "eureka" moment and starts play.

Archimedes passes to Socrates, later to Heraclitus, then sets up a perfect header that Socrates buries in the back of the net. The German goalie, Leibniz, "never had a chance." The Germans protest the goal in their own obscure philosophical terminology, but the Greeks win the day. A viewer can get the joke without having read any Greek or German philosophy—famous philosophers playing football is ridiculous enough on its surface. I own a Greek national jersey for the player Sokratis, which instantaneously transforms itself into a joke inside a philosophy classroom.

Imagine, in the same spirit, a group of philosophers attending a dinner party. No, really, go ahead and imagine it as if someone asked you to write a skit. What would they eat—stale crusts of grainy bread, individually peeled grapes, thin soup, exotic fish? What about the costumes—berets, togas, black turtlenecks, wide-wale brown corduroy? Would they argue with one another, and about what—the possibility of knowledge, whether the table *really* exists, the definition of gravy, whether the angels dancing on the edge of their wine glass prefer the waltz or the twist? Perhaps one of the characters would drunkenly stare at his hands and then exclaim, "Hands exist. I insist—just look, will you!" Would they laugh, or would they take themselves entirely too seriously?

It turns out "philosophers attend a dinner party" was a remarkably common source of comedy in Greek and Roman antiquity, and the Epicureans played a special role in the fun. Athenaeus, in the second century CE, composed a lengthy work entitled *The Learned Banqueters*, which depicts a days-long dinner party attended by a wide variety of intellectual luminaries that terminates with a list of tasty fishes in alphabetical order, including a discussion of the best ways to prepare them. The work quotes liberally from a veritable encyclopedia of comedic sources of philosophers at table.

Athenaeus notes that Epicurean characters regularly serve as the unapologetic gluttons. Their hedonism makes Epicureans ideal "helpers" when poets want to depict someone manifesting wanton disregard for self-restraint, the Greek for "helpers" in this passage being *epicourous*, a play on Epicurus' name.[2] Other philosophers, who are with few exceptions quite hostile to pleasure, often come across as comically hypocritical, as dispositional killjoys seeking to justify their rare culinary indulgences with sophistic terms like "the Paris exception."[3] Epicureans, hedonists to their core, are by contrast easy to caricature as indiscriminate pleasure-seekers who relish delicacies unreflectively and with unrivalled speed and vivacity. For example, the following anecdote from *The Learned Banqueters*:

> When an eel was served, an Epicurean who was dining with us said, "The Helen of dishes has arrived; so I shall be Paris." And before anyone else could reach for the eel, he fell upon it and gobbled it down to the bone.[4]

The passage continues by recounting how the Epicurean trained himself to eat searingly hot food so that he could wolf it all down before his non-Epicurean dining companions even began. Everyone else found themselves feebly waiting for the dish to cool.

The association of Epicurus with the ridiculous elements of fine dining also appears in a peculiarly quirky feature of Greek comedy—the stock character of the conceited chef, or *mageiros*. As Pamela Gordon puts it, the *mageiros* is "a braggart chef whose comic role centers on his propensity to flaunt his knowledge of cookery in contexts where he is out of place."[5] One memorable *mageiros* claims that his superiority comes from close reading of Democritus and Epicurus, including two years and ten months studying (and presumably cooking) at the Garden. He bandies about some obscure Epicurean terminology to suggest that he alone has extended Epicurean natural science into the kitchen. Other chefs merely cook food, but he understands the science! The Epicurean *mageiros* concludes: "So whenever you meet a chef who has not read all of Democritus, and the canon of Epicurus, smear him with dung and kick him out, like he flunked out of philosophy school!"⁶ Philosophers in the role of pompous chefs could just as well be a Monty Python skit.

Epicurus as unapologetic foodie has proven his most emblematic and longest-running identity. Even during his lifetime, Epicurus' views on the pleasures of eating were an object of public, largely good-natured ribbing. In France, gourmet grocery stores still bear Epicurus' name, and epicurious.com is one of the largest repositories of recipes on the internet. I have eaten at a restaurant named for Epicurus, and I recently ordered a local craft beer named "Epicurus" simply because I felt obligated to honor the brewer's sentiment. Even though Epicurus, as far as we can tell, never wrote "Eat, drink, and be merry for tomorrow we die," it is commonly associated with his philosophy. When I say I am writing a book about Epicurus, people usually respond, "Who?" But other times I get, "Oh, he's the food guy, right?" The equation of "Epicurean" and "foodie" is so pervasive that one can't help thinking it must contain a germ of truth when properly understood.

It seems to me that Epicurus often suffers from two misrepresentations at opposing extremes—the inveterate foodie or the smug hunger artist. Defenders of Epicurus have good reason to resist the impression that Epicurus was an insufferable foodie. Epicurus himself bitterly denies the charge, claiming that those who equate Epicurean hedonism with the "pleasures of consumption" do so "either from ignorance and disagreement or from deliberate misinterpretation."⁷ He writes that "barley cakes and water provide the highest pleasure when someone in want takes them" and that that "simple flavours provide a pleasure equal to that of an extravagant life-style when all pain from want is removed."[8] Epicureans think "sober calculation," not "consuming fish and the other dainties of an extravagant table," brings happiness.[9]

These passages, with their use of "sober," "simple," and "equal," have led to a charitably motivated overcorrection that also risks misrepresenting Epicureanism. Some render Epicurus an ascetic, a hedonist in theory but an anti-hedonist in practice. For example, when I was considering whether to write this book, I attended a post-conference dinner at a nice restaurant with some of the bigger and more exotic fishes of the Ancient Greek philosophy profession. One of my pleasant dinner companions, an intensely clever and mildly intoxicated British philosopher, stridently dismissed Epicurus as worthy of such a book. Why write about someone who hated pleasure so much?! Epicurus, he insisted, would scorn the very meal we were eating. It seems one must choose between Epicurus as glutton or champion of gruel.

It makes good sense that Epicurus would build his philosophy to account for tranquility under conditions of scarcity. He lived in Athens during a time of periodic grain shortages, when extensive trading was difficult because the Macedonians controlled the main Athenian port of the Piraeus. Attica also suffered periodic military incursions that destabilized the food supply because the invading armies tried to time their efforts so they could eat from the fields as they advanced. We have a historical record of the Garden rationing beans, and Epicurus wrote a foreign friend to thank him for selling him scarce grain at a fair price.[10] When he writes that barley-cakes taste good for a hungry person, he speaks from experience. Sometimes gruel is the only option, and Epicurus insists that a good hedonist will find pleasure in such a life. Consider how some people responded to brief food shortages and the temporary closure of restaurants during the pandemic. Epicureans would number among those happy to leave the store with a bag of dried beans.

But times were not always hard for the Garden. There are fishes in the sea, and Epicurus liked cheese.[11] Epicurus also explicitly denies that we should seek to "make do with few things under *all* circumstances" because some circumstances allow for a great deal more.[12] Epicureans should prepare for difficult times, not live as if all times are difficult. Too much "parsimony" is as bad as too much indulgence.[13]

Remember, too, that the ability to make do with less increases our appreciation of having more. Epicureans are "genuinely convinced that those who least need extravagance enjoy it most."[14] In this fashion, Epicurus does perhaps come across as a variation on a superior foodie, as if announcing when seated at a fine restaurant, "I will enjoy this amazing meal more than anyone here because I don't make a habit of eating so well and can happily do without it!" Then perhaps he would pounce on the eel. Epicureans, for all their rejection of intellectual snobbery, do think their way of living is better and more pleasant, and anyone who claims to live better than others will perpetually run the risk of exuding snobbery.

To what extent then, are the Epicureans foodies, and what sort of attitude do they adopt toward eating? They are clearly not food and wine snobs in the most common manner of snobs. Epicurus would not catalogue his extravagances as a mark of pride or judge people who do not share or appreciate them. Epicurus would not care that some people like Bud Light and others like Belgian sours—to each their own as long as neither considers beer necessary for happiness nor derides the other's preference. He would accept the food and drink that people serve him as a mark of respect and gratitude to hosts. He would not, in short, argue about the food and wine.

While Epicureans are not obsessed with having superior taste in extravagances and lording it over others, they are nevertheless committed to thinking of a particular kind of eating as best and as conducive to secure well-being. Specifically, they are foodies in that they value shared dining because it builds relationships and provides opportunities for memorable gratitude and joy. The Garden's Epicureans dined together with great, even ritualistic regularity. They celebrated many special events annually, including Epicurus' birthday, as well as the twentieth of every month. Their social dining habit no doubt lies behind Seneca's labeling them a "shade-loving clan of philosophizing banqueters."[15] Seneca is welcome to his own views, but I find it difficult to dislike someone who encourages me to step out of the harsh sun to eat and talk with friends.

The Epicurean commitment to the value of shared and social dining seems so unthreatening to most people because it is so obviously true. Yet its truth does not always translate into action. America, and perhaps some other places less familiar to me, illustrates how we can fail to prioritize one of the most important forms of collective pleasure and what it costs us. For many Americans, eating together in leisure has been crowded out and discouraged by relentless market and cultural forces. A place with access to some of the best food is among the worst places to eat because so many people eat fast, quiet, and alone.

That is not to say that Americans want to eat alone or silently! In fact, many Americans seem almost obsessed with the idea of the dinner party. I would wager, though, that ninety-five percent of all American dinner parties take place in magazines, newspapers, and commercials. I once opened an article in the *New York Times* with the alluring title, "How to Throw a Festive Korean-Inspired Dinner Party."[16] That indeed seemed "festive," but I quickly realized it was way out of my league on pretty much all fronts. The more general *New York Times* dinner party instructions, "How to Host a Dinner Party," begin two weeks prior to the event and include words like *mise en place*, aperitif, and place cards.[17] Don't get me wrong, those sound and look like excellent events, but if this is what counts as a "dinner party," it's no surprise we attend so few.

It's not only the food that keeps us apart, since we sometimes worry whether our home furnishings will inspire admiration or at least benign approval. Every summer home improvement store commercial makes me think, "We can't have people over because we don't have an attractive outside dining space!" The unintended result of this false standard of great food in an admirable home is that we don't invite people over at all. Who has the time to present themselves as paragons of taste and style?

What of restaurants, then, if not homes? In America, few restaurants encourage social engagement because they are designed for turnover and profit. Sometimes we spend more time picking a restaurant that is hot, new, an "overlooked gem," definitely not a chain, than we spend talking to our friends when we get there. And in the dash and crush for what everyone wants right now, we go places where we're pressured out the door right after we eat because there's a waitlist and we're just sitting there like stubborn talking cows who refuse to make space for weary, hungry cows. The acoustics are horrible in most bustling restaurants, so those who struggle to hear struggle to converse. Soundproofing has been sacrificed to the aesthetic of concrete floors and high-ceilinged warehouses that echo into an unruly din. The better option for social dining is usually in our homes, but again, we no longer do that sort of thing.

Finally, Americans have a problem with overscheduling and overworking, which for some results from brutal necessity, for others from a lifestyle choice born of ambition and acquisitiveness. Before the COVID-19 pandemic, it was against the law to eat at your desk in France. Against the law! Article R.4428-19 of the French labor code (fittingly titled, the *Code du Travail*) made it illegal not only for a boss to require, but also to permit, an employee to eat at their desk. The French, consummate café and social diners that they are, deeply regretted that COVID-19 required them to save lives by doing what Americans choose to do all the time. No wonder Epicurus features so prominently in their grocery markets.

Americans not only break French law by eating at their desks at work. They also eat alone or on the run in their free time. Families rarely share meals. Some families cannot eat together because every adult works two jobs and they still find themselves living on the edge. They are robbed by practical necessity of the opportunity for shared dining. Other families could eat together but they choose to overschedule themselves in hopes of promotions or overschedule their children in hopes of getting them into elite colleges. In Epicurean terms, they sacrifice the core pleasures for the corrosive ones. Shared meals, such as they are, often happen silently in front of the television or with at least one person stolidly operating their smart phone. I say all of this not from judgment so much as from experience. After all, I am an American.

When I was chaperoning those twenty-six Duke students in Greece, the mechanic of a boat the program rented said he had spent a year in America training for a professional qualification. He was appalled that when he asked the guys he worked with about their weekend plans—they had none. As he put it, "They said they were going to eat Subway and watch television." He insisted that they bring drinks and something for the grill to his place to spend the afternoon together, and as he told it, it was some sort of revelation of possibility. As if people could live this way! The boat mechanic shook his head with an expression of pity that seems so common when foreigners discuss American eating habits.

Simply eating together with a friend in conversation counts as an Epicurean meal, whether you eat oatmeal, fire up the grill, or converse for hours over a six-course tasting menu with wine pairings. For me, this Epicurean conception of what matters in eating crystallized at a rare and welcome dinner party attended by eight people, some of whom had never met. Everyone had a wonderful time, and the hosting couple served frozen pizzas and a simple green salad on compostable plates. The drinks were tasty and abundant, and no one wanted to go home. In the same vein, some of the best and most meaningful conversations I have had were in dive bars or in the equivalent of a Chili's. It's not about the furnishings, the price, or even the food—it's about the people, the time, and the spirit.

Imagine, then, what some proper Epicureans eating together might look like and make it happen, maybe even on the twentieth of the month to be festive. Throw a "twentiether." And just don't be so serious about it—Epicurus says we must laugh, even as we philosophize and take care of life's daily necessities like keeping ourselves fed.[18] In some sense, then, Epicureans dining together are truly funny, but they are not so much the joke itself—they are the source of fun.

19 | SCIENCE AND ANXIETY

Imagine that a physics professor walked into a classroom on the first day and announced, "This class will diminish your suffering and anxiety, and, what's more, without it you will live out your days needlessly tormented by psychological pain!" Physicists tend to advertise the value of bridges and the nanotechnology that powers our devices. We more often market how science enables action and production rather than how it quietens the mind.

For Epicurus, science is also necessary to chill us out. In *Principal Doctrines* 11 and 12, he writes:

> If our suspicions about heavenly phenomena and death did not trouble us at all and were never anything to us, and, moreover, if not knowing the limits of pain and desires did not trouble us, then we would have no need of natural science.[1]
>
> It is impossible for someone ignorant of the nature of the universe but still suspicious about the subjects of the myths to dissolve his feelings of fear about the most important matters. So it is impossible to receive unmixed pleasures without knowing natural science.[2]

Streamlined and direct, these doctrines say that we need natural science to

- free ourselves from superstitions, including those concerning celestial phenomena;
- manage our fear of death; and
- understand the relationship between unlimited desires and pain.

We have spent most of the book thus far exploring the relationship between unlimited desires and anxious dissatisfaction. But what of these other supposed roles for natural science in our psychological economy—fighting superstition and managing our fear of death? Perhaps it would help to first get a better sense of Epicurus' natural science itself.

The most striking feature of Epicurus' natural science is how much he got right. While the Stoics were trying to predict the future by reading the entrails of sacrificial birds, Epicurus was developing a remarkably modern account of the natural world. For Epicurus, the cosmos in its entirety is composed of atoms and void. The atoms collide, come together, and break apart according to fixed causal principles with some occasional indeterminacy of the sort postulated in particle physics. Epicureans think the species that populate our earth are the ones who have proven the fittest in a fight for survival. Everything we encounter is explicable in purely physical terms. Epicurus thinks gods exist, but they do not causally intervene in the world, nor do they create, sustain, or destroy it.

The Epicurean conception of physics is also much broader than ours, in part because our word "physics" comes from the Greek word for "nature," *phusis*. Epicurean physics studies the whole of the natural world and humans as a part of that natural order. Lucretius titles his work *On the Nature of Things*, and he covers everything from the atomic structure of the universe to the biological causes of illness, the evolution of human communities, how magnets work, the nature of the divine, and the perils of romantic love. For Epicurus, natural science includes what we mean by "physics," but also biology, astronomy, psychology, medicine, religion, and politics.

This atomic physicalism at the cosmic level extends to individual humans. Our body is an elaborate structure of atoms and void, as is our conscious mind, which awards us our capacity to think, feel, and deliberate. Like most of his peers, Epicurus believes in a material mind because the mind can move our body, and only material things can move material things. Positing an immaterial soul would give us the inconsistent powers of Casper the Friendly Ghost or Patrick Swayze in *Ghost*, somehow able to both pass through walls and knock things over. Most philosophers think that because the mind makes us raise our hands and comb our hair, it must be physical.

Epicurus, though, thinks the atoms that compose our mind are more complex and fluid than the atoms that make up, say, a table. Unlike tables, the configurations of our atoms afford us distinctive capacities to think, feel, and desire that are not contained in the individual atoms themselves. In other words, none of the atoms that make us up are conscious in isolation. When suitably organized, though, these non-conscious psychological atoms give rise to our sensory awareness and powers of reason. Such capacities "emerge" from the structure, not entirely unlike locomotion becomes possible when all the necessary parts of a train are properly assembled.

We differ importantly from tables because we have some control over what we do, a kind of agency that tables clearly lack. We can alter our desires in response to judgments about what benefits us. These judgments are at least partially informed by our capacity to articulate and entertain reasons about what benefits and harms creatures like us. A table cannot say, "After much thought, I have decided to pursue a career in a corporate boardroom." Unlike tables, we are not purely subject to the external forces of nature. Epicurus does, by hook or by crook, intend to preserve space for some measure of effective rational agency within a mechanistic world, though perhaps not radical freedom.[3]

At root, though, we remain physical "stuff," and when that "stuff" breaks apart at death, the consciousness arising from our atomic structure likewise dissipates. We are sophisticated atomic creatures, but we eventually lose some of the atoms that keep the house of cards standing. An essential part of the engine gets removed. At that point, the complex structure of atoms scatters and our conscious awareness ends. Because we are not consciously aware once dead, Epicurus thinks being dead can neither benefit nor harm us—pleasure and pain depend on the capacity for conscious awareness, and death removes that capacity. We will focus on that specific argument about death in a few chapters.

In its broadest outline, then, Epicurean natural science rejects non-physical explanations of the world, the existence of an immaterial soul, and the prospect of the postmortem survival of our own individual consciousness. We are in many respects far more sophisticated animals than wolves and birds, although we resemble them in our fundamental drive to live securely and pleasantly. Epicurus thinks living securely and pleasantly as a human being requires understanding the science of the natural world we occupy. Otherwise, we will cause ourselves harm and increase our anxiety.

Let's return, then, to the question of whether natural science as Epicurus understands it lessens our anxiety in the ways he suggests. It is certainly to Epicurus' credit that his atomism greatly resembles a modern scientific account, especially because he postulated the existence of atoms he could not see and atomic swerves before we built a Hadron Collider. Natural science's effects on our anxiety, though, seem mixed at best. Most of us hardly think about atoms in our daily lives, so you could easily think they have no real impact on our tranquility.

Natural science frees us from anxious superstitions—on this point Epicurus is clearly right. Talk of superstitious fear of celestial phenomena sounds quaint. We don't worry that a streaking comet portends the end times because we understand that comets are rocks we can measure and predict, not updates from a god registering displeasure at our failings. Astrology is a crackpot theory. Things that go bump in the night are the house settling, a rodent in the attic, or a burglar, not the Ghost of Christmas Past. In that sense, natural science does free us of superstition, and most of us are Epicureans already. We do not fear ghosts or comets, chiefly because Epicurus eventually won the day against his competitors.

It is not clear, however, that Epicurean natural science helps diminish our fear of death, and scientific truth might give rise to its own anxieties. It might even seem that people who affirm opposing views—an immaterial soul, postmortem survival, a divine hand at work in the world—are less anxious. Perhaps those who deny the climate consensus or consider COVID-19 a hoax navigate the world with less fear. Some people fear that the planet will kill us off because we are poisoning it; others are indifferent to death and global destruction because heaven awaits. Those conducting their normal business without concern for contagion might seem less anxious than those who refuse to venture out. Epicurus needs to do some work if he hopes to show that those who reject science are more anxious than those who accept it.

Take a simple medical case. I boarded a flight to Portland when the press was engaged in a bit of fear mongering about an Ebola outbreak in Africa. I was unconcerned because Ebola is not spread through air, food, or water, but an older couple a few rows ahead of me were wearing face masks and using hand sanitizer for reasons of their own. I noticed, though, that each time they used the hand sanitizer, the woman seated next to me opened a little bag of essential oils and rubbed some on either herself or her young child. I assumed she had a sensitive nose. Eventually she turned to me to complain about the hand sanitizer, but for reasons I had not anticipated. The couple, she asserted, should be using essential oils to protect themselves instead, proudly adding that she had recently replaced all the items in a friend's medicine cabinet with "natural" medicine.

The woman had reassured her husband that morning that she and their daughter would be fully protected against Ebola while flying because she had packed her oregano oil, which she carried with her when she visited the plane's bathroom. We had three hours remaining in the flight, and suddenly those hours stretched out endlessly. As we disembarked, she accosted the older couple with her bag of oils in hand like some modern-day huckster riding the medicine-show farm circuit. Neither the woman nor the elderly couple were going to get Ebola on that plane. The couple, though, were anxious, and the woman trumpeting pseudo-pharmaceutical tinctures seemed brazenly confident.

If Epicurus thinks bad science causes anxiety, then he must explain why he considers her as anxious as she was imprudent. In response, he might claim that false beliefs are inadvisable because they tend to have bad long-term consequences. Chances are that the woman on the plane might eventually confront a situation where she or her child had a choice between antibiotics or sepsis. Her friend with the medicine cabinet of oils probably came to regret that decision for the waste of funds alone. Maybe somebody she knows got a nasty case of tetanus.

By the same long-term token, the effects of climate change will eventually prove undeniable. As I write this sentence, cold parts of Canada are being immolated by a meteorological phenomenon NASA describes as "the fire-breathing dragon of clouds."[4] People who convince themselves smoking does not cause lung cancer often end up with lung cancer. Some people pass up vaccines and end up dead. In other words, denying the truth often has bad long-term consequences.

Bad long-term consequences just establish imprudence, though, not anxiety. That pain comes eventually does not establish anxiety now. Remember, though, that Epicurus thinks that correcting intellectual errors is a kind of frank speech. People who encounter scientific truth often perceive it as painful and a threat, thereby causing them to lash out in defensiveness, frustration, or anger. It is also cognitively and emotionally exhausting to ignore the truth and defend a lie. Someone calmly reporting the truth or pointing to a factually accurate chart will often meet hostility, even wrath. Galileo was almost killed for arriving at the scientific truth that the sun is the center of our universe. Epicurus would likely consider such defensiveness and close-mindedness a symptom of a deeper insecurity that gives rise to such reactionary denials of the truth.[5] I kept my mouth shut about the oils because I was not in the mood to weather the woman's angry defense.

Still, those who accept the truth have their own reasons for anxious despair, and for that reason it seems difficult to just accept Epicurus' view and move on. In some cases, anxiety seems to attend both the acceptance and denial of science. Epicurus might simply set up a game of whack-a-mole. Smash the anxiety of denying the truth—up pops the anxiety of accepting it. Those who affirm climate science might not fear the truth, but they generally fear climate change. They might not get angry at the epidemiologists or the mask mandates, but they do fear COVID-19.

In addition, accepting natural science can give us reason to fear the people who deny it. The oil-bearing woman on the plane posed no threat to me, so she never gave me a moment's pause. By contrast, Galileo was up against the Inquisition. Climate science deniers keep us from averting climate change. Vaccine deniers keep us from eradicating diseases, and in America some of them carry guns in the streets and into legislative sessions. Ask the wrong person to wear a mask and you could end up dead. So again, we might endorse natural science and still fear what it promises us or worry about the threat of people who deny it. Disagreements about science can, as we have seen during the pandemic, rip at the social fabric and cause rifts in our relationships with friends and family.

Someone might reasonably raise an additional objection to Epicurus' claims about the benefits of scientific knowledge. We should not overlook that natural science in the hands of wicked people is very, very bad. After all, natural science gave us nuclear weapons, Zyklon B, eugenics, and the Tuskegee trials. Science can be as much a weapon as a balm. In the language of earlier chapters, some kinds of natural science are conditional goods—beneficial when used well, destructive when used viciously. Our advances in scientific understanding only benefit us within a system that already has a set of prudential and ethical values that govern science's use.

Epicurus thinks he offers such a system. In fact, his ethics is itself a part of his natural science. In the end, though, Epicurus might oversell science's power to diminish anxiety, at least for individuals who find themselves enmeshed in a powerfully anti-science environment. I suspect he is right that those who reject science and embrace superstition carry around more fear and anger, like volcanoes always on the verge of eruption. Living among fearful and angry people, however, might itself be a legitimate source of anxiety, like living in the vicinity of an active volcano. Epicurus insists that the problem is not science itself, but the people who misuse or malign it. As with science, it turns out, so also with religion, to which we now turn.

20 | THAT OLD TIME RELIGION

Epicurus was his own man when it came to religious questions, but his core commitments were remarkably traditional. He claims that "god is an indestructible and blessed living being" and that Epicureans should never "ascribe to god anything foreign to his indestructibility or repugnant to his blessedness."[1] While Epicurus never weighs in on the number of gods, using the singular and plural seemingly interchangeably, he insists that "gods do exist, since we have clear knowledge of them."[2] He calls this knowledge a "basic grasp," which helps us discern the fundamental truths about divine nature. Epicurus lists the existence and blessedness of gods as the first Epicurean commitment in both his *Letter to Menoeceus* and the *Principal Doctrines*.

Given that Epicurus regularly puts these theological commitments front and center, it might seem bizarre that he has been both celebrated and reviled as an atheist. On the celebratory front, Christopher Hitchens chose a passage from Lucretius for the first chapter in his *Atheist Reader*, though Lucretius also defends at length the Epicurean view that gods exist. The Apostle Paul, far less keen, considered the Epicureans his prime target when he preached in Athens against the atheists, and generations of subsequent Christian intellectuals followed suit, producing their own attacks on Epicurean atheists.[3] Yet, as we have seen, Epicurus makes quite clear he is no atheist.

Even when not misunderstood as an atheist, Epicurus is commonly maligned as a heretic. The seventeenth-century Jewish philosopher, Baruch Spinoza, for example, was excommunicated and labeled an *apikoros*, Epicurus' own name transformed into a Hebrew word for "heretic."[4] In the *Inferno*, Dante lets other "pagan" philosophers gad about pleasantly in limbo, but he makes Epicurus the arch-heretic of the Sixth Circle of Hell. Epicurus' *Vatican Sayings* were discovered in the library's collection of heretical texts, and while Cicero acknowledges that Epicurus was clearly not an atheist, he fails to understand why not. Epicurus might as well be an atheist for all the difference it would make.

In short, while Epicurus clearly considers piety central to his way of life, important enough to appear first among his commitments, many have mistaken him for an atheist. Others consider him a dangerous heretic, and still others are simply perplexed about what, exactly, Epicurus thinks the gods do. As a general principle, no one motivates centuries worth of invective without having said something interesting and difficult to casually dismiss. Epicurus' criticisms of some long-standing and deeply embedded features of religious practice remain just as relevant today, so they still elicit their fair share of confusion and resentment.

Perhaps the best way to understand what perplexes and sometimes enrages people about Epicurean theology is to draw attention to what Epicurean gods *don't* do. First, Epicurean gods did not create the universe, they are not active in the world, and they will not play any role in bringing about our world's inevitable destruction. An Epicurean god, in other words, is not an agent of creation or change. As we saw in the previous chapter, Epicurus thinks the world results from the regular and occasionally spontaneous interplay of atoms and void, not from design. Second, Epicurean gods do not concern themselves with human beings, at least not enough to care about what we do. Lastly, the gods do not reward or punish human beings, whether now or in an afterlife. Rewarding and punishing humans during life would involve intervening in the world, which the gods are neither able nor interested in doing. Epicurus denies personal immortality, so the gods also do not oversee an afterlife. In briefest outline, Epicurean gods do not create, care, reward, or punish.

You could see why someone would wonder what part of religious belief remains. If gods do not create, care, reward, or punish, what do they do? For Epicurus, they serve as perfect instantiations of the tranquil life of satisfaction. Many religious believers hope to reflect, to whatever extent possible, their conception of divine nature in their own lives—people aim to live like the Buddha, in the spirit of Jesus, etc. They emulate God. In that respect, Epicurus is no different, since he also thinks the gods help us understand the good life by modeling it. We benefit from the gods because we can aspire to approximate their nature and life, not because they act in our lives, rewarding our proper attention or administering divine justice. For Epicurus, the perfectly tranquil life of the gods determines what features we can piously attribute to them. We cannot, for example, attribute jealousy to a divinely tranquil being, and by the same token, we should not be jealous.

That might help clear up some of the confusion about the role of the gods in Epicurean piety, but it does not explain the widespread animosity. Some of the resentment stems directly from what

Epicurus denies—that the afterlife exists and that the gods reward or punish human beings. Dante's *Inferno* depicts the landscape of divine punishment, raging hellfire hammered out in elegant sestinas, and Epicurus features prominently in the Sixth Circle because he denies the afterlife, as well as divine punishment more broadly. The Apostle Paul likewise scorned the Epicureans because they denied personal immortality and the rewards of the afterlife that Paul anticipated. The exact cause of Spinoza's excommunication remains unclear, but one of the more likely explanations is that he doubted immortality and divine judgment.[5]

What gives full-flower to Dante and Paul's animosity, though, is not that Epicurus would consider the *Inferno* scientifically impossible, but that Epicurus would consider it impious. The *Inferno*, or any depiction of divine judgment, is an insult to God, or in Epicurus' words, "repugnant to his blessedness." Such beliefs are not only impious—they also create more anxiety than they ameliorate. For Epicurus, people who believe in divine judgment suffer from an underlying psychological insecurity, an insecurity that they also impiously attribute to the gods. That might seem counterintuitive, as many religious believers report that their belief in an afterlife diminishes rather than reveals their anxiety. Epicurus might, as I explore below, consider some expressions of the desire for immortality harmless, but most on his view are not.

Again, Epicurus would not earn so much hostility if he were not presenting a serious challenge worth our attention. So, let's explore his reasons, focusing on his theological and prudential arguments because we have already explored his physics and natural science. Religion, in his view, departs from the "basic grasp" of divine nature when it suggests that gods make people successful and healthy or unsuccessful and sick, when it fosters and sustains fear of the afterlife, and when it motivates anger and violence. Religious belief and practice of that sort is both impious and psychologically unhealthy. It misrepresents the gods as anxious, angry, and unsatisfied, transforming divine beings into a reflection of human anxiety, anger, and dissatisfaction—just the sort of things we should aim to avoid.

For Epicurus, the greatest impiety and anxiety stems from viewing the relationship between humans and the gods as transactional, as a market exchange where both parties seek something they desire. On a transactional model, the gods bestow rewards on those who believe, pray, and worship correctly. Humans who fail to satisfy the gods suffer bad outcomes, whether now or after death. Thinking that God plays a role in windfalls and misfortunes is "repugnant to his blessedness" because it violates our "basic grasp" of a god as perfectly good, fully tranquil, indestructible, and self-sufficient.

The transactional model undermines the gods' self-sufficiency and tranquility because it makes them want things from us, whether recognition, praise, sacrifice, or ethical action. The gods have some desire or other, and we can choose whether to satisfy it. Our willingness or refusal, though, gives us in effect the power to control the gods' emotions, to either upset or secure their tranquility. In other words, we can *make* the gods upset when we fail to satisfy their desires. We can cause a god pain. Depending on human beings for divine pleasure and satisfaction leaves the gods vulnerable, their tranquility at the mercy of fickle and inferior creatures. For that reason, Epicurus thinks the gods cannot care what humans do and at the same time preserve their tranquil self-sufficiency. *Principal Doctrine* 1 distills the point:

What is blessed and indestructible has no troubles itself, nor does it give trouble to anyone else, so that it is not affected by feelings of anger or gratitude. For all such things are a sign of weakness.

Anger results from frustrated desire, and gratitude results when we appreciate having our desire met. If gods are perfectly self-sufficient and tranquil, then they lack reason for anger or gratitude in relation to human beings. Either emotion would give us power to influence divine emotions, making the gods in some fashion dependent on us. In the *Letter to Herodotus*, Epicurus writes that "troubles and concerns and anger are not consistent with blessedness."[6] The gods, then, do not concern themselves with what we do.

The transactional model also casts the gods in the role of rewarding and punishing people, whether in this life or the next. Epicurus thinks gods cannot intervene because that would violate scientific principles, but even if they could intervene, Epicurus thinks they would not. Again, he resists attributing certain kinds of desires to divine beings. Take first the relatively benign example of a football player who thanks Jesus for delivering a Super Bowl victory, as though Jesus thinks the New England Patriots are especially deserving this year. On this assumption, Jesus seems like the most fair-weather of fans, rooting this year for Liverpool or Manchester City, on rare occasion for Leicester. Either way, the celebration attributes to the gods a desire for someone to win. Considering the graver question of which soldiers survive a war rather than who wins at football, the musician Tom Waits asks, "And tell me how does God choose? Whose prayers does he refuse?"[7]

On the financial front, Epicurus thinks those who identify God's favor as the source of their excessive wealth impiously imply divine endorsement of the corrosive desire for money and honor. It remains relatively common, though, to think God awards great wealth and material success to those who believe rightly and pray fervently. In recent years, this mindset has gained force within the Christian evangelical tradition in the form of the stunningly non-fringe "Prosperity Gospel," whose adherents believe Jesus wants them to have bigger houses and more expensive cars. Setting aside the fact that Jesus was no fan of mixing money and religion, it also attributes empty and corrosive desires to both humans and God. For Epicurus, Joel Osteen's many expensive cars are not a sign of God's favor. They are instead manifestations of anxiety and dissat-isfaction. If God were in the business of rewards, the benefit would hardly be an insatiable desire for possessions.

Far more troubling, though, is the other side of the coin, the one entailing that some people deserve to lose, to be poor or sick. Recall Lucretius' frustration with religious authorities who cause the "widespread belief" among the regrettably childless that they have lost favor with the gods, their petitionary sacrifices sadly "in vain."[8] The idea that physical illness is divine punishment also re-mains stunningly non-fringe. I remember a church member telling my youth group that she had recently attended the funeral for a friend's son who had died young. She initially felt sad, but she reported quickly recovering once she remembered that "AIDS is God's punishment for homosexuality." Such patterns of reasoning stretch across religious traditions. A colleague reports that some of his relatives in Sri Lanka refuse to seek medical attention for serious diseases, assuming they deserve their illness because of actions in their prior or current life.

Kate Bowler, now a professor at the Duke University Divinity School, was suffering from a painful physical condition while writing her dissertation on the Prosperity Gospel. Leaders at the churches she visited often noticed her visible pain. In her recent memoir, *Everything Happens for a Reason: And Other Lies I've Loved*, she writes, "Sometimes I received an invitation to a quiet room to go over a checklist of sins I might have committed that would have opened the door to the ministrations of demons with names like Python, Sitri, and Vassago." She was in the company of people for whom "illness is a symptom of unconfessed sin."[9] Epicurean science would of course reject divine causation of illness on physicalist grounds, but Epicurean theology judges it impious for independent, non-scientific reasons.

Epicurus' aversion to a transactional conception of the divine also drives his related worry about postmortem punishment and reward. Again, he rejects the afterlife on scientific grounds, but also on grounds of piety and psychological well-being. Religious authorities often use the afterlife as a carrot and a stick, promising a delayed justice or threatening an inescapable punishment. Lucretius regrets that people are "terrorized by the fearsome pronouncements of the fable-mongers," whose efforts prove "capable of confounding your calculated life plan of life and clouding all your fortunes with fear."[10] I have heard six-year-old children avow complex religious commitments from fear of hell, only to have a roomful of people joyfully respond, "Amen." The idea of a final reckoning can also encourage us to kick the can of justice down the road, to make it, in effect, no longer the responsibility of the living. For example, I heard a prominent theologian casually dismiss the harms of slavery because slaves benefited eternally from the Christian conversion that slavery itself made possible.

For Epicurus, promises of rewards and punishments meted out eternally are unnecessary because virtuous people can live satisfied lives, while the vicious make themselves miserable. As Lucretius puts it, the vicious reveal that the horrors of the "abysm of Acheron actually exist in our life." He thinks the person chasing excess wealth or political power has created a psychological hell for themselves already.[11] Like Epicurus, Lucretius considers ethical living pleasant and joyful. We already have reason enough to live virtuously, and a strong desire to live forever, whether on earth or in an afterlife, encourages the attitude that nothing is ever enough.

Finally, Epicureans object to religious violence and the anxiety it manifests. Lucretius worries that his unorthodox religious beliefs will be misunderstood, telling Memmius, "I fear that you may perhaps imagine that you are starting on the principles of an irreligious philosophy and setting out on a path of wickedness. But in fact more often it is that very superstition that has perpetrated wicked and irreligious deeds." He recounts how Agamemnon sacrificed his daughter Iphigenia because he believed the gods would put wind in the sails of his ships bound for war. "Such heinous acts could superstition prompt."[12] Epicurean gods would never desire anything from a human, much less a sacrifice of that sort.

While child-sacrifice is now mercifully uncommon (though it still happens), religious wars, both internecine and interfaith, are ongoing. The Greeks did not seem to fight wars over religion itself, but they believed their wars were matters of divine interest and activity, enough that the gods required prayer and sacrifice to secure divine favor in battle. Plutarch, perhaps the staunchest critic of Epicurean theology, gleefully reports a possible indication of providence that when the Romans slaughtered the German Cimbri tribes, the abundance of corpses produced such rich manure for their orchards that the trees yielded fruit and wine better than ever before.[13] Epicurus would consider Plutarch's conjecture as impious as it is gruesome.

There are, for what it's worth, some expressions of the desire for an afterlife that I'm not convinced Epicurus has prudential reason to resist, and some he might in fact endorse. Someone could theoretically treat the desire for an afterlife as extravagant, one of those desires we would welcome should it occur, but that we could quite happily do without. Epicurus thinks we do not need to see the gods punish the unjust, certainly not eternally, to make our life content. We also do not need to live forever to make our life content. Yet he might not have reason to rule out an extravagant desire for friends to remember us, for the natural world's continued protection, or even for some continuance of our own person, at least on the condition that such desires prove harmless, and we do not consider their satisfaction of any import.

But Epicurus and Lucretius take themselves to have made the case that a great deal of religious doctrine feeds harmful, corrosive desires that increase anxiety and dissatisfaction. It also impiously imputes similar desires to gods. Much of what concerns Lucretius continues today, sometimes even more pronounced. Religious fervor still motivates and supposedly licenses wide-scale animosity and violence. People do in fact justify their greed and express indifference to poverty on grounds that the balance sheet is exactly as God intends. Bereaved parents hear that God allowed their child to die for some good reason that will always lie beyond their own comprehension. Religious figures kill, overthrow governments, and yell at one another until they are blue in the face over religious doctrine of no real consequence that causes very real violence. Epicurus might reasonably look around and say, "You know, I see a lot of anxiety and animosity there, and that does not look psychologically healthy to me. Surely that is inconsistent with the basic grasp of God."

Epicurus thinks that religious believers should have a vested interest in a conception of the divine that clears the low bar of not licensing violence in the name of religion, blaming the sick and poor, encouraging rapacious greed, and ignoring suffering that can be fixed in this life by our own efforts. He thinks we should not frighten children with hell or confuse God for some kind of cosmic moneychanger. To that extent, the Epicurean religious critique remains relevant, even if his bare bones theology might leave some people uninspired or, contrary to his intention, anxious rather than comforted.

21 | EXPERIENCING DEATH

Some might say I am an expert in the fear of death. I do not mean that I am an expert *at* fearing death, but that most of my published research addresses the fear of death in Ancient Greek Philosophy. Academics who do not know one another often kick off their introductions with, "So what do you work on?" My answer, "the fear of death," tends to elicit a variety of responses, ranging from, "Oh, excuse me, I think I see a friend across the room," to, "Maybe let's talk about my work instead of yours." On a rare occasion, it has motivated philosophers renowned for their cold, calculating reason to express unexpectedly profound emotion. Two older philosophers told me quietly and with feeling about the recent death of their wives.

The current consensus among public intellectuals is that Western societies are not very good at discussing death or facing it. These two points are often related because it is difficult to face something you will not even discuss. American doctors have long reported receiving little to no training in how to discuss death with terminal patients. When a proposed 2009 American health care bill offered compensation for doctors who had voluntary discussions with older patients about advanced medical directives, some politicians called these discussions "death panels." The idea that doctors should be encouraged to discuss death with patients became political kryptonite. Like most of his philosophical peers, Epicurus considers it prudent to discuss and prepare for death. In Plato's *Phaedo*, Socrates even defines philosophy itself as "preparation for death."[1]

As an example of the importance of prudent preparation, consider the fact that roughly eighty percent of Americans want to die at home, yet roughly sixty percent of natural deaths occur in institutional care, twenty percent on ventilators.[2] In *Being Mortal*, the surgeon Atul Gawande appeals to data showing that terminal patients on average live longer in home hospice, and their family members report healthier grief outcomes. He recounts his own struggles talking to a patient about her impending death, writing, "My solution was to avoid the subject altogether." The most prudent strategy for avoiding an undesirable death is to develop a plan with doctors and family members. Yet most people report having had no conversations of this sort. We cannot prepare collectively for what we will not discuss. We need to manage our fear at least well enough to make some plans.

In an earlier chapter about death, we explored why Epicurus opposes the desire to live forever and why he does not consider death a harmful deprivation of opportunities for future pleasure. Epicurus thinks that accepting life's limits, our essential mortality, increases daily satisfaction with the joys of life, which could very well be right. Perhaps we can rid ourselves of whatever resentment we might feel when we consider the expanse of time the human condition puts out of our reach. Removing our desire to live forever or to see death as a deprivation of good things, though, does not address every reason we might fear death.

We might also fear, for example, dying painfully, dying alone without human touch, dying violently, dying plugged into machines in a hospital, or simply the idea of being dead. All of these are ways one might be thought to "experience death." Epicurus thinks the first four fears can only be effectively managed with prudence, distraction, and friends. Those fears cannot be eliminated, and we will return to them at the close of the chapter.[3] The last one—fear of being dead—Epicurus considers incoherent. By "being dead," Epicurus means something like being in one's coffin, in the ground, or stirring about as a ghost. To tackle that specific fear, he offers what many have considered an effective argument.

Epicurus' argument that "death is nothing to us" is one of his most recognized influences on subsequent philosophy, though he was not the first to introduce the argument itself. Credit there goes, so far as I can tell, to Aristotle, who also anticipated the argument's best objection. Let's look at two of Epicurus' formulations of the argument, the first from the *Principal Doctrines* and the second from the *Letter to Menoeceus*:

Death is nothing to us. For what has been dissolved has no sense-experience, and what has no sense-experience is nothing to us.[4]

Get used to believing that death is nothing to us. For all good and bad consists in sense-experience, and death is the privation of sense experience.[5]

It might help to unpack the terms of the argument. By "sense-experience," Epicurus means all the ways we are aware of pleasure and pain. That includes not only our sensory awareness of what we see, hear, smell, and touch, but also the pleasures and pains attending thought and activity more broadly. By "what has been dissolved," Epicurus refers to our conscious mind, without which "sense-experience" is impossible. Remember that Epicurus thinks our conscious mind results from the structural organization of material atoms, and when death occurs, that structure breaks apart, removing consciousness in its wake. Death is the "privation of sense experience," so death removes our ability to feel pleasure and pain. No pleasure or pain, no harm. No harm, no fear. In that respect at least, Epicurus thinks death is "nothing to us."

While most contemporary philosophers grant Epicurus' claim that death is the end of experience, they disagree with Epicurus that we must experience something for it to harm us. Epicurus says that "all good and bad consists in sense-experience," and his opponents think otherwise. To see how Epicurus' argument might play out with an opponent, imagine a conversation between two friends, Mary and Todd:

TODD: I find myself thinking a lot about death these days, and I'm not going to lie, Mary, I'm terrified.

MARY: Don't be silly, Todd. It's no big deal. It's not like you're going to be around to experience it. You won't be lying there in your coffin thinking, "Ah, god, but it sucks to be dead." That would be like if some rock in a field was talking to itself saying, "It sucks to be a rock." There is no good or bad for rocks because . . . well . . . they're rocks! You being dead is like you being a rock. No awareness, no problem.

Mary should be a touch more patient with Todd, but she's got Epicurus' argument right. For Epicurus, sensory experience depends on our being non-rocks who experience pleasure and pain, and corpses rot like rocks erode. Epicurus' argument continues with a general claim that we should not fear something that is not bad:

TODD: That doesn't help at all, Mary. Because it's that very thing, being nothing more than a rock, that I fear.

MARY: But that doesn't make sense either! Fear is about bad things, and I've just told you being dead isn't bad. It's not anything at all! No pleasure, no pain, so nothing good or bad. Fearing being dead is like fearing a dental surgery you know you'll have. If you can't ever experience it, it can't ever harm you. And if there's no harm, there's no reason to be afraid. Like I said already.

Mary has advanced the whole of Epicurus' argument. Now, though, imagine that Todd pushes back:

TODD: I guess I disagree that you have to be aware of something for it to harm you. Like, imagine that some friend is deceiving you, like stealing your money or shagging your spouse, and you don't know about it. Or I say horrible things about you behind your back (not that I would do that). Aren't you still being harmed, even if you're not aware of it? So yeah, I can suffer harm from being dead even if I never discover it. I will have lost my life and all I care about. It doesn't matter whether I'm aware of that fact once I'm dead. It's still a harm, just one I'm not currently experiencing.[6]

MARY: No—unless you discover that your spouse is cheating or your money is gone, no harm because no pain. And it's not like when you turn into a rock you can experience the pain of discovering your bank account is empty or that your friend was never your friend at all. Discovery is impossible for the dead!

Mary offers a response to Todd entirely in keeping with Epicurean hedonism. For Epicurus, what makes something good is that it is pleasant; what makes something bad is that it is painful. If there is no pleasure or pain for the dead, then there is no good or bad either. Todd, on the other hand, thinks we can be harmed in ways that have nothing to do with experiencing pain, whether physical or psychological. In that sense, Mary and Todd are at loggerheads, and their dispute might prove irresolvable.

Note, though, that Todd has a rougher road when it comes to decoupling harm from experience. Epicurus has the easy task of tethering harms to our consciously lived experience. Todd might need to explain why we do not harm a rock when we break it to bits or a blade of grass when we mow the lawn. If the Mona Lisa suffers water damage after the great extinction of humankind, has anyone been harmed? Harms that are independent of anyone experiencing them or having the capacity to experience them can get a bit "woo."

Again, though, the argument that "death is nothing to us" only shows that the state of being dead does not harm us because we do not experience it. We do, however, usually experience dying itself, so let's return to the discussion from the chapter's opening. Dying is often painful, slow, costly, smelly, and gross. Sorry, I know reading that last sentence is a bit discomfiting. The process of dying can seem so frightening that most of us would prefer not to consciously experience dying at all. People report wanting to die peacefully in their sleep, perhaps because their intuition aligns with Epicurus' that something you do not experience does not harm you.

Yet, given the choice, many people would still prefer, in some fashion at least, to "experience" death. Sometimes it feels best to slip out of the party unnoticed, but more commonly we like to say a proper goodbye. For that reason, many of us imagine a death surrounded by friends and family, ideally at home. As a matter of practice, though, we often make that result unlikely, sometimes impossible, by asking the doctor for every life-saving intervention, even when terminally ill. We tell the doctor, "Do everything you can." We do not stop treatment. As a result of these documented and legally binding preferences, though, we are far more likely to die sedated while plugged into loud, beeping machines than at home. In sum, we often have con-flicting desires—we simultaneously do and do not want to die painlessly and peacefully.

Epicurus cannot casually dismiss our fear of a painful death be-cause he thinks pain is genuinely bad and dying is often painful. Epicurus generally rejects suicide, so he is disinclined to solve the problem of a painful death by recommending euthanasia, ex-cepting rare circumstances.[7] He must show, then, that the pains of death can be counterbalanced with sufficient pleasure to make it imprudent to hasten death, at least in most cases. As we might ex-pect, Epicurean friends help supply the requisite "counterbalance." Epicurus writes that "of the things which wisdom provides for the blessedness of one's whole life, by far the greatest is the possession of friendship."[8] One part of "one's whole life" is the part where one dies.

Epicurus reiterates this point in his very next *Principal Doctrine*. He writes that "security" among unavoidable pains "is most easily achieved through friendship."[9] Prudence can help us steer clear of some kinds of pain, but other kinds lie beyond our control, and we find ourselves most grateful for friends in such moments. For Epicurus, the basis of Epicurean friendship is reliability, even in crisis, so an Epicurean would not abandon a dying friend. The resolve to maintain reciprocal concern under the duress involved in caring for the dying develops through trust and time spent together. Epicurean prudence enjoins us to cultivate that resolve in ourselves and seek it out in others.

The support and company of friends, though, is not the only role friendship plays in helping us confront our mortality. Remember that Epicurus thinks memories play a key role in helping us manage misfortune. While his view that memories counterbalance great physical pain surely overstates the power of memory, Epicurus has, as we have seen, reason to think that distracting ourselves with memories of shared experiences with friends can help us in hard times. Epicurus claimed to employ this strategy while he died, writing to Idomeneus:

> On this blissful day, which is also the last of my life, I write this to you. My continual sufferings from strangury and dysentery are so great that nothing could augment them; but over against them all I set gladness of mind at the remembrance of our past conversations.[10]

Philosophers have historically made their dying a focal manifestation of their philosophical practice. An uncharitable critic might say philosophers make a show of their deaths, which could explain why Diogenes Laertius transmits so many absurd narratives about how philosophers died. For example, he relays a report that Pythagoras, who believed for some reason that beans are divine, was killed by an angry mob who caught up with him only because he refused to escape by running across a field of beans.[11] This practice of performing one's mortality began at least as early as Plato's recounting of Socrates' death in the *Phaedo*. Athens sentenced Socrates to death for impiety, yet Plato has Socrates spend the afternoon with friends discussing and anticipating a long-cherished immortality in the company of the gods.[12] By contrast, the Scottish economist Adam Smith wrote with admiration of the death of his good friend David Hume, an inveterate heretic, who cheerfully anticipated annihilation.[13]

Hume's case is particularly relevant, due in part to his various affinities with Epicurus.[14] Smith published his account of Hume's death as the *Letter to Strahan*, which drew immediate, virulent backlash.[15] Many chastised Smith for attributing virtue, in fact as much virtue as humans might attain, to someone who did not believe in the afterlife. More shockingly, they accused Smith of lying, insisting that Hume must have died in terror. Some spread rumors he had undergone a deathbed conversion, as if they found it entirely impossible that someone could live and die joyfully within the recognized limits of a lifetime.[16]

The public might have taken a similarly prurient interest in Epicurus' death, no doubt curious whether a hedonist could handle the pains of dying, whether he would experience terror, perhaps take a sudden, keen interest in the afterlife. It seems that Epicurus, like Hume, spent his last days in the company of friends, recounting the various pleasures of their lives together. I suspect that most of us fancy that kind of death for ourselves if possible, and that is why few people report wanting to die on a ventilator. If so, not to belabor the point (though why not belabor it, really?), we should prepare by crafting a life of joy with the recognition that time is limited.

While we might struggle to keep our mortality in mind, Epicurus reminds us that our attitudes toward death can help anchor our life of prudence and joy. In the *Letter to Menoeceus*, he writes that "he who advises the young man to live well and the old man to die well is simple-minded, not just because of the pleasing aspects of life but because the same kind of practice produces a good life and a good death."[17] One and the same way of life makes life pleasant and death bearable, even meaningful.

For Epicurus, living pleasantly and prudently extends throughout life—prudence is both a daily activity and a long game. In the opening of the *Letter to Menoeceus*, Epicurus claims that "both young and old must philosophize, the latter so that though old he may stay young in good things owing to gratitude for what has occurred, the former so that though young he too may be like an old man owing to his lack of fear of what is to come."[18] Our full appreciation of our daily joys and pleasures, our memories and gratitude for those joys and pleasures, and our daily realization that we have what we need make death easier when it comes. It takes practice to live that way, practice in living for pleasure.

22 | PANDEMICS AND OTHER COMFORTING HORRORS

Let's just bring this out into the open—some people think Lucretius struggles with arrogance. Others think Lucretius does not struggle with arrogance at all. Instead, they think he gives free and eager rein to his arrogance, like some drunk reading his poems aloud at your party, and his poems feature you as a central character, and you are depicted as an idiot. Still others think Lucretius has not a mean-spirited bone in his poetic little body. Okay, sure, he might indulge in some good-natured mockery of fools in love, and he lays it on thick describing the exploits of perpetually dissatisfied rich people, but that is all in jest. He would never ridicule people in peril, certainly not, for example, a community in the grips of a deadly plague.

Before turning to the plague, let me set before your eyes a passage that reveals the origins of the complaint that Lucretius is smug and callous. At the opening of Book Two of *On the Nature of Things*, Lucretius adopts the rhetorical vantage point of a dispassionate witness to nature's destruction, human violence, and anxious ambition. He writes:

It is comforting, when winds are whipping up the waters of the vast sea, to watch from land the severe trials of another person: not that anyone's distress is a cause of agreeable pleasure; but it is comforting to see from what troubles you yourself are exempt. It is comforting also to witness mighty clashes of warriors embattled on the plains, when you have no share in the danger.

But nothing is more blissful than to occupy the heights effectively fortified by the teaching of the wise, tranquil sanctuaries from which you can look down upon others and see them wandering everywhere in their random search for the way of life, competing for intellectual eminence, disputing about rank, and striving night and day with prodigious effort to scale the summit of wealth and to secure power. O minds of mortals, blighted by your blindness!

Perhaps you can already see why someone could consider this passage perverse. Cyril Bailey, for example, notes that most readers think it has "an unpleasant taste of egoism, even of cruelty." Martin Ferguson Smith responds in Lucretius' defense that he "is careful to stress that pleasure is derived not from the suffering of other people, but from the thought that one is not sharing it, and surely what he says is true."[1] Smith is no doubt correct that we feel relieved not being party to a shipwreck.

That said, if Lucretius feels much sympathy for the plight of the sailors or soldiers, he does not register it here. Some of us have been in peril at sea, in the air, or in battle, and I suspect Lucretius reveling in his safety might win him a nasty glare at best. Those of us unfamiliar with immediate threats to life and limb also might not welcome his condescension toward the daily climbing and ambition we can all fall prey to, some of us struggling against it more often than we might like. We're trying our best, and there Lucretius is, just looking down at us with his "comfort" and "bliss," calling us "blighted."

Lucretius has two readerships, the converted and the unconverted, those Epicureans already hanging out with him at the overlook and those pondering a trip up the hill.[2] It might seem Lucretius encourages his fellow Epicureans to join him and watch the show, appreciate their shared comfort, pass around some popcorn around a cozy fire. By contrast, he shows the unconverted what their fevered lives look like from his position of safety. He sees them striving to scale the mountain of popularity, intellect, power, and wealth. Even if they climb to the pinnacle of popularity, triumph as the smartest person in the room, or lead the free world, he will nevertheless be looking down on them as they anxiously rise and fall.

We might think Lucretius has only himself to blame if readers suspect he adopts that same smug perspective on other human suffering, drawing perpetual comfort from remaining safely above the fray. He condescends to soldiers and sailors fighting for their lives in battle or at sea. He even seems to suggest that corrosive desires for money, honor, and power played a role in their collective peril, the war fought for power and honor, the merchant's vessel constructed in search of riches. What might Lucretius see if he focused his keen eye on human beings in the grips of some other brutal force of nature? Imagine, for example, that a virulent plague suddenly descended on a wealthy, powerful, and proud city, populated by people hostile to science, secretly anxious, who suffer from seemingly insatiable desires.

Lucretius entertains exactly that scenario. The sixth and final book of *On the Nature of Things* begins with a picture of Classical Athens at its financial and cultural apex. Such is the nature of apexes that they foreshadow decline. Lucretius meets his reader's expectations on that front by abruptly concluding the book and the work itself with a lurid account of a plague that ripped through Athens and exposed the weak underbelly of a decadent society. The plague of Athens was no fiction. Lucretius lifted his details from the historian Thucydides, who not only witnessed the plague's social effects, but also caught it and survived.[3]

Scholars disagree about whether Lucretius intended to end *On the Nature of Things* with the plague. The scene breaks off mid-action, more like a modern novel than a well-rounded tale. The work's last sentence tells of bloody fights that broke out when people capitalized on their neighbor's funeral pyres to commemorate their own dead, like someone tossing their deceased father into the casket you just built for your dead mother. Lucretius does not roll the credits of *On the Nature of Things* with a sunset, a happily ever after. Just fights over space for the dead.

Some ancient readers wildly speculated that Lucretius failed to finish the book because he killed himself from despair or jilted love, but most recent scholars agree he intended to end with the plague. One interesting interpretation suggests that Lucretius considers the plague some sort of final exam for the newly minted Epicurean. He asks his reader, "When you watch the plague wreck a decadent and superstitious society, like a boat in a storm, like an army in battle, like petty back-stabbers competing for trifles, how do you feel? Safe?" I agree that the plague serves as Lucretius' final lesson in Epicureanism, but I suspect he intended to include a few more key details.

Lucretius opens Book Six with the story of Epicurus' arrival in Athens. Epicurus, as Lucretius tells it, looked about town and was impressed that "everything that necessity demands for subsistence had been already provided" and that "life was, so far as possible, established in security."[4] Athens deserved credit for agricultural advances that kept its people fed and for writing and enforcing laws that gave order to society. Epicurus set up shop within striking distance of the walls that protected the city, presumably happy to take shelter from external threats. Food and physical security through law are two natural and necessary desires that Athens used its scientific and prudential ingenuity to satisfy as best it could.

While Epicurus found much to admire, Lucretius claims he also saw their unhappiness. They "possessed power, with wealth, honor, and glory, and took pride in the good reputation of their children." They considered this wealth among the greatest benefits of living in a flourishing city. Epicurus, though, found that "not withstanding this prosperity, all of them privately had hearts racked with anxiety which, contrary to their wish, tormented their lives without a pause, causing them to chafe and fret."[5]

The problem was the "vessel itself," which might represent the psychologies of individual Athenians, or the hive mind of the city itself. Whatever the exact nature of the vessel, it was leaky because of insatiable desire. Pour as much pleasure into a leaky vessel as you want, and it will never remain full. Worse, Lucretius writes that the leaky vessel somehow "corrupted within it all things, even good things, that entered it from without." Pleasures that someone with a sounder vessel might have fully enjoyed became instead "contaminated with a foul flavor." In the terms of this book, corrosive desires broke holes in the vessel and poisoned otherwise harmless extravagances. Epicurus set about trying to help the Athenians shore up and detox the vessel.

In the passages between the opening description of Athens and the plague that struck it, Lucretius discusses the physical causes of various meteorological and mineral phenomena. Meteors, thunder, and lightening are physical events, not encoded messages from the divine. He explains the mysterious power of magnets. Finally, Lucretius turns to the natural origins of diseases. His account is astute for its time, including that some diseases arise after excess rains and the putrefaction produced by the sun's heat, while we catch other illnesses that hover "in the atmosphere itself, so that, when we inhale the infected air, we inevitably absorb the germs in our body at the same time."[6] Such was the plague of Athens. In the words of Blind Willie Johnson, "It was an epidemic, it floated through the air."

Lucretius borrows his account of the plague almost full cloth and in the same order of exposition from the Greek historian Thucydides, including some very disgusting details about secretions, rotting limbs, dead dogs, and putrefaction.[7] Thucydides' account is dreadful enough, and Lucretius embellishes it. Scholars seem to have overlooked, though, that Lucretius breaks off his own rendering of Thucydides just where it gets good, right when Thucydides' Athenians start acting like Epicureans.[8] The missing section captures the lessons of Epicureanism so effectively that it seems unlikely that Lucretius intended to leave it out.

According to Thucydides, once the Athenians saw that they could die at any moment, they abandoned their desire for honor and great wealth, instead giving in to pleasure. They "did just what they pleased." They "resolved to spend quickly and enjoy themselves," realizing that saving up for the future was ridiculous when the future was so uncertain. They abandoned grand ambitions and the desire for great honor for the same reason. Why make such sacrifices to pursue something so volatile when death revealed their efforts as a waste of time? Thucydides claims that death "hung ever over their heads," and they vowed that "before this fell it was only reasonable to enjoy life a little." They "settled on the present enjoyment."

The plague also impacted the survivor's religious beliefs, chiefly because they recognized that death did not discriminate between the pious and impious. They saw "all alike perishing" and concluded religious sacrifices and prayers made no difference. Thucydides reports that in the early stages of the plague, the Athenians tried desperately to please the gods with "supplications in the temples, divinations, and so forth," all such efforts proving fruitless. Once it became clear that the gods were not in the business of preserving or ending life or of otherwise intervening in the natural world, Thucydides says they lost their "fear of gods."

Thucydides most likely considers these lapses into impropriety regrettable, a breakdown of social norms to be righted once the plague retreats. Lucretius, had he finished his recounting of Thucydides, might very well have turned that assessment on its head. After all, the plague transformed the Athenians into something more closely resembling Epicureans, and Lucretius might recommend they make the change permanent. If in fact Lucretius had access to Thucydides' full text, I suspect he intended to add something about the Epicurean lessons Athens learned from the plague.[9] We cannot, of course, settle that question, but we can use this fuller account of Athens under viral siege to explore the Epicurean response to similar events in our own backyards.

We have had—indeed, at the time of this writing, we are still having—firsthand experience of a worldwide pandemic, and we face a future filled with crises, some inevitable and others unforeseen. Lucretius describes what happens when a decadent, anxious, and superstitious people encounter an indiscriminate plague. If Lucretius intends the plague of Athens to serve as a final exam in Epicureanism for his reader, as the testing ground for all lessons and exercises, we might wonder how we have fared during our pandemic.

Did we develop a greater appreciation for the simple pleasures of life shared safely with friends and family, respect the truths of science, recognize the shallow pursuit of greed as a recipe for dissatisfaction, calmly accept the temporary loss of opportunities for extravagant pleasures, work to strengthen communal trust? For those of us who reached new Epicurean conclusions, who reassessed how much time we should spend working or fretting, who now more clearly see the importance of the underappreciated people who keep society running at grave risk to themselves, will those changes become permanent, or will we just slip back into the mindset of wherever we were before the contagion?

As for how Lucretius, perched on his overlook, might describe the pandemic if he gave full rein to his darker impulses, well, there's plenty of material. He would certainly note the rejection of science and the politicians who encouraged it—people calling the virus a hoax, killing each other over masks, refusing a vaccine because of something they saw on YouTube, the empty shelves of horse dewormer, the charlatans peddling ridiculous cure-alls. And all those exhausted and traumatized doctors and nurses ministering to the health of people calling them liars, dying of a ferocious illness they have long denied.

He might marvel as parishioners piled into churches at the behest of ministers, as though God would save them but choose to kill others, as if God or viruses worked that way. He might see people dying alone, only just now realizing they have failed to take time to really live. And then the pain of those so dependent on satisfying their extravagant desires for restaurants, travel, and parties that they screamed bloody murder about being unable to indulge for an insignificant amount of time. Entire groups of people erupting in rage at someone reporting facts, so much anger that that they carried guns through the streets or screamed at children in masks.

Lucretius, surveying all that anger and anxiety, superstition and indulgence, loneliness and self-involvement, might very well feel relieved to be free of such consternation and dissonance. And if he did feel relieved, would that make him smug and arrogant? Asking for a friend.

23 | THE FOURFOLD REMEDY

We have covered a lot of ground, so now seems like a good time to start tying threads together, distilling all these ideas into something short and memorable. Humans often rely on and benefit from simple expressions of complex and important ideas. The sort of mantra a person can chant to themselves, though, rarely contains its own justification. For example, I once fell into the quirky, possibly deranged, habit of chanting "despair is a vice" to myself, though I was not at all confident that I would emerge victorious in an argument about the moral appropriateness of despair. If someone demanded that I explain myself, though, I had reasons for throwing in my lot with hope.

Epicurus himself did not condense his practical philosophy into something so brief and chantable as "despair is a vice," but his followers wished he had, so they did it for him. Drawing upon, among other things, a passage from the *Letter to Menoeceus* and a smattering of *Principal Doctrines*, they produced "The Fourfold Remedy" (the "tetraphamakos").[1] From Philodemus:

> God presents no fears, death no worries; the good is easy to get, the bad easy to endure.

Imagine that I had opened the book by telling you that Epicurus espoused these four claims, rather than putting them here, at the end. I assume that every reasonable person would likely dismiss one or more claim out of hand. The Classicist Fiona Hill, for example, writes that "the third remedy may provoke a cynical snort in any reader struggling to make ends meet, unless they have no dependents and are temperamentally ascetic."[2] And in some sense she's clearly right. Taken in isolation, the Fourfold Remedy serves at best as a promissory note for difficult arguments, an IOU for a hefty sum unlikely to be met.

By this point, though, I hope you feel like you have the tools to piece together Epicurus' reasons for supporting all four claims. Not that Epicurus thinks you need such arguments ready at hand as you traverse the rocky path of daily living or that you must feel prepared to triumph in an argumentative battle of skill, but it helps to have confidence that such arguments exist. Let's briefly recap, then, the general outlines of the Epicurean commitments that undergird the Fourfold Remedy, somewhat like the greater part of the iceberg that lies below the surface of the water.

Epicurus cannot, of course, offer just any old argument for the Fourfold Remedy's ingredients. A suitable justification must cohere with his hedonism and his natural philosophy, and it should also produce tranquility, preferably more effectively than competing philosophies of living. With that in mind, let's turn to the Remedy's first *pharmakos*.

<u>God Presents No Fears:</u> There are at least two common ways to reach the conclusion that "God presents no fears," both of which we now know Epicurus rejects. Some people, atheists, maintain that no divine being exists, which means that of course "God

presents no fears." We would have no reason to fear the actions of a non-existent being. Epicurus, though, thinks gods exist, in part because humans share a common conception of divine existence—a "basic grasp" of a perfection around which we can orient our lives and values.

Another non-Epicurean way to conclude that "God presents no fears" would involve believing that God actively rewards the virtuous, whether on earth, in the afterlife, or both. On this way of thinking, God created and now sustains the universe providentially, so that everything that occurs is part of a divine, perfectly good plan. If something does not seem good to us now, we should assume it will turn out well over the long haul or is good from a divine vantage point not accessible to us. In the end, the virtuous receive rewards in an afterlife. Epicurus, as we saw in the chapters on science, misfortune, and theology, also rejects this avenue for removing religious anxiety.

On the scientific front, Epicurus denies divine activity in the world because he claims that the universe is infinite, composed of both atoms and void. The regular and sometimes spontaneous motions of these atoms gave rise to our world by a mixture of regularity and chance. Atomic interactions, again both regular and occasionally spontaneous, structure and drive our current experience of the world, and they will eventually result in our shared world's destruction (though the atoms themselves are eternally preserved and will eventually find themselves of use for other worlds and beings). Atomic motions are not created, sustained, or interrupted by divine nature, nor are they purposive or aimed at the good. Thus, for Epicurus, divine beings do not cause fear, in part because they do not actively cause anything.

Even were a person to reject his physics, though, Epicurus has independent reason to think "God presents no fears." Specifically, he considers it impious to attribute such attitudes and actions to God. Recall that Epicurus thinks a divine being is self-sufficient and needs nothing from human beings, certainly not praise or worship. As such, the gods have no reason to feel gratitude or anger about human actions. God's feelings of pleasure do not in any way depend on us, and humans surely cannot cause the sort of pain that gives rise to anger in a perfectly happy being.

The greater impiety, though, is supposing that the gods reward humans with material wealth or success, not only because it attributes corrosive interests in wealth and status to divine beings, but also because it suggests that others suffer from divine neglect for reasons beyond their understanding. For Epicurus, God neither brings about the death of a child nor ensures its survival for a cosmic purpose. Nothing divinely well-ordered accounts for the suffering in the world. The non-providential interactions of atoms result in setbacks to human interests, and suffering is neither a punishment nor a test of faith.

In sum, Epicurus argues on religious grounds that divine beings "present no fears" because it is beneath them to invest themselves in human affairs and above our station to think they do. In addition, his physics would render divine intervention impossible, even if the gods had an interest in intervening (which, he argues, they don't).

<u>Death Presents No Evils:</u> Here again, Epicurus places some theoretical limitations on how we should determine that we lack reason to fear death. For example, many people assuage their fear of death by focusing on the prospect of personal immortality, a

commitment often conjoined with religious beliefs of the sort Epicurus rejected a few paragraphs ago. If life were to never properly end, then it would not make sense to fear death. If I were immortal, then death, understood as the end of me, would never happen. I would not fear irrevocable separation from my family because I would see them again.

Epicurus, though, thinks the principles of natural science rule out such immortality, and perhaps more controversially, he considers it psychologically unhealthy to desire immortality. Epicurean natural science maintains that each of us is composed of physical atoms whose elaborate structure gives rise to conscious thought and experience. Our mind is made of matter, albeit matter with some very sophisticated powers. When those relevant atoms break apart at death, our consciousness is extinguished, and we no longer suffer either pleasure or pain. A hedonist like Epicurus thinks pain is the only evil we can suffer, so being dead is no evil because it involves no pain. Non-existence is neither good nor bad. In his words, death is "nothing to us."

Immortality is ruled out by Epicurean science, but he also thinks desiring limitless life is itself psychologically damaging. Even those who accept Epicurean science and deny postmortem survival often nonetheless desire to live much longer, perhaps forever, in their mortal condition. For Epicurus, a limitless desire for more time is like any other unlimited desire, whether for wealth, power, or acclaim. A desire for immortality contains within itself the idea that "this is never enough," that life satisfaction depends on an uncertain future and must be perpetually delayed, always incomplete. Epicureans view the finitude of life as no cause for alarm because they fully value each day and cultivate gratitude for past and current pleasures; they welcome more time as an extravagance, but never as necessary for a life lived well.

As every astute philosopher has pointed out, though, the fear of being dead is only one among many death-related fears, and arguably not the most anxiety-provoking for the average person. We often fear our own non-existence much less than we fear witnessing and living past the death of those we love. We might likewise fear a violent death, death while intubated, death alone, or a painful death. Epicurus needs more than one nifty argument that "death is nothing to us" to help us diminish or eliminate those various manifestations of the fear of death because they involve pain, and he considers pain the only thing harmful in itself. As such, he must weave his approach to our pain-related anxieties about death into the larger fabric of the Epicurean way of life, into the way we pursue what's good and avoid what's bad. That brings us to the final two ingredients of the Fourfold Remedy.

The Good Is Easy to Get: For Epicurus, what produces and sustains our tranquility is relatively easy to get, and painful misfortune can be strategically endured. Of course, we know that by "good," Epicurus does not mean things like great wealth and power. While the objects of corrosive desires might produce transient pleasures, dissatisfaction comes along for the ride. A distinguishing feature of harmful desires is in fact that their objects are difficult, not easy, to acquire and keep. By contrast, the things necessary for our happiness—food, shelter, an appreciation of knowledge, a community of trusting friends—are within reach.

Yet simple observation suggests otherwise. Many people struggle to make it through the day with enough to eat, insecure about the basic necessities of life, their needs unfulfilled and ignored by others. Epicurus (unlike the Stoics) considers unrelieved hunger a genuine source of harm that makes tranquility difficult, sometimes perhaps impossible. Confidence that we will not starve is not a mere convenience. An Epicurean can often find ways to endure such misfortunes should they arise, but painful deprivations of necessary desires are harmful, not a matter of indifference as for the Stoics. To say that "the good is easy to get" and "the bad easy to endure" risks blaming those in desperate need for failing at something easy.

The more cavalier dismissals of Epicureanism, though, tend to overlook that when Epicurus says "easy to get," he does not mean easy to get on your own steam, entirely alone. Remember that Epicurus thinks tranquility requires building a community of supportive friends. He and his followers lived in the Garden together, and while they had private possessions and unequal resources, the community protected its members from material and physical peril. When we think about our friends, we tend to focus on our intimate friends, but Epicurus thinks a civic community is also a community of friends. Locating and building a community of concern, whatever its size, provides the greatest source of confidence that we are protected from the pains of unmet needs. When people share the benefits and burdens of life and look out for each other, Epicurus is optimistic about their chances. "Easy to get" must be put in context.

But still, misfortunes happen—we do not command the earth and rule the sea. Having what's good, however easily we might acquire it, does not entirely secure protection against what's bad. Epicurus thinks we can use many of the same mechanisms to handle misfortune that we use to achieve stable pleasure. His conception of "easy to endure," though, will again require context and qualification.

<u>The Bad Is Easy to Endure:</u> We tend to measure the merits of a philosophy of living in part by how it advises us to manage the misfortunes of life. How does it help us navigate life's difficulties? People who do more than dip their toe in the water of a philosophy discover that each tradition addresses suffering within their larger system, not as a few tidy and easily implemented pieces of advice. Buddhism requires adopting a new perspective on personal identity, one that expands, even erases, the self. Stoicism, at least traditional Stoicism, likewise requires seeing oneself as situated within a cosmos of meaning organized by a divine hand. The doctrines of time-tested philosophical schools hang together as a whole, so we cannot cherry-pick advice.

For example, the Stoic rejection of negative emotions requires adopting their view that virtue is the only benefit and vice is the only harm. As such, a child's existence or death does not benefit or harm a parent because a child is neither virtue or vice. The only genuine harm a Stoic can suffer is the loss of virtue, so the loss of anything else, person or object, does not count as a harm. It is irrational for a Stoic to grieve the death of a child because grieving what does not harm us is irrational. *That* is why Stoics reject grief as irrational. A subscriber to Stoicism needs to grapple with the Stoic system of value (only virtue is good) to reach the Stoic conclusion about indifference to misfortune. For all my reservations about Stoicism's theory of value, I respect their admirable systematicity and do not like to see it chopped up for parts.

Epicureans, unlike the Stoics, cannot redescribe physical pain or significant misfortunes as harmless, primarily because they are hedonists. The very definition of hedonism contains the view that pain is genuinely bad, just as pleasure is genuinely good. Epicureans, then, must give their advocates advice for managing misfortune rather than denying its existence, for counterbalancing physical and psychological pain. As we saw in the chapter on misfortune, Epicurus considers grief a natural outgrowth of attachment to the people with whom we share pleasures and form bonds of trust. While we are rarely injured beyond possible repair, Epicurus does not deny that can happen.[3] Nevertheless, Epicurus remains optimistic that cultivating certain habits of living provides resources for managing the inevitable misfortunes of life.

While the Fourfold Remedy's authors over-sell their pain-enduring wares as "easy," they also use the word "endure," and no one endures without practice. Endurance does not fall from the heavens into the fiber of our being. Epicureans, though, do not recommend building endurance by practice at suffering pain, by courting physical or psychological difficulty to build up a pain muscle. We should not dwell on the bad things that might at some point befall us, or "pre-rehearse" for misfortunes as some ancient philosophies recommend.

Epicureans instead prepare for misfortune by living pleasantly with friends and by cultivating gratitude for the daily pleasures that living pleasantly affords. When we fall on hard times, whether through physical incapacity or the loss of those we love, we draw on gratitude's resources, largely in the form of pleasant memories and the support of the friends we are grateful to have in our lives. In some fashion, we distract ourselves by recalling our pleasures until we make peace with a misfortune that lies beyond our control. Epicureans do not reconceive their loss as a matter of indifference (as a Stoic might), nor do they reject all possibility for future pleasure, even joy. Finding pleasure in living, even in hard times, is easier (though not exactly "easy") for a person who makes it a life-long habit to seek and cherish available pleasures, especially in the company of friends who share an approach to life.

The Fourfold Remedy is the core of a much larger nexus of Epicureanism's philosophical commitments, the kind of complex nexus that undergirds any philosophy worth considering. We should never let anyone convince us of an overnight magic elixir, that a coin in our pocket with a catchphrase will make life manageable, that a quick fix will engender a fundamental life reorganization. Something like the Fourfold Remedy can only serve as a handy reminder of a deeper system of value and way of living that we fully inhabit and express.

True, you can remember distillations like the Fourfold Remedy in a way that you could never remember this chapter. It would prove fruitless, though, to chant it over and over in isolation of its argumentative context, and perhaps that is why the distillation does not come from Epicurus himself. Distillations are for people who already know the "why," and Epicurus was in the business of providing the "why." At this point, you know the "why," at least in broad outline and within the context of modern life. You have the tools to evaluate the project writ large as a system of value and decide for yourself.

Yet a philosophy is to be lived, not simply evaluated in the cold light of reason, or squabbled over among scholars in a stuffy hotel conference room. Epicurus does not think it is enough to merely chant the words, nor even to understand the arguments he uses to support his claims. We must also internalize and act on them.

At the end of his *Letter to Menoeceus*, Epicurus directs his readers to "practice these and the related precepts day and night, by yourself and with a like-minded friend, and you will never be disturbed either when awake or in sleep."[4] We might wish Epicurus had said a bit more about what he means by "practice." How might a person practice Epicureanism, or short of that, incorporate a few Epicurean principles into their daily life?

24 | PRACTICING EPICUREANISM

I initially pitched this book to settle a disagreement among friends. We went out for drinks at a conference, and we were discussing Oxford's new book series on philosophy as a way of life. I have welcomed the recent resurgence of interest in philosophy as an approach to living, an idea that fell out of favor among Anglo-American philosophers in the early twentieth century for reasons no one can fully explain. I chose to study the Ancient Greek philosophers for two reasons—they resisted the modern impulse to over-specialize and they thought philosophy could help us make sense of our lives.

At some point in our conversation, my friends asserted, entirely without justification, that Epicureanism was a non-starter for the series. In fact, one of them asked incredulously, "Who would possibly write a defense of Epicureanism?!" I sensed this was a rhetorical question, and as a philosopher, I am honor-bound to challenge rhetorical questions. I also felt compelled to resist what I considered an entirely unfair assessment of Epicurus. I found myself offering a spirited and mildly inebriated defense of Epicureanism.

By the end of the evening, I had convinced myself that not only should someone write a book about Epicurus, but that perhaps it should be *me*. I told my students of the friendly dispute, and they, too, thought Epicureanism required an advocate. So, I contacted the editor, developed a proposal, and was offered a contract. Still, my intention at the time was to defend Epicureanism as a way of life, not live like an Epicurean. I was no promoter, just a spirited defender. As much as I knew about Epicureanism as a scholar, I had never given much thought to the question of what it's like to be an Epicurean.

Just as I started writing this book in earnest, the pandemic hit. I thought, "Perhaps this is not the best time to be writing a book about pleasure in the absence of anxiety!" In fact, it seemed a bit perverse, possibly unethical. One of my proposed chapters was about restaurants and dinner parties! Then it got worse. I watched my country erupt in protests over racial injustice long ignored, sometimes entirely denied. Months later, I watched a mob come dangerously close to ending a great democratic experiment. I taught distressed students Stoicism, Epicureanism, and Skepticism online as best I could, and they learned as best they could. I was isolated from friends and family. Then I got a vaccine and began to see my family and friends again. In the interim, many, many people got very sick and died.

In all that time, I struggled to write, not only because pleasure seemed a hard sell, but also because I was swamped with other things to do. It takes a lot of effort to learn to teach online and in an entirely new way, and I was on a lot of committees. But I also realized that if I was going to write a book about living as an Epicurean, I needed to take the philosophy out for a spin and see how it handled. And what better time for a philosophical stress test than a worldwide pandemic and great civil unrest?

I also realized that failing to try living the philosophy would violate Epicurus' own commitments. He writes that we "must not pretend to philosophize, but philosophize in reality. For we do not need the semblance of health but true health."[1] I did not (and will probably never) attain the "true health" Epicurus (or any philosopher) teases, but my impression is that he encourages people to do the best they can, and in that sense I can say that Epicurus has good things to offer. If, in reading this book, you've found yourself intrigued by what Epicurus says about living well, or at least living better, then you are already thinking like an Epicurean. As for living like an Epicurean, I have a few suggestions, some drawn directly from Epicurean texts, others extrapolated from ancient texts for modern purposes.

This one might sound a bit obvious, of course, but the first thing to do is to **read Epicurus**. Though his writing is terse, what remains of his work is not voluminous. Trying to read Epicurus, at least most Epicurus, is not like trying to read Kant or Hegel. The Hellenistic Philosophers, especially the Roman ones, wrote to be read. Epicurus intended the *Letter to Menoeceus*, *Principal Doctrines*, and *Vatican Sayings* to be clear and easy to consult. If Epicurus' prose disappoints, then choose Lucretius, who tries as best he can to faithfully reflect Epicurus' views, but with charm, meter, and a wit finely attuned to human foibles. Lucretius claimed that his poetry was like putting honey on the cup of a glass of medicinal wormwood to make swallowing it easier. Think of Epicurus as a whiskey neat, and Lucretius as a tasty cocktail. People tend to prefer one over the other, but they both serve their purpose.

Some critics of Epicurus thought he encouraged Epicureans to unreflectively memorize and recite his writings without concern for comprehension. Among the many uncharitable objections to Epicureanism, I consider that accusation the most unfair. Reading, even memorizing, Epicurus is insufficient. You need to take the philosophy apart and see how it works, develop a fuller understanding, reflect on how it applies to living, especially in the context of your own life. Thankfully, you can plow through Epicurus multiple times without losing a single month of your life—try that with Kant!

Less obvious is the Epicurean advice to **write some Epicurus** of your own. In his *On Gratitude*, Philodemus recommends that we write our own texts.[2] Remember that Epicureans think we all have individual natural dispositions and that our life histories and circumstances make us who we are. Some of us struggle more with pride, others with self-effacement. Some with greed, some with parsimonious asceticism. Some with a desire for honor, some with a disdainful indifference to the approval of good people. Some of us express gratitude for people who harm us, while others of us are prone to ingratitude for those who help.

Philodemus recommends that those liable to ingratitude, for example, should not only attentively revisit Epicurean texts concerning gratitude, but they should also write their own text against ingratitude. So, if you recognize that you struggle with something—envy, greed, resentment, fear, snobbery—read some Epicurean texts and then sit down and write about why those emotions, and the desires from which they arise, rob us of joy. Don't just write that it is harmful, like some schoolboy ordered to copy sentences, but determine exactly why you oppose it, offering principled reasons and some examples from your own life. That task, I have discovered while writing this book, will take a while and be more difficult than you might expect. But writing it for your-self hammers it home. While I do not struggle with some of the things I wrote about in this text, I do struggle with many of them. Writing helped clarify things.

Some psychological research supports this strategy. When subjects sought advice from experts about how to overcome their struggles, they improved less than when they wrote advice to others they were told struggled with the same weakness.[3] Researchers found that "strugglers who gave advice, compared with those who received expert advice, were more motivated to save money, control their tempers, lose weight, and seek employment." So why not do both? Read some advice, and then write some. If there was a chapter in this volume that got you thinking, write your own version that better fits your circumstances. Maybe write it as a "letter to a friend" when the friend is yourself. Or to an actual friend, as Epicurus wrote his *Letter to Menoeceus*. Epicurus never cared how people express themselves, so use your own natural voice.

Reading and writing about Epicurus can be useful for big-picture concerns, but what about the challenges of daily living? Remember that Epicureanism is fundamentally about evaluating our desires to determine whether they benefit or harm us and whether they merit our energies. On this front, I recommend the Epicurean advice that we **ask ourselves two questions** about what we want. Epicurus writes that "one should bring this question to bear on all one's desires: what will happen to me if what is sought by desire is achieved, and what will happen if it is not?"[4] A briefer rendering: *What happens if I get this, and what happens if I don't?* Note that these are two meaningfully different questions that can result in two different mistakes:

- *We often assume that if we get what we want, it will be good. Never assume that.* Getting what we want can require sacrificing things of greater worth (personal integrity, time with children, relationships, the truth); it can leave us perpetually unsatisfied because we find ourselves wanting more; it can alienate us from our community. Many of the most angsty rock songs are about making it big and not really liking it much (see, "Unsatisfied," Billie Eilish; "Unsatisifed," The Replacements; "(I Can't Get No) Satisfaction," The Rolling Stones).

- *We often believe that not getting what we want will diminish our prospects for happiness. That's rarely the case.* Epicurus thinks an inability to satisfy our necessary desires is a legitimate threat to our tranquility. If we cannot feed ourselves and our children or feel safe in our home, then our prospects for tranquility and life satisfaction are in fact diminished. Can a person who is rejected from Harvard live a happy life? Of course. For Epicurus, tranquility and a satisfied mind lie within reach of those who have what they need and can recognize it as enough.

But what do we need, again? While Epicurus thinks tranquility requires much less than we often think it does, it also requires more than we sometimes realize. Many of the things we need are psychological and social goods, not material goods. For that reason, people ranging from the very poor to the very rich can lack one or more of the necessary components of tranquility. It helps, then, to regularly remind ourselves of what we need so that we can determine where to direct our efforts. When we find ourselves with competing desires, we should remember that necessary desires get priority. I found the following checklist helpful:

- Do I have food and shelter and confidence that I will continue to have them?
- Do I have friends I can rely on in a time of crisis who understand what really matters in life?
- Do I have confidence that I will be rescued from remediable peril?
- Do I understand enough science to reliably tell a real scientist from a fake scientist, a good explanation from a bad one?
- Am I willing to sacrifice non-necessary things of material cost to protect friends and the members of my community from physical and material peril?
- If I have the other things on this list, am I grateful for having what I have and do I see it as enough?

Sometimes we fail to satisfy a necessary desire through no fault of our own—misfortune strikes. For the most part, though, Epicurus thinks the greatest impediment to securing our necessary desires, as well as the necessary desires of our friends and community, are corrosive desires. For that reason, we must weed out corrosive desires. Corrosive desires disregard natural limits because they tell us that "it is always better to have more." More status, more money, more power, more clicks, more likes, more life. Epicurus thinks we can never be satisfied unless we place limits on our desires. Greed takes many forms, all of which put satisfaction out of reach.

While some people are magical sparkleponies of tranquility, the rest of us struggle with some form of unlimited desire—for power, for status, for attention, for wealth. We should assess with clear eyes how these things make us anxious and insecure, lead us to neglect things of greater value, alienate us from others, and make us "slaves to the mob" or the powerful. Then, whatever your particular concern, you could follow the first two pieces of advice and read Epicurus and write your own Epicurus.

Ridding ourselves of corrosive desires, or at the very least diminishing them, is insufficient. We must use the resulting free time and headspace to get and maintain what we need, especially what Epicurus considers the greatest source of tranquility—friendship. We must make and keep good friends, which well-seasoned adults realize is more difficult than it sounds. Remember that Epicureans consider reciprocity, mutual concern, and shared values the bedrock of friendship.

The Epicureans have been derided for considering trust and mutual assistance the core of friendship. Some critics consider it devoid of feeling, and others think it treats friends as mere instruments, as an investment in walking, talking insurance. On this point, though, I think the Epicureans have the better account. Granted, powerful feelings and unconditional attachment often produce great art, but they can also invite people to kick us in the teeth and call it friendship. And yes, it might seem nobly self-sufficient to help friends without ever expecting anything in return. As we saw in the chapter on friendship, though, that kind of self-reliance risks transforming a friend with needs into the weaker party. We risk condescension. For Epicurus, all humans have needs—the frailty is the point. Mutual protection and shared values allow friends to acquire both security and joy on equal terms.

Paying attention to the essential features of Epicurean friendship can help us identify good friends and be better friends. Using Epicurean standards, we might locate beneficial friendships and weed out harmful relationships along the following lines:

- If someone makes us insecure about our intellect, taste, status, or attractiveness, jump ship.
- If someone abandons us or others in crisis, they cannot be trusted.
- If we do not like who we become around someone (e.g., we become petty, mean, judgmental, gossipy, or status-conscious), the relationship does not benefit us.

Our friends should not measure us by the metrics of corrosive desires, give us the sense they will abandon us when we become inconvenient, or bring out the worst in us.

Nor should we behave that way or have that effect on others! Friendship is a two-party relationship, so we need to understand other people might sometimes have reason to sever friendships with us. I have certainly dropped the ball in important friendships, sometimes in ways that continue to haunt me. We might have failed to support, even actively neglected, a friend. Maybe we left someone behind in our quest for a shallow aim or got lost in an extravagance, convinced somehow that pursuing something inconsequential merited eroding an essential value. The only solution when we fail is to seek forgiveness and hope it comes, then take up our share of the labor of friendship. At root, we know that a good friend is a reliable friend and that we fail our friends if we ignore their genuine needs.

When we deliberate about how to spend our time, then, our default setting should be to prioritize friends. When offered a choice between time with friends and an inconsequential waste of time, choose friends. I started this book just as social action ground to a halt. For many of us, the most difficult part about the

COVID-19 shutdown was the sudden and prolonged loss of time with friends and family. Some people responded by moving in together or forming "bubbles." I spoke to an Epicurus expert whose mother became his neighbor. Those of us without that option, though, wondered whether we would ever again have the secure feeling of spending time safely with those we love.

At the same time, many of us also acknowledged the uncomfortable truth that we might not have prioritized our friends and family as much as we should have. Their absence made us realize we had not fully appreciated their presence. This was most true, I suspect, for those of us with older parents. My parents are in their late seventies in Arkansas, a twelve-hour drive from where I now live. The reprieve of vaccines made many of us rush to see our friends and family, which was an intense pleasure of the sort Epicurus loves—the pleasure resulting from the removal of pain, giving rise to joy in one another's company.

Still, we can too easily fall back into our habit of doing much less important things than spending time with friends and family. I wonder even whether I should have spent the summer relaxing with the people I love rather than writing this book, as surprisingly pleasant as it was to write. Striking a balance between projects and social time is difficult. As a rule of thumb, accept as many opportunities to spend time with good friends as possible and avoid wasting valuable time prioritizing people you know are unfit for Epicurean friendship.

In case of emergency, practice gratitude. Epicurus writes that "he who forgets the good which he previously had, has today become an old man."[5] I noticed an interesting trend when the pandemic initially hit and we found ourselves with time on our hands.

I had friends who reconnected with people from their *elementary* schools. People reached out to old friends to reminisce. Epicurean gratitude is my favorite part of the philosophy. We clearly practice it somewhat naturally when we engage in reminiscence, but we can also develop deeper reservoirs of pleasant memories by making gratitude part of how we live.

I try to focus on three things on a daily basis: (1) a short bit of time at the end of the day when I remember at least one exceptionally pleasant experience from my life in as much detail as I can. When I have the energy, I write it down. (2) I try, at least when I remember, to prioritize doing at least one thing worth remembering every day, jotting it down. It could be as simple as a good conversation with a friend or as momentous as a beautiful hike on a fall afternoon. (3) I remind myself as often as I can that the pleasures most worth remembering involve other people. If you want to give the people you love lasting joy, give them something they can remember.

Change can hurt (at least at first). Epicurus writes that "in a joint philosophical investigation he who is defeated comes out ahead in so far as he has learned something new."[6] Most of us do not find being defeated pleasant, especially when the defeat concerns something that cuts close to home. For Epicurus, the only way to improve ourselves is to recognize that we err and are sometimes very wrong. That realization can sting, even when it greatly benefits our long-term well-being. Sometimes, though, we should confront truths, whether about our own values and behavior, intellectual mistakes, scientific errors, ignorance of historical events, or mistreatment of others. My life changed radically for the better years ago when a close friend informed me that I had an inexcusable temper, which I already in some sense knew, but had never been required to acknowledge. Refusing to recognize our failings and work on them has long-term consequences that render us miserable, defensive, sometime alone.

That said, we should not abuse others or ourselves with the truth. We will sometimes miss the mark, but we should always seek to employ frank speech judiciously or we will do more damage than good—we will harm ourselves or others. Looking at the social and political landscape during my time exploring Epicureanism revealed just how much frank speech in the public arena is mean-spirited and counterproductive. We are doing frank speech horribly, horribly wrong by Epicurean standards. It is as if people wanted to cut each open with no concern to stitch each other up. Frank speech is a painful, though often necessary, step towards self-improvement. Proceed with caution.

One of the places I struggled with Epicureanism was with its political advice to live unnoticed. I had trouble even figuring out what it meant, honestly.[7] Even when I got some sort of grip on Epicurus' intention, I was unsure whether it was good advice. When it comes to high-octane politics, the caution seems almost trivially true. Epicurus thinks fulfilling the desire for major political power usually requires the kind of machinations that transform people into shameless lackeys, petty tyrants, or actual tyrants. Those who resist abnegating their core values are chewed up by the system, sometimes at the cost of their lives. The current political environment does little to undermine Epicurus' assessment on this front, what with so many public figures casting aside their moral compass to stay in power by hook or by crook.

But what of other kinds of political engagement—campaigning against injustice, caring for the weak, asserting our own core values in the public sphere? If Epicurus discourages that sort of political activity and risk, then the criticism that his advice to "live unnoticed" is insular, disengaged, and selfish might have some merit. On my reading, Epicurus does not discourage political involvement on the ground, but he does set some controversial limits on our political priorities. Our natural desire for tranquility requires living in a community bonded by trust that ensures mutual protection against remediable distress. Our core political aim, then, should be to prioritize our community's necessary desires.

Epicurean politics focuses on building communal trust and securing the needs of the imperiled, and that kind of political activity is in some measure available to all of us, elected or not. Very little of mainstage politics, though, focuses on meeting needs or increasing trust, opting instead to encourage pointless fights and moral grandstanding, generally about things that do not require anyone to sacrifice their own material resources or limit their desires for the good of others. If, as I have come to think, Epicurean politics is about meeting people's greatest needs without making a show of it, then I find myself with fewer misgivings about the advice to "live unnoticed."

For more mundane advice, we should eat and drink together whenever possible. Sit at the table, even if it is a coffee table or a cardboard box and talk to one another. Turn off the television and put away your phones. Get some "start a conversation" cue cards if you need to. The fact that culture and practical necessity often make shared meals difficult is regrettable, so we should carve out time when we can. We have so much to gain from taking time to communicate and enjoy one another's company.

As awkward as it is to end a book on this note, we need to remember that we will die, whether unexpectedly and soon or, fortune permitting, further down the road. In an article for *The Atlantic*, Hana Schank recounts her medical and cognitive struggles after a horrific traffic accident her family suffered during a vacation. Among other things, she found herself less motivated to exercise: "I have always been a regular exerciser. Now I can't imagine wanting to do a burpee, let alone 10 of them. I always ate healthy things. But did you know that you can eat whole grains and still get hit by a truck?"[8] She's right; you can.

We might initially be unsettled by recognizing the fragility of our life, but Epicurus thinks prudence directs us to face mortality because it helps us anchor our days and our relationships. If you find yourself chasing corrosive desires instead of finding joy in your days with friends, you might have lost sight of the natural limits of a lifetime, not a minute of which is promised to us. Epicurus never, at least so far as we can tell, wrote "eat, drink, and be merry, for tomorrow we die." But he might as well have.

Epicurus was accused of being insufficiently rigorous, of not concerning himself with the metaphysics and abstractions of other philosophers. He wanted to help people, and he wore that as a badge of pride, writing:

> Vain is the word of a philosopher by which no human suffering is cured. For just as medicine is of no use if it fails to banish the diseases of the body, so philosophy is of no use if it fails to banish the suffering of the mind.[9]

Only you can determine whether you think Epicurus wrote in vain. See for yourself whether any of his advice about what matters and how to live "banishes the suffering" of your mind. For a philosophy focused on pleasure, it makes a lot of demands, but he thinks meeting those demands pay dividends in tranquility and joy, for both individuals and communities. At its least, Epicureanism offers a diagnostic tool for why decadence does not bring satisfaction. At its best, it offers a path out of the woods.

ACKNOWLEDGMENTS

I would like to thank the Bitove Family and the Wake Forest Humanities Institute for awarding me time and funds to complete this project. For editorial support, thanks to Lucy Randall and Stephen Grimm, who rounded off my sharp edges and told me when my jokes fell flat. For bolstering my work ethic, a shout-out to my Acroprint punch clock.

As befits a book on Epicureanism, my greatest debt is to friends, students, and colleagues. My Spring 2019 Hellenistic Philosophy students convinced me to write this book, and my Spring 2021 students motivated me to finish it. Special thanks to Ben Rider and Kelly Arenson for comments on the entire manuscript. For never asking me to stop my incessant talk of Epicurus, thanks to Matthew Campbell, Lara Kammrath, and Brian Warren. For getting me hooked on Epicurus years and years ago, Clerk Shaw and my doctoral adviser, Eric Brown. Finally, thanks to all my teachers.

NOTES

CHAPTER 1

1. The Waffle House anecdote is not mine. It was inspired by Sturgill Simpson's contribution to the Waffle House jukebox, "No shirt, No Shoes, No Knuckleheads."
2. *Letter to Menoeceus* 128. All translations of Epicurus' *Letters* are from Inwood and Gerson (1988).
3. *Letter to Menoeceus* 132.
4. *Letter to Menoeceus* 129.
5. *Vatican Sayings* 41. All translations of Epicurus' *Vatican Sayings* are from Inwood and Gerson (1988).

CHAPTER 2

1. Clay (2009) and Oliver (2007).
2. Clay (2009).
3. I agree with Clay (2009, 24–25) that the aim of such rituals was to foster and sustain social cohesion, especially when celebrated after Epicurus' death.
4. For a careful and highly readable account of Epicurean women, see Gordon (2012, esp. 75–80).
5. Gordon (2012, 76), her translation of *On the Nature of the Gods* 1.93.
6. Clay (2009, 28).
7. Diogenes Laertius, *Lives of Eminent Philosophers* 7:185.
8. Diogenes did not copy the texts of any other philosophers, so his uncommon generosity gives us reason to suspect he was sympathetic to Epicureanism, a conjecture further supported by his claim that those who slandered Epicurus' character were "out of their minds" (Diogenes Laertius, *Lives of Eminent Philosophers* 10:9; trans. Mensch [2018]).
9. For an exposition of this intellectual and cultural debt to Lucretius for non-scholars, see Greenblatt (2012). See also Wilson (2008).
10. For an argument that Memmius was friendly to Epicureanism, see Morgan and Taylor (2017). For an argument that the Memmius who owned Epicurus' property in Melite is not the same Memmius as the addressee of *On the Nature of Things*, see Hutchinson (2001).

11. See Brembs (2011) for discussion of indeterminancy in particle physics and in spontaneous brain activity, along with an explanation of why spontaneous behavior in animals is evolutionarily adaptive. I would like to thank Brembs for taking time to patiently explain the basics of spontaneous neural activity and its possible bearing on free action to an Epicurus scholar.

12. For Lucretius as satirist, see Gellar-Goad (2020).

13. For a scholarly study of Philodemus, especially his ethics, see Tsouna (2007).

14. Bourne (1977) argues that Julius Caesar was an Epicurean; see Mulgan (1979) for the opposing view.

15. Smith (1993, 48) provides our best resource on the inscription, and he makes a case for dating it as early as 120 CE.

16. For a thorough and accessible account of Cicero's philosophical commitments, see Woolf (2015).

17. See Griffin (1976, 350) and Schiesaro (2015, 241).

18. See Schiesaro (2015, 243) for Seneca's mixed attitudes toward Epicureanism.

19. See Gordon (2012) for a lively discussion of charges that Epicureanism was insufficiently manly. Her translation here of *Ben.* 4.1.3.

20. For Plutarch's criticisms of Epicurus, see Kechagia-Ovseiko in Beck (2014).

CHAPTER 3

1. Kraut (1979, 187–189).

CHAPTER 4

1. *On Moral Ends (DF)* 1:30.

2. *On the Nature of Things (DRN)* 5:223–228.

3. *On Moral Ends (DF)* 2:16.

4. *Letter to Menoeceus* 129.

5. *Letter to Menoeceus* 128.

6. I here follow Woolf (2004), who convincingly defends the view that Epicurus is a psychological hedonism against Cooper (1999), who denies that Epicurus is a psychological hedonist. However, I am philosophically sympathetic to both positions. I think Epicurus believes we cannot act contrary to what we consider most pleasant, but even if we could, I think he would advise against it. In other words, he thinks we either must or should pursue our own pleasure. His philosophy remains relevant either way because he thinks our life will improve if we use our reason to assess and change what we consider most pleasant.

7. *Principal Doctrines* 14.

8. This is a non-specialist text, so I have chosen not to wade into the dispute about katastematic and kinetic pleasures in the body of the text. A specialist will recognize

that I am adopting a view roughly in line with Gosling and Taylor (1982) and Arenson (2019). On my reading, katastematic pleasures are sensory pleasures that issue from confidence in one's ability to satisfy one's necessary desires and an awareness of one's healthy psychological functioning; choice-worthy kinetic pleasures are the various pleasures consistent with maintaining healthy functioning, and those pleasures vary, but do not increase healthy psychological functioning.

9. *Letter to Menoeceus* 132.

10. Aristotle, *Nicomachean Ethics* 10:8.

11. The empirical adequacy of psychological hedonism lies beyond the scope of this book, and I think Epicureanism does not rise or fall on the question. All ancient ethicists thought we aim at our own happiness, so in that sense they all struggle to make sense of exclusively other-regarding concern; what distinguishes Epicurus from other eudaimonists is that he thinks we all aim at our own pleasure. See Batson (2019) for empirical support for altruism. For discussion of the strengths and limitations of empirical evidence for altruism, see Doris, Stich, and Walmsley (2020).

12. See Mischel (2014) for a book-length exposition of the marshmallow experiment by the original researcher.

13. Watts, Duncan, and Quan (2018); Calarco (2018).

14. See Morton (2017) for an argument that norms of practical reasoning alter according to an agent's circumstances, including factors like "cognitive capacity, context, and ends" (544).

15. This banking example drawn from Buttigieg (2020, 48–49).

CHAPTER 5

1. *Vatican Sayings* 63.

2. I have some misgivings about renaming the natural and unnecessary desires "extravagant" because that might mistakenly suggest that such desires are excessive or inappropriate. I eventually settled on "extravagant" in light of Inwood and Gerson's apt translation of πολυτελείας at *Letter to Menoeceus* 130 as "extravagance," especially as theirs is the translation I suggest for readers of this volume.

3. *Letter to Menoeceus* 127.

4. *Principal Doctrines* 30.

5. *Principal Doctrines* 21.

6. *Letter to Menoeceus* 130.

CHAPTER 6

1. *Vatican Sayings* 52.

2. *Principal Doctrines* 27.

3. *On Moral Ends (DF)* 2:80.

4. *Principal Doctrines* 28, accepting Inwood and Gerson's brackets.

5. *Vatican Sayings* 34.

6. *Vatican Sayings* 56–57.

7. Aristotle, *Nicomachean Ethics* 8:4.

8. Wiseman, R. (2002).

9. Saunders (2017).

10. As noted in the chapter on hedonism, I here accept Woolf's (2004) qualified defense of "psychological hedonism" against Cooper's (1999) "ethical hedonism."

11. Seneca, *Letters on Ethics* 9.8 (175U), trans. Inwood and Gerson.

12. Ibid.

13. *Vatican Sayings* 39, accepting Inwood and Gerson's brackets.

CHAPTER 7

1. Though I will, with great reverence, use the Konstan et al. (1998) text and translation of Philodemus' work, I have rendered the title and practice as *On Frank Speech*, rather than as *On Frank Criticism*. Philodemus suggests that some frankness is not criticism, but disclosure, openness, and joint philosophical inquiry into beliefs and values. I accept all the translators' brackets to avoid distraction for the reader.

2. Fr. 28, 45.

3. Fr. 15, 37.

4. Fr. 43, 57.

5. Fr 43, 57.

6. Col. IVb, 97.

7. Col Va, 99.

8. Fr. 12, 35.

9. *On the Nature of Things (DRN)* 3:308–322.

10. *On the Nature of Things (DRN)* 3:300.

11. *On the Nature of Things (DRN)* 3:308–322.

12. *On the Nature of Things (DRN)* 4:1072–1073.

13. See Duckworth (2016) for the importance of grit; see Morton and Paul (2019) for reservations about encouraging grit in all circumstances.

14. Fajkowska et al. (2018).

15. Hudson et al. (2019).

16. Ibid. 849–850.

17. See Morton and Paul (2019) for discussion of how encouraging grit indiscriminately can also backfire.

18. Fr. 35, 51.

19. Fr. 20, 39.

20. Fr. 46, 59.

21. Fr. 81, 85.
22. Col XVb, 115.
23. Col XVIb, 115.
24. Col. VIIb, 117.
25. Col. VIIIb, 105.
26. Fr. 78, 83.
27. *Principal Doctrines* 13, 14.
28. The sense of "irony" here is admittedly unclear, in part because the text is fragmentary, but also because "irony" itself seems to take so many forms.
29. Fr. 26, 43.
30. Col. Ib, 93.

CHAPTER 8

1. Ted Sorenson, Kennedy's speechwriter, admits to having drafted most of the book, though Kennedy apparently wrote the opening and closing chapters largely on his own. Sorenson received no credit for the book at the time, while Kennedy won the Pulitzer Prize. See Sorensen (2009).
2. *On Moral Ends (DF)* 1:23; n. 26.
3. Perri, T. (2013).
4. *Letter to Menoeceus* 132, also *Principal Doctrines* 5.
5. *On Moral Ends (DF)* 1:35.
6. *Principal Doctrines* 34, accepting Inwood and Gerson's brackets.
7. *Vatican Sayings* 7.
8. *Principal Doctrines* 35, accepting Inwood and Gerson's brackets.
9. *On Moral Ends (DF)* 2:53.
10. In Cicero (2001, 19, n38), Woolf notes: "Cicero seldom resists the chance to make a favourable reference to his consulship in 63, during which he uncovered an attempted coup by the disaffected aristocrat Lucius Sergius Catalina."
11. *On the Nature of Things (DRN)* 5:1159.
12. Detectives used the Ancestry.com database to identify the Golden State Killer. The practice remains under legal and ethical scrutiny.
13. *On Moral Ends (DF)* 1:49, my emphasis.
14. *On Moral Ends (DF)* 1:51.
15. *Principal Doctrines* 17.
16. *Vatican Sayings* 79.
17. The Epicurean might in some cases break the law, for example to fulfill a necessary desire. In such desperate cases, though, Epicurus would likely consider the law itself unjust. See Robitzsch (2016) for sustained exploration of such circumstances.
18. *Rep.* 1:351d–e.

19. Aristotle, *Nicomachean Ethics* 9:6 1167b, 9:4 1166a–b. There is some indication that Aristotle might elsewhere countenance the possibility of some harmoniously vicious people (see *Nicomachean Ethics* 7:8).
20. John 15:13.
21. *Vatican Sayings* 56–57.
22. https://www.youtube.com/watch?v=RYxMRiftYuY.
23. This puzzle also arises from Epicurus' decision to write a will that included, among other requests, directions for celebrating his birthday in perpetuity. For discussion, see Warren (2001).

CHAPTER 9

1. *60 Minutes*, April 30, 2006, https://www.cbsnews.com/news/the-colbert-report/.
2. *Vatican Sayings* 45.
3. *Vatican Sayings* 58.
4. Seneca, *On the Shortness of Life* (2005, 20–21).
5. Plato, *Protagoras* 347c–348b.
6. Blank (2009, 222–223).
7. Bloom (1987, 81).
8. Blank (2009, 221).
9. *On the Nature of Things (DRN)* 1:930–950.
10. *On Moral Ends (DF)* 1:26.
11. *On Moral Ends (DF)* 1:15.
12. *On Moral Ends (DF)* 1:27.
13. Plato, *Gorgias* 452d–e.
14. *On Moral Ends (DF)* 1:52.

CHAPTER 10

1. Plato, *Gorgias* 491e–492a, trans. Zeyl.
2. Diogenes Laertius, *Lives of Eminent Philosophers* 7:33.
3. Plato, *Republic* 416c–417b.
4. Diogenes Laertius, *Lives of Eminent Philosophers* 6:20, see Brown, E. (2014).
5. Griffin, M. (1976, 286).
6. Griffin, M. (1976, 77–79).
7. Seneca, trans. By Butler-Bowden and D. Robertson (2021, 19–20).
8. Diogenes Laertius, *Lives of Eminent Philosophers* 10:11.
9. *Vatican Sayings* 63.
10. *Principal Doctrines* 7; *On the Nature of Things (DRN)* 5:1120ff.
11. *The Principal Doctrines* 14.
12. *Vatican Sayings* 67.

13. *Vatican Sayings* 43.
14. Plato, *Apology* 36b–c.
15. In 2019, some CEOs signed Business Roundtable's "Statement on the Purposes of a Corporation," a public-facing pledge to serve "stakeholders" (e.g., workers, the community, the environment) as well as "shareholders." While many considered this announcement significant, Bebchuk and Tallarita (2021) demonstrate that the relevant companies have not revised any internal documents to privilege stakeholder interest *over* shareholder interest. Companies continue to concern themselves with "stakeholders" only when doing so is consistent with maximizing value for "shareholders." Bebchuk and Tallarita conclude that the Roundtable statement is "mostly for show."
16. There is some dispute about whether corporations are legally obligated to maximize "profit" over other "values," but cashing out shareholder value in terms of profit is the safest path for corporations. For competing interpretations of the legal obligation to focus on the interests of investors, see Yosifon (2015) and Stout (2015).
17. https://abc.xyz/investor/founders-letters/2004-ipo-letter/.
18. For example, the program for the 2021 World Economic Forum covered topics including global reforestation, saving the seas, global inequality, and global mental health crises.
19. See Giridharadas (2019) for discussion of what he calls the "elite charade of changing the world," and Bregman, Giridharadas, and Byanyima (2019) for a roundtable discussion concerning the political fallout from Bregman and Byanyima's panel about tax avoidance at the World Economic Forum at Davos in 2019.
20. *On Moral Ends (DF)* 1:51–52.
21. https://www.mtv.com/video-clips/nadsyi/tupac-talks-trump-and-greed-on-mtv-news-in-92
22. For example, Caitlyn Jenner reported that a friend with a private jet told her, "I'm moving to Sedona, Arizona. I can't take it here anymore. I can't walk down the street and see the homeless." https://www.foxnews.com/transcript/caitlyn-jenner-ive-watched-california-crumble-right-before-my-eyes.
23. *Vatican Sayings* 53.
24. "A Satisfied Mind," Joe Hayes and Jack Rhodes (writers).

CHAPTER 11

1. See Roskam (2007a) for a scholarly account of what Epicurus and later Epicureans meant by "live unnoticed."
2. Following Roskam (2007b, 50n25), who claims that Cicero considered his sudden affinity for Epicureanism as a "sad irony" rather than a "real conversion."
3. See *On Leisure* in Seneca et al. (2014, 219–229).
4. Everitt (2003, 319).

5. Griffin (1976, 386–387).

6. *Vatican Sayings* 56–57.

7. http://www.cnn.com/TRANSCRIPTS/2104/27/cnnt.01.html.

8. *The Principal Doctrines* 31.

9. *The Principal Doctrines* 33, 36. While Epicurus thinks rationality itself is a universal norm, he unfortunately suggests that some groups might lack the capacity to employ reason to make contracts (*The Principal Doctrines* 37).

10. *On the Nature of Things (DRN)* 5:959–962.

11. *On the Nature of Things (DRN)* 5:998–1011.

12. *On the Nature of Things (DRN)* 5:1018–1027.

13. See Odell (2019, esp. 61) for a recent depiction of Epicureans as the sort of people who drop out of politics to spend their time "contemplating potatoes."

14. See Long (2006, esp. 178–180) for discussion of Epicurus' view that satisfying necessary desires is necessary for happiness, making happiness thereby dependent to some extent on good fortune.

15. Epicureanism's enlightened self-interest seems to have inspired Adam Smith as much or more than it did any socialist. See Smith and Kaakonssen (2002), *Adam Smith: The Theory of Moral Sentiments*, Part VII, Chapter 2. For Smith's complicated relationship with Epicureanism, see Leddy and Lifschitz (2009, 183–205).

16. *Letter to Menoeceus* 131.

17. *Letter to Menoeceus* 127.

CHAPTER 12

1. *The Principal Doctrines* 7.

2. *Vatican Sayings* 67.

3. *Vatican Sayings* 45.

4. *Vatican Sayings* 67.

5. *Vatican Sayings* 81.

6. See, for example, Audie Cornish's (2021) NPR interview with Andy Carvin on the tenth Anniversary of the "Arab Spring." Carvin puts it succinctly: "And in many ways, I think the Arab Spring was a very naïve time."

7. *The Principal Doctrines* 7, my emphasis.

8. *Vatican Sayings* 64.

CHAPTER 13

1. Williams (2019).

2. If Kahneman and Deaton (2010) are correct, that number circa 2010 in America was a household income of roughly $75K. See Price (2020) for an account of

the good things that happen for workers when a CEO increases the salary of his employees to $70K.

CHAPTER 14

1. Quote from the original play, Williams and Albee (2004, 91), instead of from slightly altered film script.
2. Diogenes Laertius, *Lives of Eminent Philosophers* 2:86, 93–96.
3. *Letter to Menoeceus* 126.
4. *Vatican Sayings* 35.
5. *Letter to Menoeceus* 126.
6. *The Principal Doctrines* 2; *Letter to Menoeceus* 124–125.
7. Williams (2011).
8. See Scheffler (2013) for a clear explanation of Williams' argument that living forever would become tedious.
9. *On the Nature of Things (DRN)* 3:42–59.
10. *Letter to Menoeceus* 129.
11. *On the Nature of Things (DRN)* 3:60–70.
12. Friend (2017).
13. *On the Nature of Things (DRN)* 3:65–70.
14. Plato, *Gorgias* 492e.
15. *Vatican Sayings* 55, 66; *The Principal Doctrines* 40.
16. *The Principal Doctrines* 19.
17. *The Principal Doctrines* 20.
18. *Letter to Menoeceus* 130.
19. *Vatican Sayings* 47; Plutarch *Tranquility of Mind* 474c, trans. Sedley.

CHAPTER 15

1. Diogenes Laertius, *Lives of Eminent Philosophers* 10:22, trans. Hicks.
2. Algra (2003, 171–172), qtd. from Plutarch *St. rep.*
3. Seneca, *Letters from a Stoic*, Letter 9: "On Philosophy and Friendship."
4. *On the Nature of Things (DRN)* 2:167–183; 5:156–234.
5. Plutarch, *A Pleasant Life* 1101ab (120U); Plutarch's suggestion that the Epicureans will indulge in lamentations overstates things, which we might expect given his general hostility to Epicureanism. Epicurus himself specifically discourages lamentations (*Vatican Sayings* 66).
6. "On Living in an Atomic Age," in Lewis (2017, 91–102).
7. *Consolation to Helvia*, in *On the Shortness of Life* (2004, 60–61).
8. *Vatican Sayings* 55.
9. *Vatican Sayings* 66.

10. See Rider (2019) for the central role of gratitude and its cultivation in Epicureanism.

11. *On Moral Ends (DF)* 1:62.

12. Philodemus, *On Death* 25.2–25.10, in Philomedus and Henry (2009).

13. See, for example, Carver, Scheier, and Weintraub (1989).

14. Seneca, *Consolation to Helvia*, in *On the Shortness of Life* (2005).

15. See, for example, Waugh, et al. (2021).

16. Lieberman (2021); Wood, Froh, and Geraghty (2010).

17. Wood, Froh, and Geraghty (2010, 897).

18. *The Principal Doctrines* 27.

19. *The Principal Doctrines* 14.

20. *Vatican Sayings* 31 (Metrodorus fr. 51).

21. *The Principal Doctrines* 40.

CHAPTER 16

1. "Special Report: Sex Week at the University of Tennessee-Knoxville," https://comp troller.tn.gov/content/dam/cot/orea/advanced-search/2019/SexWeek_FullReport.pdf.

2. Athenaeus *Deipnosophists* 12, 546ef (67 U, 22 [1]A).

3. *Letter to Menoeceus* 129.

4. https://www.thehotline.org/.

5. *Vatican Sayings* 51, trans. Arenson (2016).

6. *On Moral Ends (DF)* 1:32.

7. *Principal Doctrines* 18.

8. See Gellar-Goad (2020, esp. 63–68, 197–198) for discussion of Lucretian satire.

9. *On the Nature of Things (DRN)* 4:1038–1044.

10. *On the Nature of Things (DRN)* 4:1208–1209.

11. *On the Nature of Things (DRN)* 1075–1077.

12. *On the Nature of Things (DRN)* 4:1072–1074.

13. As best I can tell, "women be shopping" originates from a character played by the comedian Dave Chapelle in *The Nutty Professor* (1996).

14. *On the Nature of Things (DRN)* 1122–1141.

15. *On the Nature of Things (DRN)* 4:1279–1287.

16. *Vatican Sayings* 18.

17. Plato, *Republic* 10:607e. In context, Socrates here compares unhealthy romantic desire to the desire to attend the theater.

18. *On Moral Ends (DF)* 1:30.

CHAPTER 17

1. Diogenes Laertius, *Lives of Eminent Philosophers* 10:119, trans. Inwood and Gerson, who reject the emendation by Causabon and Gassendi. Accepting Inwood and Gerson's brackets.

2. Ibid., trans. Hicks, who accepts the emendation by Causabon and Gassendi.

3. See Chilton (1960), Brennan (1996), and Arenson (2016) for competing views.

4. Freeman (1947), Fr. 277, 116.

5. Senior (2010).

6. Diogenes Laertius, *Lives of Eminent Philosophers* 10:19.

7. Diogenes Laertius, *Lives of Eminent Philosophers* 10:26.

8. *On the Nature of Things (DRN)* 4:1234–1236.

9. *On the Nature of Things (DRN)* 4:1252–1254.

10. *On the Nature of Things (DRN)* 4:1260.

11. *On the Nature of Things (DRN)* 5:1012–1023.

12. Diogenes Laertius, *Lives of Eminent Philosophers* 10:20, trans. Hicks.

CHAPTER 18

1. The announcer calls Epicurus the number six, but the lineup lists him as the number seven. I consider him best suited for the seven.

2. See Gordon (2012) for Epicureanism in the *Learned Banqueters*.

3. The "Paris exception" is an anachronistic example inspired by the contemporary philosopher Peter Singer.

4. Athenaeus, *The Learned Banqueters* 7.298d–e, trans. Gordon (2012, 72).

5. Gordon (2012, 23); for sustained discussion of the *mageiros*, see Wilkins (2000).

6. Athenaeus, *The Learned Banqueters* 3.102a–b, trans. Gordon (2012, 25), my exclamation point.

7. *Letter to Menoeceus* 131.

8. *Letter to Menoeceus* 130.

9. *Letter to Menoeceus* 132.

10. Oliver (2007).

11. Diogenes Laertius, *Lives of Eminent Philosophers* 10:11.

12. *Letter to Menoeceus* 130, my emphasis.

13. *Vatican Sayings* 63.

14. *Letter to Menoeceus* 130.

15. Seneca, *On Benefits* 4.1.3, (trans. Gordon, 136).

16. Bew (2019).

17. https://www.nytimes.com/guides/tmagazine/how-to-host-a-dinner-party.

18. *Vatican Sayings* 41.

CHAPTER 19

1. *The Principal Doctrines* 11.
2. *The Principal Doctrines* 12.
3. Most interpreters agree that Epicurus thinks the capacities for thought and deliberation arise from physical atoms. The disagreement largely concerns whether those powers reduce to the atoms and whether the emergent features have independent causal efficacy, and if so, how much. For a sustained account of Epicurus on freedom, see O'Keefe (2005).
4. Finneran (2010).
5. Thanks to Ben Rider for this point.

CHAPTER 20

1. *Letter to Menoeceus* 123, Inwood and Gerson modified, substituting "living being" for "animal."
2. I will also use the singular and plural interchangeably and largely without design to reflect Epicurus' casual and seemingly unprincipled shifts. Plato also tended to use the singular and plural seemingly interchangeably.
3. See chapter three, "Atheist Epicurus," in Sheppard (2015).
4. Deutsch (1907). Thanks to Adrian Bardon for drawing my attention to this point.
5. See Nadler (2018, esp. 155–163).
6. *Letter to Herodotus* 77.
7. Tom Waits, "Day After Tomorrow," from the album *Real Gone*.
8. *On the Nature of Things (DRN)* 4:1233–1240.
9. Bowler (2019, 15).
10. *On the Nature of Things (DRN)* 1:104–112.
11. *On the Nature of Things (DRN)* 3:978.
12. *On the Nature of Things (DRN)* 1:80ff.
13. Plutarch, *Caius Memmius* 21, 3.

CHAPTER 21

1. Plato, *Phaedo* 64a.
2. See Cross and Warraich (2019) for the extent to which these numbers have improved in the past decade, primarily through the rise of home hospice.
3. This is admittedly a bit of a controversial view. Some scholars (esp. Warren, 15) contend that Epicurus believes all fears of death are irrational and eliminable in light of rational arguments. Austin (2012) contends that some fears result from our animal nature and can only be managed, not eliminated.
4. *The Principal Doctrines* 2.
5. *Letter to Menoeceus* 124.

6. See Nagel (1970) for discussion of "unperceived harms" like deception; Aristotle also considers the possibility of such harms, *Nicomachean Ethics* 1: 1110a.

7. *Letter to Menoeceus* 126–127; *Vatican Sayings* 38.

8. *The Principal Doctrines* 27.

9. *The Principal Doctrines* 28.

10. Diogenes Laertius, *Lives of Eminent Philosophers* 10:22, trans. Hicks.

11. Diogenes Laertius, *Lives of Eminent Philosophers* 8:39.

12. Plato, *Phaedo* 63b–c.

13. For Hume on immortality, see Levine in Radcliffe (2008).

14. On Hume's debt to Epicurus, see Jordan (2017).

15. For more on the friendship between Hume and Smith, see Rasmussen (2017).

16. The friends and relatives of Christopher Hitchens were similarly slandered. See Krauss (2016) and Cohen (2016).

17. *Letter to Menoeceus* 126.

18. *Letter to Menoeceus* 122

CHAPTER 22

1. Lucretius (2001, 35n1, translation by Smith).

2. For discussion of Lucretius' dual audience, see Gellar-Goad (2020).

3. Thucydides, *The Peloponnesian War* (1998), 2.47–2.54.

4. *On the Nature of Things (DRN)* 6:1–12.

5. *On the Nature of Things (DRN)* 6:11–16.

6. *On the Nature of Things (DRN)* 6:1129–1131.

7. Thucydides, *The Peloponnesian War* 2.47–2.54.

8. I say "seem to have overlooked" only because I have not seen this point in print. I am not asserting its originality.

9. Also missing from Lucretius' account is Thucydides' final commentary on the competing interpretations of a prophecy that the gods would unleash a plague (2.54).

CHAPTER 23

1. Epicurus offers a particularly long-winded version of the Fourfold Remedy at *Letter to Menoeceus* 133. While the first four *Principal Doctrines* contain most of the remedy's claims, the notion that "the good is easy to get" is found elsewhere, especially in *Principal Doctrine* 21.

2. Hall (2021).

3. This claim is admittedly contentious when it comes to an Epicurean sage, and I cannot defend it here. The chief supporting evidence comes from Lucretius (*On the Nature of Things* 3:1040–1042) and Cicero (*On Moral Ends* 1:49).

4. *Letter to Menoeceus* 135.

CHAPTER 24

1. *Vatican Sayings* 54.
2. Tsouna (2007, 74–87) was an invaluable resource for writing this chapter, especially on this point.
3. Eskreis-Winkler, Fishbach, and Duckworth (2018).
4. *Vatican Sayings* 71.
5. *Vatican Sayings* 19.
6. *Vatican Sayings* 74.
7. Roskam (2007) provides a sustained scholarly exploration of how various Epicureans likely interpreted the advice to "live unnoticed."
8. Schank (2021).
9. Usener fr. 222.

SUGGESTED FURTHER READING

ANCIENT EPICUREAN TEXTS

For those seeking an English translation of Epicurus' major extant writings, including testimony from Ancient Greek and Roman advocates and critics, I recommend:

The Epicurus Reader: Selected Writings and Testimonia. 1994. Translated and Edited by Brad Inwood and L. P. Gerson, with introduction by D. S. Hutchinson. Indianapolis: Hackett Publishing.

Those interested not only in Epicureanism, but also in Stoicism and Skepticism, might instead choose an expanded text from the same editors:

Hellenistic Philosophy: Introductory Readings. 1997. 2nd edition. Translated and Edited by Brad Inwood and L. P. Gerson. Indianapolis: Hackett Publishing

Lucretius' *On the Nature of Things (De Rerum Natura)* is without question the best source for rounding out one's understanding of Epicureanism. Lucretius wrote in verse, although I have quoted from the following prose translation:

Lucretius, 2001. *On the Nature of Things*. Translated by Martin Ferguson Smith. Indianapolis: Hackett Publishing.

For those interested in reading an English translation in verse, I recommend:

Lucretius, 2009. *On the Nature of the Universe*. Translated by Ronald Melville. Introduction by Don Fowler and Peta Fowler. Reissue edition. Oxford: Oxford University Press.

SCHOLARSHIP FOR NON-SCHOLARS

The following texts are written by trained scholars and require no working knowledge of Greek or Latin. For Epicurus and Epicureanism more broadly:

O'Keefe, Tim. 2009. *Epicureanism*. London, UK: Taylor & Francis Group.

Warren, James, ed. 2009. *The Cambridge Companion to Epicureanism*. Cambridge: Cambridge University Press.

For Lucretius, including his intellectual and cultural influence on the Renaissance and Enlightenment:

Gillespie, Stuart, and Philip Hardie, eds. 2007. *The Cambridge Companion to Lucretius*. Illustrated edition. Cambridge, UK; New York: Cambridge University Press.

Greenblatt, Stephen. 2012. *The Swerve: How the World Became Modern*. New York: W. W. Norton & Company.

STOICS, SKEPTICS, AND EPICUREANS

Epicureanism's chief philosophical competitors were Stoicism and Skepticism, all three schools flourishing during the Hellenistic Period (323–331 BCE). I recommend beginning with following:

Sellars, John. 2018. *Hellenistic Philosophy*. Oxford: Oxford University Press.

Cicero, Marcus Tullius. 2001. *Cicero: On Moral Ends*. Edited by Julia Annas. Translated by Raphael Woolf. Cambridge; New York: Cambridge University Press.

REFERENCES

Algra, Keimpe. 2003. "Stoic Theology." In *The Cambridge Companion to the Stoics*, edited by Brad Inwood, 153–178. Cambridge: Cambridge University Press. https://doi.org/10.1017/CCOL052177005X.007.

Algra, Keimpe, Jonathan Barnes, Jaap Mansfeld, and Malcolm Schofield, eds. 1999. *The Cambridge History of Hellenistic Philosophy*. Cambridge: Cambridge University Press. https://doi.org/10.1017/CHOL9780521250283.

Annas, Julia. 1992. *Hellenistic Philosophy of Mind*. Vol. 8, *Hellenistic Culture and Society*. Berkeley: University of California Press.

Annas, Julia, and Gábor Betegh. 2015. *Cicero's De Finibus: Philosophical Approaches*. Cambridge, UK: Cambridge University Press.

Arenson, Kelly E. 2016. "Epicureans on Marriage as Sexual Therapy." *Polis: The Journal for Ancient Greek Political Thought* 2, no. 33: 291–311. https://doi.org/10.1163/20512996-12340095.

Arenson, Kelly. 2019. *Health and Hedonism in Plato and Epicurus*. New York: Bloomsbury Academic.

Arenson, Kelly E. 2020. *The Routledge Handbook of Hellenistic Philosophy*. Milton: Taylor & Francis Group.

Aristotle. 1999. *Nicomachean Ethics*. Translated by Terence Irwin. 2nd edition. Indianapolis, IN: Hackett Publishing Company, Inc.

Asmis, Elizabeth. 2009. "Epicurean Empiricism." In *The Cambridge Companion to Epicureanism*, edited by James Warren, 84–104. Cambridge: Cambridge University Press. https://doi.org/10.1017/CCOL9780521873475.006.

Austin, Emily A. 2012. "Epicurus and the Politics of Fearing Death." *Apeiron* 45, no. 2: 109–129. https://doi.org/10.1515/apeiron-2011-0003.

Batson, C. Daniel. 2019. *A Scientific Search for Altruism: Do We Care Only about Ourselves?* New York, NY: Oxford University Press.

Bebchuk, Lucian A., and Roberto Tallarita. 2021. "Will Corporations Deliver Value to All Stakeholders?" SSRN Scholarly Paper ID 3899421. Rochester, NY: Social Science Research Network. https://doi.org/10.2139/ssrn.3899421.

Beck, Mark, ed. 2014. *A Companion to Plutarch*. 1st edition. Chichester, West Sussex, England; Malden, MA: Wiley-Blackwell.

Bew, Sophie. 2019. "How to Throw a Festive Korean-Inspired Dinner Party." *The New York Times*, July 22. https://www.nytimes.com/2019/07/22/t-magazine/rejina-pyo-korean-dinner-party.html.

Blank, David. 2009. "Philosophia and Technē: Epicureans on the Arts." In *The Cambridge Companion to Epicureanism*, edited by James Warren, 216–233. Cambridge: Cambridge University Press. https://doi.org/10.1017/CCOL9780521873475.013.

Bloom, Allan. 1987. *The Closing of the American Mind*. New York: Simon and Schuster.

Bourne, Frank C. 1977. "Caesar the Epicurean." *The Classical World* 70, no. 7: 417–432. https://doi.org/10.2307/4348711.

Bowler, Kate. 2019. *Everything Happens for a Reason: And Other Lies I've Loved*. Reprint edition. New York: Random House Trade Paperbacks.

Bregman, Rutger, Anand Giridharadas, and Winnie Byanyima. 2019. "Fightback Against the Billionaires: The Radicals Taking on the Global Elite." *The Guardian*, February 7. https://www.theguardian.com/books/2019/feb/07/rutger-bregman-winnie-byanyima-anand-giridharadas.

Brembs, Björn. 2011. "Towards a Scientific Concept of Free Will as a Biological Trait: Spontaneous Actions and Decision-Making in Invertebrates." *Proceedings of the Royal Society B: Biological Sciences* 278, no. 1707: 930–939. https://doi.org/10.1098/rspb.2010.2325.

Brennan, Tad. 1996. "Epicurus on Sex, Marriage, and Children." *Classical Philology* 91, no. 4: 346–352.

Brown, Eric. 2009. "Politics and Society." In *The Cambridge Companion to Epicureanism*, edited by James Warren, 179–196. Cambridge: Cambridge University Press. https://doi.org/10.1017/CCOL9780521873475.011.

Brown, Eric. 2013. "Cynics." *Routledge Handbooks Online*. https://doi.org/10.4324/9781315871363.ch28.

Bruehlman-Senecal, Emma, and Ozlem Ayduk. 2015. "This Too Shall Pass: Temporal Distance and the Regulation of Emotional Distress." *Journal of Personality and Social Psychology* 108, no. 2: 356–375. https://doi.org/10.1037/a0038324.

Buttigieg, Pete. 2020. *Trust: America's Best Chance*. Illustrated edition. New York: Liveright.

Calarco, Jessica McCrory. 2018. "Why Rich Kids Are So Good at the Marshmallow Test." *The Atlantic*. June 1. https://www.theatlantic.com/family/archive/2018/06/marshmallow-test/561779/.

Carver, Charles S., Michael F. Scheier, and Jagdish K. Weintraub. 1989. "Assessing Coping Strategies: A Theoretically Based Approach." *Journal of Personality and Social Psychology* 56, no. 2: 267–283. https://doi.org/10.1037/0022-3514.56.2.267.

Chilton, C. W. 1960. "Did Epicurus Approve of Marriage? A Study of 'Diogenes Laertius X', 119." *Phronesis* 5, no. 1: 71–74.

Cicero, Marcus Tullius. 2001. *Cicero: On Moral Ends*. Edited by Julia Annas. Translated by Raphael Woolf. Cambridge; New York: Cambridge University Press.

Clay, Diskin. 1999. *Paradosis and Survival Three Chapters in the History of Epicurean Philosophy*. Ann Arbor, MI: University of Michigan Press.

Clay, Diskin. 2009. "The Athenian Garden." In *The Cambridge Companion to Epicureanism*, edited by James Warren, 9–28. Cambridge: Cambridge University Press. https://doi.org/10.1017/CCOL9780521873475.002.

Cohen, Nick. 2016. "Deathbed Conversion? Never. Christopher Hitchens Was Defiant to the Last." *The Guardian*, June 4. https://www.theguardian.com/commentisfree/2016/jun/04/deathbed-conversion-christopher-hitchens-defiant-to-last.

Cooper, John M. 1999. *Reason and Emotion: Essays on Ancient Moral Psychology and Ethical Theory*. Princeton, NJ: Princeton University Press. http://www.tandfonline.com/toc/rwhi20/.

Cornish, Audie, Art Silverman, and Sarah Handel. 2021. "As Arab Spring Unfolded on Twitter, Social Media Gained Foothold At NPR." *NPR*, May 4. https://www.npr.org/2021/05/04/993605477/as-arab-spring-unfol ded-on-twitter-social-media-gained-foothold-at-npr.

Cross, Sarah H., and Haider J. Warraich. 2019. "Changes in the Place of Death in the United States." *New England Journal of Medicine* 381, no. 24: 2369–2370. https://doi.org/10.1056/NEJMc1911892.

Deutsch, Gotthard. 1907. "APIḰOROS." *JewishEncyclopedia.com*. https://jew ishencyclopedia.com/articles/1640-apikoros.

Diogenes Oenoandensis, Martin Ferguson Smith, and Istituto Italiano per gli Studi Filosofici. 1993. *The Epicurean Inscription*. Napoli: Bibliopolis.

Doris, John, Stephen Stich, and Lachlan Walmsley. 2020. "Empirical Approaches to Altruism." In *The Stanford Encyclopedia of Philosophy*, edited by Edward N. Zalta, Spring 2020. Stanford, CA: Metaphysics Research Lab, Stanford University. https://plato.stanford.edu/archives/spr2020/entries/altruism-empirical/.

Duckworth, Angela. 2016. *Grit: The Power of Passion and Perseverance*. Illustrated edition. New York: Scribner.

Epicurus, and Cyril Bailey. 1989. *The Extant Remains*. Hildesheim; Zürich: G. Olms.

Epicurus, and Hermann Usener. 2010. *Epicurea*. Cambridge: Cambridge University Press. https://doi.org/10.1017/CBO9780511711077.

Erler, Michael. 2009. "Epicureanism in the Roman Empire." In *The Cambridge Companion to Epicureanism*, edited by James Warren, 46–64. Cambridge: Cambridge University Press. https://doi.org/10.1017/CCOL9780521873475.004.

Eskreis-Winkler, Lauren, Ayelet Fishbach, and Angela L. Duckworth. 2018. "Dear Abby: Should I Give Advice or Receive It?" *Psychological Science* 29, no. 11: 1797–1806. https://doi.org/10.1177/0956797618795472.

Evans, Matthew. 2004. "Can Epicureans Be Friends?" *Ancient Philosophy* 24, no. 2: 407–424.

Everitt, Anthony. 2003. *Cicero: The Life and Times of Rome's Greatest Politician*. Reprint edition. New York: Random House Trade Paperbacks.

Fajkowska, Małgorzata, Shulamith Kreitler, Wiebke Bleidorn, Christopher J. Hopwood, and Richard E. Lucas. 2018. "Life Events and Personality Trait Change Life Events and Trait Change." *Journal of Personality* 86, no. 1: 83–96.

Finneran, Michael. 2010. "NASA—Fire-Breathing Storm Systems." October 19. https://www.nasa.gov/topics/earth/features/pyrocb.html.

Fish, Jeffrey, and Kirk R Sanders. 2015. *Epicurus and the Epicurean Tradition*. Cambridge: Cambridge University Press.

Foster, Edith. 2009. "The Rhetoric of Materials: Thucydides and Lucretius." *American Journal of Philology* 130, no. 3: 367–399.

Freeman, Kathleen. 1947. *Ancilla to the Presocratic Philosophers: A Complete Translation of the Fragments in Diels, Fragmente Der Vorsokratiker*. Oxford: Basil Blackwell.

Friend, Tad. 2017. "Silicon Valley's Quest to Live Forever." *The New Yorker*, March 27. http://www.newyorker.com/magazine/2017/04/03/silicon-valleys-quest-to-live-forever.

Gawande, Atul. 2015. *Being Mortal*. Main edition. London, UK: Profile Books Ltd.

Gellar-Goad, T. H. M. 2020. *Laughing Atoms, Laughing Matter. Lucretius' De Rerum Natura and Satire*. Ann Arbor, MI: University of Michigan Press.

Gill, Christopher. 2009. "Psychology." In *The Cambridge Companion to Epicureanism*, edited by James Warren, 125–141. Cambridge: Cambridge University Press. https://doi.org/10.1017/CCOL9780521873475.008.

Giridharadas, Anand. 2019. *Winners Take All: The Elite Charade of Changing the World*. Reprint edition. New York: Vintage.

Gordon, Dane R., and David B. Suits. 2003. *Epicurus: His Continuing Influence and Contemporary Relevance*. Rochester, NY: RIT Cary Graphic Arts Press.

Gordon, Pamela. 2012. *The Invention and Gendering of Epicurus*. Ann Arbor, MI: University of Michigan Press. https://doi.org/10.3998/mpub.1826277.

Gosling, J. C. B. and C. C. W. Taylor. 982. *The Greeks on Pleasure*. 1st edition. Oxford: Oxford University Press.

Greenblatt, Stephen. 2012. *The Swerve: How the World Became Modern*. New York: W. W. Norton & Company.

Griffin, Miriam T. 1976. *Seneca: A Philosopher in Politics*. Oxford: Clarendon Press.

Hall, Edith. 2021. "The Fourfold Remedy by John Sellars Review—the Secret of Happiness." *The Guardian*, January 8. https://www.theguardian.com/books/2021/jan/08/the-fourfold-remedy-by-john-sellars-review-the-secret-of-happiness.

Hitchens, Christopher. 2007. *The Portable Atheist: Essential Readings for the Nonbeliever*. 1st edition. Da Capo Press.

Hudson, Nathan W., Daniel A. Briley, William J. Chopik, and Jaime Derringer. 2019. "You Have to Follow Through: Attaining Behavioral Change Goals Predicts Volitional Personality Change." *Journal of Personality and Social Psychology* 117, no. 4: 839–857.

Hutchinson, G. O. 2001. "The Date of *De Rerum Natura*." *The Classical Quarterly* 51, no. 1: 150–162.

Inwood, Brad. 2009. *Reading Seneca: Stoic Philosophy at Rome*. Oxford: Clarendon Press.

Inwood, Brad, and Lloyd P. Gerson, trans. 1998. *Hellenistic Philosophy*. Second Edition. Indianapolis, IN: Hackett Publishing Company, Inc.

Irvine, William Braxton. 2009. *A Guide to the Good Life: The Ancient Art of Stoic Joy*. Oxford: Oxford University Press.

Johnson, Monte Ransome. 2003. "Was Gassendi an Epicurean?" *History of Philosophy Quarterly* 20, no. 4: 339–360.

Jordan, Alexander. 2017. "David Hume Is Pontiff of the World: Thomas Carlyle on Epicureanism, Laissez-Faire, and Public Opinion." *Journal of British Studies* 56, 3: 557–579.

Kahneman, Daniel, and Angus Deaton. 2010. "High Income Improves Evaluation of Life but Not Emotional Well-Being." *Proceedings of the National Academy of Sciences of the United States of America* 107, no. 38: 16489–16493.

Kechagia-Ovseiko, Eleni. 2013. "Plutarch and Epicureanism." In *A Companion to Plutarch*, edited by Mark Beck, 104–120. Malden, MA: Wiley-Blackwell.

Konstan, David. 2013. "Lucretius and the Epicurean Attitude towards Grief." In *Lucretius: Poetry, Philosophy, Science*. Oxford: Oxford University Press. https://doi.org/10.1093/acprof:oso/9780199605408.003.0008.

Krauss, Lawrence M. 2016. "The Fantasy of the Deathbed Conversion." *The New Yorker*, June 6. https://www.newyorker.com/culture/culture-desk/the-fantasy-of-the-deathbed-conversion.

Kraut, Richard. 1979. "Two Conceptions of Happiness." *The Philosophical Review* 88, vol. 2: 167–197. https://doi.org/10.2307/2184505.

Laertius, Diogenes. 1925. *Diogenes Laertius: Lives of Eminent Philosophers*, Volume II, Books 6–10. Translated by R. D. Hicks. Cambridge, MA: Harvard University Press.

Leddy, Neven, and Avi Lifschitz. 2009. *Epicurus in the Enlightenment*. Oxford: Voltaire Foundation.

Lewis, C. S. 2017. *Present Concerns: Journalistic Essays*. Reprint edition. New York, NY: Harper One.

Lieberman, Charlotte. 2021. "Why We Romanticize the Past." *The New York Times*, April 2. https://www.nytimes.com/2021/04/02/smarter-living/why-we-romanticize-the-past.html.

Long, A. A. 2001. *Hellenistic Philosophy: Stoics, Epicureans, Sceptics*. London, UK: Duckworth.

Long, A. A. 2006. *From Epicurus to Epictetus: Studies in Hellenistic and Roman Philosophy*. Oxford: Clarendon Press.

Long, A. A., and D. N. Sedley. 1987. *Translations of the Principal Sources, with Philosophical Commentary*. Vol. 1, *The Hellenistic Philosophers*. Cambridge, UK; New York: Cambridge University Press.

Long, A. A., and D. N. Sedley. 1989. *Greek and Latin Texts with Notes and Bibliography.* Vol. 2, *The Hellenistic Philosophers.* Reprint edition. Cambridge, UK: Cambridge University Press.

Lucretius. 2001. *On the Nature of Things.* Translated by Martin Ferguson Smith. Indianapolis, IN: Hackett Publishing Company, Inc.

Mensch, Pamela, and James Miller. 2018. *Lives of the Eminent Philosophers. By Diogenes Laertius.* Oxford: Oxford University Press.

Mischel, Walter. 2014. *The Marshmallow Test: Mastering Self-Control.* First edition. New York: Little, Brown and Company.

Mitsis, Phillip. *Epicurus' Ethical Theory: The Pleasures of Invulnerability.* Ithaca, NY: Cornell University Press. https://www.jstor.org/stable/10.7591/j.cttq45fk.

Morgan, Llewelyn, and Barnaby Taylor. 2017. "Memmius the Epicurean." *The Classical Quarterly* 67, no. 2: 528–541. https://doi.org/10.1017/S0009838817000672.

Morton, Jennifer M. 2017. "Reasoning under Scarcity." *Australasian Journal of Philosophy* 95, no. 3: 543–559.

Morton, Jennifer M. n.d. "Resisting Pessimism Traps: The Limits of Believing in Oneself'." *Philosophy and Phenomenological Research* preprint. Accessed September 18, 2021. https://doi.org/10.1111/phpr.12809.

Morton, Jennifer M., and Sarah K. Paul. 2019. "Grit." *Ethics* 129, no. 2: 175–203. https://doi.org/10.1086/700029.

Mulgan, R. G. 1979. "Was Caesar an Epicurean? (Sallust, BC 51.20)." *The Classical World* 72, no. 6: 337–339. https://doi.org/10.2307/4349066.

Nadler, Steven. 2018. *Spinoza: A Life.* 2nd edition. Cambridge; New York: Cambridge University Press.

Nagel, Thomas. 1970. "Death." *Noûs* 4, no. 1: 73–80. https://doi.org/10.2307/2214297.

Nussbaum, Martha C. 1994. *The Therapy of Desire: Theory and Practice in Hellenistic Ethics.* Vol. 2, *Martin Classical Lectures. New Series.* Princeton, NJ: Princeton University Press.

Odell, Jenny. 2019. *How to Do Nothing: Resisting the Attention Economy.* Brooklyn, NY: Melville House.

O' Keefe, Tim. 2001. "Is Epicurean Friendship Altruistic?" *Apeiron* 34: 269–306.

O' Keefe, Tim. 2005. *Epicurus on Freedom*. Cambridge, UK: Cambridge University Press.

O' Keefe, Tim. 2009. *Epicureanism*. London, UK: Taylor & Francis Group.

Oliver, G. J. 2007. *War, Food, and Politics in Early Hellenistic Athens*. Oxford: Oxford University Press. https://doi.org/10.1093/acprof:oso/9780199283507.001.0001.

Perri, Timothy J. 2013. "The Evolution of Military Conscription in the United States." *The Independent Review* 17, no. 3: 429–439.

Philodemus, and W. Benjamin Henry. 2009. *On Death*. Atlanta, GA: Society of Biblical Literature.

Philodemus, David Konstan, Diskin Clay, Clarence E. Glad, Johan Carl Thom, and James Ware. 1998. *Philodemus on Frank Criticism*. First Edition. Atlanta, GA: Scholars Press.

Plato. 1997. *Plato: Complete Works*. Edited by John M. Cooper and D. S. Hutchinson. Indianapolis, IN: Hackett Publishing Co.

Price, Dan. 2020. *Worth It: How a Million-Dollar Pay Cut and a $70,000 Minimum Wage Revealed a Better Way of Doing Business*. Seattle, WA: Gravity Payments, Inc.

Radcliffe, Elizabeth Schmidt. 2008. *A Companion to Hume*. 1st ed. Hoboken, NJ: John Wiley & Sons, Incorporated.

Rasmussen, Dennis C. 2017. *The Infidel and the Professor: David Hume, Adam Smith, and the Friendship That Shaped Modern Thought*. Princeton, NJ: Princeton University Press.

Rider, Benjamin A. 2014. "Epicurus on the Fear of Death and the Relative Value of Lives." *Apeiron* 47, no. 4: 461–484. https://doi.org/10.1515/apeiron-2014-0001.

Rider, Benjamin A. 2019. "The Ethical Significance of Gratitude in Epicureanism." *British Journal for the History of Philosophy* 27, no. 6: 1092–1112. https://doi.org/10.1080/09608788.2019.1568229.

Robitzsch, Jan Maximilian. 2016. "Epicurean Justice and Law." PhD diss., University of Pennsylvania. http://gateway.proquest.com/open

url?url_ver=Z39.88-2004&rft_val_fmt=info:ofi/fmt:kev:mtx:dissertat
ion&res_dat=xri:pqm&rft_dat=xri:pqdiss:10190393.

Roskam, Geert. 2007a. *Live Unnoticed: On the Vicissitudes of an Epicurean Doctrine*. Leiden: Brill.

Roskam, Geert. 2007b. *A Commentary on Plutarch's de Latenter Vivendo: De Latenter Vivendo*. Leuven, Belgium: Leuven University Press.

Saunders, George. 2017. *Congratulations, By the Way: Some Thoughts on Kindness*. London, UK: Bloomsbury Publishing.

Schank, Hana. 2021. "I Know the Secret to the Quiet Mind. I Wish I'd Never Learned It." *The Atlantic*, June 17. https://www.theatlantic.com/health/archive/2021/06/car-accident-brain-injury/619227/.

Scheffler, Samuel. 2013. *Death and the Afterlife*. Edited by Niko Kolodny. 1st edition. Oxford; New York, NY: Oxford University Press.

Schiesaro, Alessandro. 2015. "Seneca and Epicurus: The Allure of the Other." In *The Cambridge Companion to Seneca*, edited by Alessandro Schiesaro and Shadi Bartsch, 239–252. Cambridge: Cambridge University Press. https://doi.org/10.1017/CCO9781139542746.022.

Sedley, David. 2009. "Epicureanism in the Roman Republic." In *The Cambridge Companion to Epicureanism*, edited by James Warren, 29–45. Cambridge: Cambridge University Press. https://doi.org/10.1017/CCOL9780521873475.003.

Sedley, David. 2011. "Epicurus' Theological Innatism." In *Epicurus and the Epicurean Tradition*, edited by Jeffrey Fish and Kirk R. Sanders, 29–52. Cambridge: Cambridge University Press. https://doi.org/10.1017/CBO9780511921704.003.

Seneca. 2005. *On the Shortness of Life: Life Is Long If You Know How to Use It*. Translated by C. D. N. Costa. 1st edition. New York: Penguin Books.

Seneca, Lucius Annaeus, Elaine Fantham, Harry M. Hine, James Ker, and Gareth D. Williams. 2014. *Hardship and Happiness*. Chicago, IL: University of Chicago Press.

Seneca, Tom Butler-Bowdon, and Donald Robertson. 2021. *Letters from a Stoic: The Ancient Classic*. Newark, UK: John Wiley & Sons, Incorporated.

Senior, Jennifer. 2010. "Why Parents Hate Parenting." *New York Magazine*, July 2. https://nymag.com/news/features/67024/.

Sheffield, Frisbee, and James Warren, eds. 2018. *Routledge Companion to Ancient Philosophy*. 1st edition. London, UK; New York: Routledge.

Sheppard, Kenneth. 2015. *Anti-Atheism in Early Modern England 1580–1720: The Atheist Answered and His Error Confuted*. Leiden: Brill.

Smith, Adam, and Knud Haakonssen. 2002. *Adam Smith: The Theory of Moral Sentiments*. Cambridge, UK: Cambridge University Press.

Sorensen, Ted. 2009. *Counselor: A Life at the Edge of History*. Illustrated edition. New York: Harper Perennial.

Stout, Lynn. 2015. "Corporations Don't Have to Maximize Profits." *The New York Times*, April 16. https://www.nytimes.com/roomfordebate/2015/04/16/what-are-corporations-obligations-to-shareholders/corporations-dont-have-to-maximize-profits.

Striker, G. 1990. "Ataraxia: Happiness as Tranquility." *Monist*, 97–110.

Thorsrud, Harald. 2011. "Sextus Empiricus on Skeptical Piety." In *New Essays on Ancient Pyrrhonism*, edited by Diego E. Machuca, 91–111. Leiden: Brill.

Thucydides, and Victor Davis Hanson. 1998. *The Landmark Thucydides: A Comprehensive Guide to the Peloponnesian War*. Edited by Robert B. Strassler. Translated by Richard Crawley. New York: Free Press.

Trump, Donald J. 2015. *Trump: The Art of the Deal*. Reprint edition. New York: Ballantine Books.

Tsouna, Voula. 2007. *The Ethics of Philodemus*. Oxford: Oxford University Press. https://doi.org/10.1093/acprof:oso/9780199292172.001.0001.

Tsouna, Voula. 2009. "Epicurean Therapeutic Strategies." In *The Cambridge Companion to Epicureanism*, edited by James Warren, 249–265. Cambridge: Cambridge University Press. https://doi.org/10.1017/CCOL9780521873475.015.

Warren, James. 2001. "Epicurus' Dying Wishes." *Proceedings of the Cambridge Philological Society*, no. 47: 23–46.

Warren, James. 2004. *Facing Death: Epicurus and His Critics*. Oxford: Oxford University Press. https://doi.org/10.1093/0199252890.001.0001.

Warren, James. 2009a. "Removing Fear." In *The Cambridge Companion to Epicureanism*, edited by James Warren, 234–248. Cambridge: Cambridge University Press. https://doi.org/10.1017/CCOL9780521873475.014.

Warren, James, ed. 2009b. *The Cambridge Companion to Epicureanism*. Cambridge: Cambridge University Press. https://doi.org/10.1017/CCOL9780521873475.

Warren, James. 2014. *The Pleasures of Reason in Plato, Aristotle, and the Hellenistic Hedonists*. Cambridge: Cambridge University Press.

Watts, Tyler W., Greg J. Duncan, and Haonan Quan. 2018. "Revisiting the Marshmallow Test: A Conceptual Replication Investigating Links Between Early Delay of Gratification and Later Outcomes." *Psychological Science* 29, no. 7: 1159–1177. https://doi.org/10.1177/0956797618761661.

Waugh C. E., C. J. Leslie-Miller, E. Z. Shing, R. M. Furr, C. L. Nightingale, and T. W. McLean. 2021. "Adaptive and Maladaptive Forms of Disengagement Coping in Caregivers of Children with Chronic Illnesses." *Stress and Health: Journal of the International Society for the Investigation of Stress* 37, no. 2: 213–222.

Wilkins, John. 2000. *The Boastful Chef: The Discourse of Food in Ancient Greek Comedy*. Oxford; Oxford University Press.

Williams, Alex. 2019. "Why Don't Rich People Just Stop Working?" *The New York Times*, October 17. https://www.nytimes.com/2019/10/17/style/rich-people-things.html.

Williams, Bernard. 2011. *Problems of the Self*. Cambridge, UK: Cambridge University Press. http://public.ebookcentral.proquest.com/choice/publicfullrecord.aspx?p=4639117.

Williams, Tennessee, and Edward Albee. 2004. *Cat on a Hot Tin Roof*. New York: New Directions.

Wilson, Catherine. 2008. *Epicureanism at the Origins of Modernity*. Oxford: Oxford University Press. https://doi.org/10.1093/acprof:oso/9780199238811.001.0001.

Wilson, J., and J. Mumpower. 2019. Special Report: Sex Week at the University of Tennessee-Knoxville. https://comptroller.tn.gov/content/dam/cot/orea/advanced-search/2019/SexWeek_FullReport.pdf.

Wiseman, Rosalind. 2003. *Queen Bees and Wannabees*. 1st Edition. London, UK: Piatkus Books.

Wolf, Susan. 1982. "Moral Saints." *The Journal of Philosophy* 79, no. 8: 419–439. https://doi.org/10.2307/2026228.

Wood, Alex M., Jeffrey J. Froh, and Adam W. A. Geraghty. 2010. "Gratitude and Well-Being: A Review and Theoretical Integration." *Clinical Psychology Review* 30, no. 7: 890–905. https://doi.org/10.1016/j.cpr.2010.03.005.

Woolf, Raphael. 2004. "What Kind of Hedonist Was Epicurus?" *Phronesis: A Journal for Ancient Philosophy* 49, 4: 303–322.

Woolf, Raphael. 2015. *Cicero: The Philosophy of a Roman Sceptic*. London, UK: Routledge. https://doi.org/10.4324/9781315724850.

Yosifon, David. 2015. "It's Law, But It Shouldn't Be." *The New York Times*, April 16. https://www.nytimes.com/roomfordebate/2015/04/16/what-are-corporations-obligations-to-shareholders/its-law-but-it-shouldnt-be.

INDEX

For the benefit of digital users, indexed terms that span two pages (e.g., 52–53) may, on occasion, appear on only one of those pages.